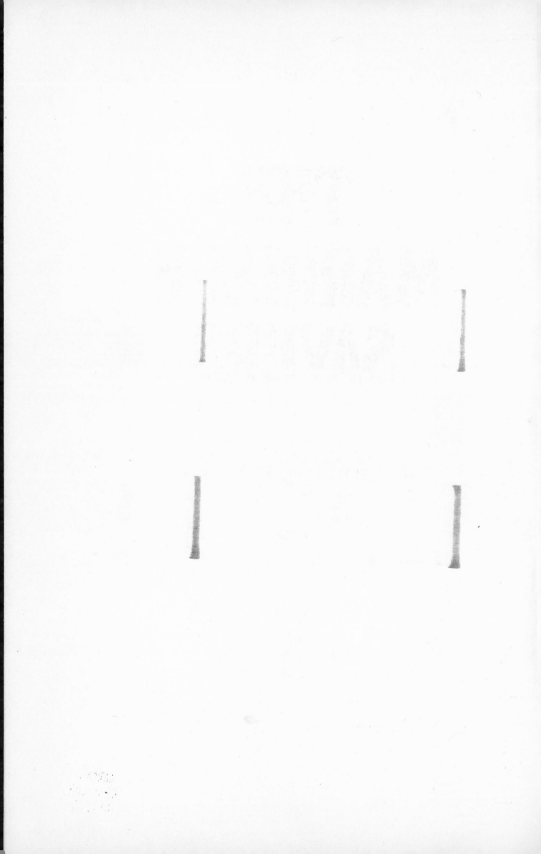

THE MARRIAGE SAVERS

Joanne & Lew Koch

COWARD, McCANN & GEOGHEGAN, INC.
NEW YORK

SBN: 698-10692-X

Library of Congress Cataloging in Publication Data

Koch, Joanne.
    The marriage savers.

    Bibliography: p.
    Includes index.
    1.   Marriage counseling—United States. I. Koch, Lew, joint author. II. Title.
HQ10.K6   1976   362.8′2   75-10479

PRINTED IN THE UNITED STATES OF AMERICA

For our parents

        Ceil Schapiro and Dr. Isadore Schapiro
        Blanche Koch and the late Sidney Koch
And for our children
        Lisa
        Rachel
        Joshua

Contents

1. Marriage Saving   13

2. Therapists   19

3. Family Therapy   67

4. Sex Clinics   113

5. Social Service Agencies   159

6. Alternatives to a Dull Marriage   203

7. Saving Yourself from the
   Wrong Marriage Counselor   231

Appendix: How to Find a Marriage Counselor   251

Notes   271

Index   278

Acknowledgments

More than 100 therapists and 200 individuals and couples were interviewed during the two years of research that went into the writing of this book. We were surprised and grateful to the couples and individuals for being willing to recount to us the most intimate and painful details of their married lives. We can't name them but they know who they are. Each person who spoke to us added invaluable insights to our understanding of marital problems and marital therapy, and we are only sorry we couldn't quote all the fine ideas and moving stories they offered.

There are many others who helped us realize this book. First were those who encouraged us to move in this direction by printing our articles and then our "Family Lib" column dealing with the new issues confronting couples and families: former editor of the Chicago *Tribune* Sunday Magazine, John Fink, and editor of the Chicago *Tribune*, Clayton Kirkpatrick. Robert Roy Metz, president of Newspaper Enterprise Association, syndicated that column and urged us to undertake a more serious and controversial approach to coping with family problems; Ross Gelbspan has edited "Coping" sensitively but never censored it.

Chicago magazine's editor, Allen H. Kelson, and publisher, Raymond Nordstrand, suggested we write an article in 1974 called "The Marriage Savers," and continue to give us opportunities, as contributing editors, to write about marriage and the family.

Our understanding of the complexities of marital and family life was made easier by three people at the University of Minnesota: Reuben Hill, Gerhard Neubeck, and Ira Reiss. Ray Fowler, the indefatigable executive director of the American Association of Marriage and Family Counselors was always helpful, and always leveled with us. Special thanks are due to therapist Jessie Potter in Chicago, Leo Jacobs and Jean Warnock, Darlene and Jack Davis, all of the Forest Hospital Sexual Dysfunction Clinic in Des Plaines, Illinois:

therapists Charles and Jan Kramer, of the Family Institute of Chicago; California-based family therapist Virgina Satir and Chicago psychiatrist F. Theodore Reid—all of whom took time to answer questions, clarify issues, and offer recommendations.

Certain people gave us sustenance during our cross-country research: Sheldon and Noreen Schapiro in Hollywood, Florida, Dr. Fred Abrams and Alice Abrams in Denver, Colorado, Peter Schrag and Diane Divoky in Oakland, California, and Jacqueline Bonnheim in Los Angeles.

Our typist Jennifer Lightner met our grueling deadlines, corrected our spelling, and offered intelligent comments as the manuscript progressed.

Others helped keep mind and body together, particularly Robert A. Wallace, Jonathan and Joan Kleinbard, George A. Ranney, Jr., Carol and Kenan Heise, and Alice Turner.

When our nerves and bank account were stretched to the limit, our agent, Timothy Seldes, taught us we could hang on for just a few more months. Our editor, Peggy Brooks, handled the unenviable job of contending with twice-weekly column deadlines, magazine deadlines, and the daily deadlines that three kids demand. She handled this with just the right mixture of sangfroid, understanding, and exasperation.

Before we actually began writing this book, a publisher suggested we focus exclusively on marriage counselors who exploited their clients. We turned down the offer, believing that this could be a false as well as disheartening view of the field. We have encountered the exploiters, but we have discovered many more therapists who were committed to facilitating growth, change, and greater understanding. We are grateful to those honest therapists who have made an immense contribution to this book and to American men and women, married and divorced.

THE MARRIAGE SAVERS

1

Marriage Saving

"Can this marriage be saved?" The question is asked every month in a popular magazine feature and millions of times a month in the privacy of offices, bedrooms, and unspoken thoughts. The question conjures up an image of a strong, heroic type, a steady pillar of strength who knows exactly what to do when those cries of "Help!" rise from the choppy matrimonial waters. He fishes out the wet and bedraggled pair and supplies them with hope, dry clothes, and words of wisdom, a favorite word being "adjustment."

We have purposely called our book "The Marriage Savers" in order to deflate this distorted and distended image of what marital therapy is, who marriage counselors are, and what it takes to help two unhappy partners to help themselves.

First, let's look at the "rescuer" who has been called the marriage counselor and is now more often termed the therapist. A therapist or therapy team may be endowed with sufficient emotional strength, insight, and experience to help you resolve a marital or sexual conflict. A therapist or therapy team may also fall into one of the following categories which represent a detriment to your marriage:

(1) The frauds. They have little or no professional training in medicine, psychology, or social work. Whether crude or supersophisticated, these charlatans are direct descendants of the patent medicine peddlers and quacks who hawked their fake cures to our unsuspecting ancestors. They can be exposed by a couple with the presence of mind to ask the right questions and to insist on recommendations.

(2) Professional mismatch. These are therapists whose training or clinical background is not suitable for your needs. Remember that a psychologist who has his PhD from a top university may have spent many years working in a laboratory with rats, mice, or monkeys—not people. An industrial psychologist may be insightful with factory workers but ineffectual with fractious housewives or philandering husbands. A psychiatrist may have spent

his or her time treating psychotics and schizophrenics. Although this is typically part of psychiatric training, you will want to know what experience the individual has had with relatively well patients. A gynecologist is not necessarily sophisticated in the area of human sexual response. Medical schools have only begun programs in this field in the last ten years, so there are thousands of practicing physicians who may be less sophisticated about sex and marital problems than you are.

(3) Personality mismatch. During the initial interview, do you find yourself frightened by the therapist, repulsed by him or her, offended by the therapist's manner or lack of consideration? You should feel comfortable with the therapist and receive assurance that he/she/they feel comfortable with you. Therapists have admitted to us that they occasionally come across a patient whom they simply can't treat. Most of them will admit this only after months of taking the patient's money. A few will ask if you feel comfortable with them. But you are the consumer here. You are paying the bill and expecting a service. Communication is absolutely vital to any form of therapy, so make sure you can talk to your marriage counselor or therapist comfortably.

(4) Exploiters. Exploitation need not be limited to frauds and phonies. In fact, it's quite easy for someone with a bit of sophistication to realize that a person with no training is an exploiter. The marriage counselor who tells you, "I reads the minds and I helps the marriage," is obviously not legitimate. It's the therapists with degrees and clinical experience who exploit their patients economically, sexually, or psychologically that are the most dangerous.

Some therapists charge exorbitant fees. Many charge for an additional hour if the couple goes five minutes over the allotted fifty-minute session. And many therapists keep patients in therapy to pay their own rent, not to help them with a particular problem.

A number of therapists exploit their patients sexually. Since therapists are not licensed in most states, they can't be disbarred or publicly dishonored or have their freedom to practice revoked. Even some of the major professional associations have not adopted any formal proscription against such unethical practices as seducing a patient.

Finally, a therapist can make use of the patient to satisfy his or her own neurotic needs. Such counselors may encourage extreme dependence. They may set themselves up as authorities and do little to encourage the self-esteem vital to helping the individual to solve his or her own problems.

In short, therapists are no better or worse than the rest of the human race. A number of them—such as Virginia Satir, Helen Singer Kaplan, William Masters, Virginia Johnson, and Carl Whitaker have made contributions which deserve our respect and gratitude. But reverence for any person calling himself/herself a therapist may cloud your judgment and prevent you from selecting a person or team that can help you with your situation.

The point is to stop seeing yourself and your spouse as that drowning couple totally dependent on a lifeline. Marital problems are inevitable. The question for a husband and wife is not whether you have marital problems, but whether or not you have the resources to deal with your problems, and ultimately whether or not you are willing to invest the time, money, and emotional outlay necessary to examine your relationship. Many couples are vaguely aware of their sick, less than satisfactory relationship, but they are afraid to examine what they've got. They don't want to start peeling the onion for fear that they will find themselves, like Peer Gynt, with nothing but layers of dry decaying skin that crumbles and leaves them bereft of even the semblance of solid life.

Others may be suspicious of marriage counselors or ignorant of what goes on at, say, a sex clinic. We have heard couples, and particularly wives, say over and over again, "I was scared to death when we went for our first session. I didn't want to admit I was going to the nuthouse. I felt we were the only ones who had a problem like this."

We hope to show you that there are effective therapists who have helped couples to rediscover, or recognize for the first time, the special qualities they can enjoy in themselves and each other.

We will show you how to avoid frauds, mismatches, and exploiters. We will give you detailed estimates of the costs of various therapies which can serve as your guidelines. We will demonstrate through the actual experiences of other couples (whose names and occupations have been changed) how various legitimate therapists operate. More important, we will report how the couples themselves contributed to the changes in their relationships.

In short, we would like you to think of yourselves as a consumer shopping for a service. You are not a freak of nature because you fight with your husband, because he doesn't talk to you, because she doesn't have an orgasm, because he ejaculates after three strokes, because your kids are misbehaving in school, because you enjoy sex wearing a leather jacket or thinking of yourself as Batman. While each marital, sexual, or psychological problem has a unique coloration, there are many universals.

We think you will recognize, in the actual stories of couples whom we have interviewed, many of your own conflicts. We hope their experiences, and the explanations of some of the top therapists in the country, will encourage you to become a discriminating shopper for marital counsel.

THE STATE OF OUR UNIONS

We have moved into an age of sexual and social relativity, which has encouraged the chronically dissatisfied couples to divorce and the complacent to be chronically dissatisfied. Though our marriages are probably just as good as Grandma's, the satisfactions we may enjoy seem dwarfed by the presence of other possibilities which religion and mores no longer exclude. It's as if we had moved our belongings from a small house into a mansion inhabited by others. In the wings are unmarried couples living together, couples who swap mates, bisexuals, homosexuals, liberated loners. The gargantuan rooms make our possessions, which once seemed attractive and ample, appear meager and shabby. We keep hearing the activities of those others in the wings, and we keep wondering how our life-style compares. We know much more about what we don't know. The periphery of our ignorance has increased, and as Alfred North Whitehead noted when comparing the learned person to the ignorant one, this increase in awareness makes us less blissful, less smug, less secure. We are reduced to humility just when the society is calling for assertiveness.

For instance, we know that we don't know about group marriages. In one of the only extant studies of this arrangement, thirty-five group marriages were identified and followed; all thirty-five had dissolved after one year. Still, we can't help speculating on the possible values of such an arrangement, no matter how illusory those rewards might be. Swinging couples, who number close to one million and have been studied more extensively, appear to give up on mate swapping after a year because the satisfactions are not commensurate with the enormous amount of time and energy spent locating new partners. Nevertheless, every housewife and househusband with a TV or newspaper *knows* about swinging, knows that that's another experience he/she has missed, and wonders if those swingers aren't having more fun. The gradual, cumulative satisfactions of marriage seem less worthy than the fast fulfillment that seems to be enjoyed by these unattached or unconventional others. Life was much less perplexing when man and God confirmed the once and final choice of matrimony as the one true way. Now even the happiest of marriages grow restive. In the personhood era, is anything or anyone worth the postponement of our individual satisfactions? That question places the whole institution of marriage in jeopardy.

Beyond this general malaise, there are predictable crisis points which are peculiar to married life in the Bicentennial period. It couldn't have been easier to grow old in the 1770's. But there were fewer people living beyond what is now retirement age. Those who did survive into their eighties, like Franklin and Jefferson, did not often do so in strict monogamy. With childbirth and illness taking a greater toll, the heartier mate might have two or three wives, or husbands, in a lifetime. Since sociology was unheard of and no one but the puritanical church elders was studying "EMS" (extramarital sex), we don't know how faithful the average colonial husband or wife was, only that "perceived opportunity" must have been low for men and practically nonexistent for women. The opportunity of living with one mate for fifty years, highly unlikely for most couples in Franklin's time, is now a common prospect for those who marry in their early twenties—a prospect which poses serious difficulties for those of us with less moral clout than the founding fathers.

Forces which once drew families together now tend to alienate them. Mobility in its present form becomes a new phenomenon on the family crisis scene. Moving from one locale to another means a loss of support from relatives, friends, and neighbors; this was true when our pioneer ancestors moved in those long arduous treks, but they had survival issues to occupy their minds. The typical move which a modern family makes from one locale to another is not accompanied by threats of Indians, famine, or disease. Often the move is made because a better job is offered, a larger home is available, a more affluent community or a more leisurely life-style beckons, so that survival becomes less of a problem. The mind is freed up to turn on the issues of alienation, emotional dissatisfactions, and latent marital conflicts.

Economic survival problems tend to take precedence over marital problems even in our era. Couples we interviewed who had serious economic difficulties usually faced them with a united front. But when the economic crisis was past, couples had the leisure to look at their relationship, to think of such things as personal fulfillment and sexual satisfaction. It was at that point, when they had made it financially, that the relationship was scrutinized and found wanting. The men often wanted to forget their past inadequacies as breadwinners by seeking out women who didn't "know them when . . ." and the women wanted to look back to those courtship days from their more affluent perspective, wishing they could keep the new comforts and have the old closeness. Thus, even though unemployment and economic reverses increase tension in the marriage, success seems a greater divider of spouses than hard times.

The temporary glue of tough times often fails to hold the marriage of a younger couple together. The self-interest of the young wife who earns almost as much as her husband, does not always make her want to stick with him to forestall the economic bind. She knows she can make it on her own. If he loses his job, he's going to become more difficult to live with. She's been trained not to take it. Her threshold for injustice is low, as is her capacity for self-sacrifice. Thus, economic necessity, which had held marriages of earlier vintage together, in the recession of the seventies becomes another cause of divorce.

As for children, they no longer keep marriages together, and they frequently intensify the marital problem or become the most visible symptom of marital ills. The childless couple is no longer an oddity; in some circles it is the couple who decides to have children who now appears foolish and wasteful. If self-interest and self-fulfillment expressed in terms of salary and status are the ultimate goals, what is the point of spending time, money, and emotional energy on dependent and useless kids? The more we have learned about children's motivations, needs and rights, the less we seem to want them around. No one wants to return to the days of the workhouse, the abuses of child labor, the cruel indentures and premature apprenticeships. But in the enlightened decades of postwar child-rearing, children have been rendered useless to adults, except as necessary possessions in the province of the acquisitive and competitive nuclear family. At the same time that we have rendered our children useless and dependent, we ourselves, the adults, have discovered that we were denied our childhood pleasures. We are picking up "vouchers" for spontaneity, creativity, intimacy. Why should a couple have to spend the money that could buy them a stereo or a vacation on Johnny's piano lessons? Why should they have to worry about the kids when they have an impulse to make love in the living room at four in the afternoon?

This state of affairs, in which parents and children are vying for similar privileges, has left many couples resenting and hating their offspring while others simply don't know what in the world to do with them. The onset of adolescence—a special period of life unheard of in the days when boys and girls of thirteen, fourteen, fifteen were working in farms, shops, mines, or mills alongside their mothers and fathers—now becomes a hurdle on which many marriages falter. When that trying adolescent period coincides with mother's menopause and father's "midolescence," most therapists declare an automatic state of emergency.

Considering these once centripetal forces which now have become centrifugal—pulling children and spouses away from the matrimonial center—it is no wonder that the divorce rate is, for the first time in our history, higher than the marriage rate.

Those of us who are still married seem to be wandering in the desert. It may not be until the next generation, when children grow up with the new notions of sex roles now in the air, that couples and families will again feel some degree of comfort and security.

In the meantime we know more about the exodus than we do about the promised land. We look for signs, portents, leaders. We look for marriage savers.

2

Therapists

We'd like you to think of marriage counseling, indeed the entire field of therapy, as a marketplace. The marketplace was once a small one with only a few versions of two basic products.

One product was psychoanalysis—a long, costly process of delving into one's past in order to free the individual of growth-stunting neuroses. The success of analysis depended upon the special one-to-one relationship between patient and analyst, a relationship from which spouse and children were excluded except as they appeared through the words and feelings of the patient.

The other product was adjustment therapy—a comparatively inexpensive, short-term process of talking about marital problems in order to have the husband and wife come to a better understanding of each other. The success of this kind of marriage counseling depended upon the couple, particularly the wife, realizing that with some concessions from the other, both could live together, and in any case, the adjusting was better than admitting failure and getting a divorce.

But look at the marketplace now. It has changed and expanded to such an extent that a couple hoping to find a cure for an ailing marriage may not even know the name brands—Gestalt, Transactional Analysis, Bioenergetics, Psychodrama, Behavior Modification, Encounter Groups, Family Therapy, Sex Clinics, Pastoral Counseling, Marriage Encounter, Feminist Therapy— to mention a few. In this chapter we'd like to familiarize you with some of the newer therapies, particularly those which come loosely under the umbrella of the "Human Potential Movement" or "humanistic" therapies. In succeeding chapters we will introduce you to family therapy and to legitimate sex clinics as well as sexploitation clinics. Elements of these approaches to therapy will appear in our examination of social service agencies which serve many mobile Americans as a substitute extended family when

emotions reach the boiling point. Finally we'll turn to a section of the therapy marketplace which may interest couples who simply want to make married life more exciting and satisfying, couples who may never have considered marriage counseling but want some insurance against the growing
threat of divorce.

In this book we focus on those therapies in which husband and wife may
participate as a couple— *conjoint* therapy as it is called. This excludes psychoanalysis, since psychoanalysis excludes spouse and family. We believe
that the marriage relationship needs to be examined as well as the needs and
neuroses of the individuals. The therapies we highlight may be used with individuals, but they have been used successfully with both partners participating. Many of the finest marital therapists in the country have been
trained in psychoanalysis but they have modified these techniques to embrace the problems of husbands and wives. As Fritz Redl, a student of
Freud and world-renowned authority on juvenile problems, told us, "I have
the feeling that if Freud were alive today, he would be a marriage counselor.
Freud always went where the action was. In Vienna, it was one on one. In
the United States it's counseling couples."

A second bias of ours excludes that kind of marriage counseling which
will not allow for divorce. We have found that the best therapy—whatever
the brand and model—helps individuals to exercise more freedom through a
better understanding of their situation and the possibilities available to them.
The possibility of divorce is not one which should be urged on couples or
glorified. But there are cases in which one or both individuals can no longer
tolerate the marriage. Coercion is not, we think, the business of marriage
counseling.

Men and women in the 1970's probably have no more marital difficulties
than they had in the 1940's or 1950's. The difference is couples today believe
they have a right to feel better. Never before in the history of marital relations have so many husbands and wives believed they were entitled not only
to be free of boredom and suffering, but free to experience, on a fairly regular basis, satisfaction, joy, and even ecstasy. This feeling of possibilities
concerning sexual and emotional satisfactions has created an unprecedented
demand for feeling good. To meet this demand, an enormous supply of gurus, therapists, trainers, facilitators, group leaders, and swamis have rushed
to the marketplace.

Unfortunately, those who have come to the bazaar of human potential
wares usually come feeling very needy, longing to find a way to resurrect the
dead senses that used to tingle at the sight of each other, or the balm for un-
bearably raw nerves, or the method to allow two people to shift gears too
monotonously meshed. They hope that a dramatic change in their behavior
and marriage will occur as if by magic. They look at the modern therapies
and think they see magic.

Take Gestalt therapy. It looks like magic when a man who has hated his father for twenty-five years can talk to an empty chair, pretending his father is sitting there and finally mustering the courage to tell that imagined father to stop running his life. It's the modern-day miracle at Lourdes, a break-through, an epiphany, what Gestaltists call a *satori.* But what will the man do after this miracle of awareness? Will this new knowledge that his father is no longer in control actually change the man's life?

It looks like magic when a schizophrenic who was deserted by her mother and exploited by her father and now can trust no man including her husband takes a tennis racket and hits a mattress with all the venom that has poisoned her life since childhood, when her husband sees the performance and under-stands that he is not the cause and tenderly holds and comforts her with new awareness. For that moment the woman is grounded, centered, whole, and the process does have the aura of magic. But will that half hour in the office of a bioenergetic therapist change that woman, that marriage? Can bioener-getics make her set aside her hangups as so many people have left their crutches and braces at Ste. Anne-de-Beaupré, healed by faith?

Therapists have no magic. What the best of them have is an ability born of natural empathy, learning, supervised training and—yes—faith in human possibilities to support your efforts to change your life. What the worst of them have is a line, a *shtick,* a patter born of the belief that people are there to be used and taken; if the right pitch is made, the snake oil will be sold. The quack may call himself a humanist, a behaviorist, a Reichian, Rankian, or Freudian, but the underlying cynicism—the wish to control and exploit—are the same.

Your best bet in making your way through this maze of therapies is: (1) Learn—by asking questions, reading, and speaking to people who have therapeutic experience—what a particular approach is supposed to do. (2) Never submit to anything—in the name of humanism, growthfulness, behaviorism, or any other "ism"—that seems humiliating.

And bear in mind that the newer therapies, which owe a greater debt than is usually acknowledged to Freud and his followers, can be very useful in marriage counseling because they tend to accelerate the process of change, dramatize the conflicts in the marriage, confront the crippling griefs, fears, and hates from the past. In theory, they reduce the authority of the thera-pist.

Above all the new therapies offer the advantage of being understandable. For example, any one of us can understand the basics of transactional analy-sis, which is why *Games People Play, Born to Win,* and *I'm O.K.—You're O.K.* sell more than all the writings of Freud. But the ease of understanding brings with it a catch. If you can understand, so can anyone else. If you are convinced that you can explain transactional analysis after reading one pa-perback, someone else can have the same conviction. He/she/they can rush with this conviction to the therapy marketplace. And since that marketplace has many stalls and few regulations, the untutored, superficial, and therefore useless or even dangerous version of TA therapy can be sold at the same price as more profound, worthwhile, learned, applicable varieties.

In a normal marketplace only children believe every merchant. Adults are skeptical, ask questions, handle the merchandise, compare goods and prices. But in the therapy marketplace we are all children.

If we have one goal in this book it is simply to have you recognize that in seeking help for your marriage, you are an adult consumer shopping for a service.

GESTALT THERAPY

In a lecture delivered to the American Association of Marriage and Family Counselors, Los Angeles Gestalt therapist Robert Resnick provided this example of the Gestalt approach. A woman comes to the therapist claiming she wants to know why she is fat. Resnick tells her, "I can't help you. I can help you to become aware of what you are doing and how you are doing it. If you want to take action based on that awareness, if you want to change what you are doing, I can help."

Gestaltists are convinced that "the purpose of therapy is not to gain a dizzying number of insights. The purpose of therapy is to change behavior, experience, or both." Resnick claims, "Behavior *is* caused and knowing the whys has nothing to do with change."[1] Resnick believes too much help can prevent the patient from standing on his own two feet.

The founder of Gestalt therapy, Fritz Perls, had an aversion to too much explanation and too little confrontation. To cut through the endless talk, Perls developed a style which included direct, often crude language and a number of techniques to discourage dependency. When he realized a patient was rationalizing to avoid confronting a problem, he would call it "mind-fucking." Resnick, a student of Perls, quotes his mentor in stating that "The essence of Gestalt therapy is allowing (by frustrating) the patient to discover that he can 'wipe his own ass.' "[2]

Marriage counselor Robert Saltmarsh, who is associate professor of educational psychology and guidance at Eastern Illinois University, practices in Charleston, Illinois. He has a PhD in psychology, two years of special training at the Gestalt Institute in Cleveland, twelve years of experience, and a willingness to utilize other approaches to therapy when they are suitable.

"One of the objects of Gestalt therapy," according to Saltmarsh, "is to reactivate a sense of responsibility for one's moment-by-moment existence." Gestalt therapy will try to remain utterly focused on the emerging surface, be it fatness, marital hostility, or sexual dysfunction. Whatever is—is. The emerging surface is the Gestalt. The Gestaltist does deal with the past, but in a present-oriented way. A woman wants to discuss her mother because she thinks her mother is profoundly affecting her marriage even though her mother died four years ago. The Gestaltist doesn't want to hear those childhood stories. He wants her to discuss her relationship with her mother only as it affects the present context.

"What I'm doing now is I'm running my life on the basis of a fear that my mother wouldn't like me unless I ran it this way. She wouldn't like a lady who chooses husband over children, pleasure over sacrifice, whim over obligation." If the woman becomes aware of what she is doing and how she is doing it—running her life based on an imagined fear and depriving herself and her husband of spontaneous pleasures—then she can make some choices. Saltmarsh sees choice-making as a critical part of the Gestalt model. Resnick calls it becoming "response-able." In fact, the goal of most responsible therapies is to make individuals, couples, families, or groups able to choose from and respond with a wider range of alternatives.

The Gestalt technique for dealing with the disapproving mother sitting on one's shoulder casting aspersions about the quality of one's personal life might be this. "We're going to put your mother over here in this chair. Just imagine that she's there, and tell her what she's been doing to you for twenty-five years." The point of this would be to bring that into the context of "Mother, what I am letting you do to me right now is having you keep me from going on vacation with my husband, letting you keep me from wearing a black negligee and garter belt which would be a turn-on for my husband but which I don't think you'd like, making me hate and berate him because he is funloving, which is one of the reasons I married him but which you never liked. Mother, we no longer have the relationship that I established for myself in my own child perceptions twenty-five years ago. This is to say good-bye to that part of you."

Saltmarsh describes this as a classic Gestalt event—saying good-bye to distorted events that have been exerting influence from the past. At that moment of breakthrough—a sudden grasping of the whole—the empty chair may seem magical. But if you are the woman in question, how do you integrate the awareness into a new process, a new way of doing things with your husband? Do you have the desire and resources for change? Can the therapist back up the empty-chair *satori* with his own acute observations? You will want to keep such a question in mind when you interview a Gestalt therapist.

The Gestaltist has license to devise "exercises"—something the therapist has done before with some kind of predictable result—and "experiments," something that has a low predictability but may heighten awareness more than just talking. Saltmarsh—this time working with his wife as his co-therapist—was treating a husband and wife who were both musicians. They both had good ears, musically. But in terms of communication the wife was demonstrating that she didn't have her own ears. Fritz Perls observed that people have holes in their way of living, holes for ears, holes for eyes, holes in their personalities. The wife in this case was refraining from doing or saying things because she was predicting they wouldn't sound right to other people. As a Gestaltist, Saltmarsh observed that the woman had taken her own ears and given them to other people. He improvised an experiment.

> I asked her to put her hands over her own ears, to clamp them tightly so she couldn't hear. She did that for a few moments and said she really didn't like it much. I asked her to go around to the other three of us and take her ears, pull as much of her ears off as she could and put them on us. She began to experience the awareness of how much she governs herself on the basis of what she thinks it's going to sound like to her husband. It was, to use Perls' term, a *satori,* a waking up. Her face became energized and radiant. We could have sat around and talked about not having ears or giving our ears to other people. But in three or four minutes of an experimental activity we got there a lot quicker. Maybe we only move, as Fritz said frequently, one ten-thousandth of a unit toward our own fulfillment, but at least we move that much. It's very likely that the woman will make the same error in the future, very likely that we will have to rework some of that. But each time we make a step forward. I am not willing to say, "You come and work with me and as a consequence of our work you're going to go out of here a changed person." I don't have that kind of power. The powers that I have are that I'm a very, very good observer of myself. And I'm a pretty good observer of you. I guess that boils down to a message that if you wish to come and spend an hour or an hour and a half with me under the conditions that we're going to observe what's going on within ourselves and between us, your chances of making more responsible choices may be increased. I predict they will. I hope that they will. But I can't take responsibility for making you do that.

Just as the couple coming to a therapist hopes to wind up with more alternatives, we would suggest that the therapist, whatever his favored approach, should have a number of alternative responses at his/her/their disposal. If he can only use the empty chair—the process conducive to a *satori*—if he can never work in a different way to suit the problem, then he seems a poor risk, considering the infinite number of problems posed by different people.

Bob Saltmarsh says:

> I've become quite impatient with the arguments between humanists and behaviorists. To me, almost all counseling is based on learning theory. In marriage counseling a couple is going to learn some things that they don't

already know, some different ways of being and doing and thinking. That's a basic part of the behavioral idea. I don't find any argument at all. If I need to work with a person by putting them on a reinforcement schedule, then I'll do that.

I remember one girl who walked into my office the second year I was there. I'd never seen her before and she seemed to be rather desperate. She said, "I've heard that you may be able to help me," and I said, "Well, I don't know if I can. What is it that you'd like help with?" She said, "Well, I screw too much." I said, "What is your frequency?" And she said during the previous week she had been to bed with fifteen different people. To use any model but a behavioral one seemed ludicrous to me, so I said, "Well, let's make a contract. Are you willing to cut that in half next week?" And she said she didn't know how she could do it. How could she say no? So we practiced a couple of ways that she could say no and we made out a form on an index card. The next week when she came in she was just beaming. She had it down to seven. We established that she had to have sexual activity. We accepted that. But what are the conditions under which she could have it constructively? Well, she wanted to find somebody where there was some caring if it was possible, and she wanted to begin to limit her number of partners. Within a space of three weeks we got her down to two. Now, these were not love relationships but there was some evidence of caring. So that's where we got her to. She had two sexual partners. She could be with either one of them as many times as she wanted to, but that's where she stayed. That's purely a behavioral approach. There are no psychodynamics involved except that the girl's walking with more pride; she's got life; she's not carrying around all this horribleness about herself and she's becoming much more productive with her academic work, and all those things which are psychodynamic, but they are indirect and contingent with her sexual behavior.

A specific behavior was presented—sexual behavior getting out of control in her life. Now, why in the hell should I have tried other therapies when there was a specific behavioral problem presented? That happens infrequently with the people that I work with. People come in feeling lonely, depressed, anxious, and so forth, and there are no behavioral specifics. But this was a case where there were. Why should I say, "Well, I'm a humanist. I don't believe in behaviorism"?

This kind of flexibility strikes us as the mark of a superior therapist. It comes of knowledge, experience, and a keen awareness of what is suitable for the situation at hand. No branch of therapy has exclusive rights to these qualities. There are no college degrees to guarantee that a therapist has these resources. You must be the judge.

There is, for example, the therapist Diane Wayne saw who thought of himself as closely aligned to Perls and the here-and-now point of view. He is the highest-priced therapist in one of this country's largest cities.

Dr. X sounded like other reputable therapists in the human potential movement. He drew heavily on the nonjudgmental, existential, present-oriented approach. He claimed to believe in the creative possibilities of each individual. In fact, he had a degree in psychiatry from a reputable school and had appeared frequently on TV because of his air of authority and his handsome appearance.

So how was Diane Wayne to suspect anything? Her boyfriend had been in therapy with Dr. X for several months. Dr. X convinced Diane, who is a beautiful woman, that she needed therapy also. Diane's youth had been stormy. Her parents had each been married four times, and at twenty-five she herself was a divorcée with a three-year-old daughter. She had not yet tapped her considerable artistic resources and so she looked for her total satisfaction to her young, rather unstable lover.

After a few months of weekly visits Diane noticed that Dr. X was becoming suggestive, then seductive, during therapy. Dr. X called Diane's apartment one evening. "There was Turkish harem music playing in the background. He suggested that I come on over. I was really shocked, shocked and confused, and I turned him down." Diane abruptly ended therapy two days later, telling Dr. X that she wasn't going to pay $35 an hour to have him make passes—especially since the therapy had been originally oriented to the goal of improving her relationship with another man. A few months after terminating treatment Diane broke up with her boyfriend. She felt confused and upset with no place to turn—both her parents lived at distant locations and were distant from her in their concerns. (After four divorces her mother was with a new man in California.) In desperation she turned to Dr. X.

"Dr. X said that I should definitely still be in therapy. He said maybe we could do both—see each other as friends and also do the therapy. He knew that I had had this rift with my boyfriend, since my boyfriend was still in therapy with him. He knew that I was vulnerable. He himself was in between marriages; I hear he's on this third marriage now. Anyway, he urged me to come over for dinner. As soon as I walked in the door, he grabbed me, started kissing me, and led me into his bedroom. The whole experience was very bizarre, very, very devastating. He tried to get me to stay the weekend, claiming that he couldn't stand to be alone. I said I had to get out and he became rude and surly. He called the next day, urging me to be his patient. He knew that I was coming undone with all the confusion in my life. He even said, 'Gee, I feel like I've dropped you on your head.' "

In fact, that's what Dr. X had done. He had exploited a beautiful woman, knowing she was psychologically vulnerable, and set her moving in a downward spiral of confusion and helplessness which would end one year later in a mental breakdown. During the four months Diane had seen him in therapy, Dr. X had opened up many issues without offering support; then he had betrayed her trust by pursuing her, catching her at a low point and leaving her bereft of hope in therapists, in men. "It's like he opened up a box of things that needed to be opened up but in a constructive, supportive manner. I came away from the experience feeling deeply troubled, helpless—none of these things had I felt when I came to him."

After a number of harrowing experiences—including one LSD trip, which left her with a recurring hallucination of the world coming to an end, and a cancer scare, which finished off her shattered nerves—Diane made the slow climb back to stability. She has remarried now, but still retains bitter feelings toward Dr. X. She is contemplating legal action but hasn't decided whether her case is strong enough.

On March 19, 1975, a woman named Julie Roy won a $350,000 damage suit against psychiatrist and then *Cosmopolitan* columnist Renatus Hartogs. Dr. Hartogs was charged by the thirty-six-year-old Ms. Roy with inducing her to have sex while she was undergoing therapy. Four other psychiatrists testified that Ms. Roy, who had been hospitalized for mental problems several times since the alleged Hartogs "treatments," was telling the truth. Several other former patients of Dr. Hartogs confirmed the psychiatrist's propensity for sexual intimacy during therapy, and one former patient stated her intention to file a separate suit.

We were curious to see how Dr. X would react to the decision in the Hartogs case. After discussing the general topic of marriage counseling with him—he now charges $50 per half hour and $100 per hour session with a couple—we asked him his opinion.

"Now, in the heyday of malpractice," said Dr. X, "any patient can turn on any doctor for anything. That girl [referring to Ms. Roy] probably was a psychopath. I wouldn't presume Dr. Hartogs was that destructive, just too friendly to that girl. It isn't only therapists who sleep with their patients. There are other doctors, lawyers, ministers who do the same. What happens is probably mutual consent, mutual attraction. The therapist may be equally vulnerable. Maybe he's got problems at home. There are schools of therapy that say their patients need this sexual experience or sexual enlightenment, though they usually don't feel such enlightenment is called for when the patient is an old, beat-up broad."

Dr. Willard Gaylin of Columbia University Medical School—one of those who condemned Dr. Hartogs' behavior in court during the case—estimates that 5 or 10 percent of psychiatrists have sex with their patients. In an interview with Philip Nobile, Dr. Gaylin noted that sexual intimacy with patients is specifically forbidden by the rules of the American Psychiatric Association. (Remember that many therapists are not psychiatrists, do not belong to this association, and thus are not subject to its rules or ethics.)

Dr. Gaylin stressed that the psychiatric code of ethics as well as the Hippocratic oath, whereby the doctor swears to do no harm, are broken when a psychiatrist takes advantage of a patient. In Dr. Gaylin's view, and in the opinion of many authorities including Sigmund Freud, mutual agreement does not absolve the psychiatrist of malpractice in such cases.[3]

Dr. X cannot be blamed for Diane's fragile mental state, any more than Dr. Hartogs can be judged totally responsible for all Ms. Roy's mental problems. But both men, who were trusted to do—at the very least—no harm, betrayed their patients when they were least able to cope with betrayal.

We would not want the Roy-Hartogs malpractice suit or this story of malpractice to serve as an excuse for high-priced therapists to claim they have to increase their rates because of the cost of insurance. Rather we see it as a warning to therapists: Sex with patients, whether the patient wants it or not, can be terribly harmful to the patient and very expensive to the therapist.

There is an interesting sequel to Diane's story. When her present husband proposed marriage to her, Diane felt they should go to a marriage counselor. Diane wanted to be sure they were making the right decision. She was afraid of being pushed over the edge again. "I wanted support and understanding. I needed to feel in control of the crazy aspects of my reality." This time Diane had better luck. She found a psychiatric social worker, purposely choosing one who was considerably older, not attractive to her, a gentle man. He accepted Diane's view that her life had been rather bizarre, saying, "I understand the duality of your flirtation with the dramatic view of life, your ambivalence. You don't want to be trapped into leading a bizarre life, but you need to feel your own individuality, your own specialness."

In Diane's view this acceptance saved a lot of time. "I didn't have to resist him. I didn't have to go through that whole thing where you have to get more crazy so you'll be taken seriously. The questions I had about Jeff, my husband, started to be settled in the affirmative. As I got stronger the relationship seemed much more positive. The therapist understood and supported my striving for strength. I started to paint—which is terribly important to me—and I began to feel strong enough to marry Jeff without believing I was dealing from weakness. It's not a syrupy happy ending. I still question things. I know I can see my therapist if I should need him. And I have a healthy relationship with Jeff."

That may not be a syrupy happy ending, but it is the kind of outcome Diane, her husband, and her counselor can be proud of.

Diane, Julie Roy, and too many other women and men are what is known in the therapy world as "casualties." They suffer a deep psychological wound as a result of their therapy, a wound which may heal—as it did in Diane's case—but which leaves noticeable scars. Unlike a battle between enemy forces, the joining of therapist and client should produce no casualties, no wounds. At the very least one should be able to declare the sessions ineffective, the pairing of counselor and client a mismatch.

But casualties do occur and they are most likely to occur when a therapist with a charismatic personality or a passionate evangelical belief in one mode of therapy evokes an emotional high—a catharsis, a letting go, or a letting down of defenses—on the part of the client. It's a classic Elmer Gantry or Marjoe revival rip-off. But men and women who consider themselves much too sophisticated to be taken in by old-time religious hucksters are uniquely vulnerable to intellectual patter, the allure of degrees, the relief of believing, and the comfort of knowing one's faith is in the exclusive and chic province of "psychology."

Ironically, the very gurus of awareness and growth often lack the awareness that they are doing harm. Eli (not his real name) had incorporated every word of the humanistic vocabulary. People should be congruent, centered, and grounded. Experience should be growthful, actualizing, and shared. One never asked why because that might lead to mind-fucking—intellectual intercourse which could never lead to a *satori*. Hirsute and heavy, Eli even looked like the founder of the Gestalt movement, Fritz Perls. Perls had brought to his work forty years of experience in the psychoanalytic and other modes of therapy. Eli had a masters degree in psychology and a sincere belief that sexual experimentation could solve most marital problems. Eli had taken the concept of *Open Marriage*—which authors George and Nena O'Neill saw as a means of maintaining self-identity within marriage—and interpreted it to mean multiple sexual alliances which couples maintain openly.[4] Eli believed that affairs outside one's primary relationship are good for every couple, and further, that those affairs must never be kept secret—that would be dishonest. In Eli's view they must be revealed even to the last detail.

Eli was certainly not the only one to take the *Open Marriage* book as a license to participate in a number of relationships. He was not even the only marriage counselor to work with couples who wanted to maintain other sexual relationships outside the marriage. He was unique, in our experience, as a therapist who advocated multiple sexual relations for *every* couple. But being a marriage counselor, Eli's misinterpretation of open marriage was particularly unfortunate since he was in a position to spread this notion as if it were gospel truth.

Ben and Brenda Parks, a young black couple with two children, happened to go to Eli for marriage counseling when he was particularly high on this open-marriage-as-interpreted-by-Eli dogma.

They had sexual problems and communications problems. Eli's therapeutic approach consisted of the following: (1) spend a half hour talking about the problem of premature ejaculation, telling the husband that he will get over it if he just stops worrying; (2) have the couple attend a weekend encounter group where they are the only blacks and the only married people; (3) suggest that they each experiment with other sexual partners as long as they promise to tell each other what they do and who they do it with.

Ben Parks' account of this therapy and its consequences illustrates a number of problems at once. It suggests the effects of isolation on the housewife, the marital strains of male ambition and female lack of fulfillment, the importance of recognizing where a couple is coming from in terms of their racial and religious backgrounds, and finally, the difference between an idea that sounds "growthful" and an idea that helps a marriage.

A friend recommended Eli. We had been having difficulty in our marriage for some years—a lack of communication, a lack of really getting into each other's heads. We were married at eighteen, and in the eleven years since then we had changed quite a bit. My wife always felt that I was somewhat dominant and that she always subjugated her personality to mine. After going to data processing school at night I landed a job at a big electronics firm.

It was a move out of a labor situation into a white-collar situation, a move that I jumped at. We moved to a suburb in which Brenda and I and our two kids made up almost half of the total black population. This was strictly a bedroom suburb. That plus the lack of blacks, plus the fact that we weren't really strong church people, made the isolation really severe for Brenda. I was so busy all day rubbing shoulders with PhD's and grooving on the prestige, I would just come home after being gone for nine, ten hours, and drop in front of the idiot tube.

We both had ambitions. We both came from middle-class black neighborhoods rather than the true ghetto. She's from a family of two. She had desires to do things, none of which were being taken care of. She had the kids to mind, no job, few friends. Then there was the sexual problem. In the beginning of our marriage I was very immature about sex—eighteen, no experience. I was uptight about performing. I wasn't relaxed at all. But I never fooled around. I never had much money in the first years, and then there was my Catholic upbringing, very strict, even in the Catholic high school, down on sex, always this underlying thing about sex; this is a thing you don't do. I remember one time when I was in high school they had this so-called retreat and they passed out St. Joseph's cords. You're supposed to tie it around your waist so that it reminds you to stay chaste, a psychological chastity belt for men. It was pretty effective for me.

My wife, Brenda, was the one who called Eli for an appointment. We weren't expecting the gentleman we met—the large body, the beard, the father-confessor voice.

He did try to get us away from accusing each other. We had two or three half-hour sessions, talking about our different problems. Then he suggested this encounter weekend. It was on the East Side, a nice apartment. The first thing we noticed when we got in there was there were no other blacks. I had anticipated a married group and thought there would be at least one other black couple. But there were no married couples and no blacks.

Eli was there when we came in, sitting in the middle of the room on a mattress looking a bit like Buddha. I thought he was high and it was confirmed later that he had been at least blowing a little smoke—which didn't bother me. I didn't have any real experience with encounters. I had seen the specials on the TV news. I had known guys that had gone to different union or company sensitivity training for racial relations, stuff which was supposed to turn a bigot around, but I didn't know what to expect.

The first thing was a sort of touching routine. You go around, you hug everybody in the room—but no one telling what their name was. Then there was the interlocking hands, pairing off and leaning backwards, and coming to a state of balance where you were depending upon the other person and the other person was depending upon you to stand up—trust falls, I think he called them. Then it was inspecting one another's palms. Then there was some transcendental meditation bag—focusing your attention on one point and then voiding your mind of all thoughts so that you would come to this great realization of the absence of thought which was supposedly very relaxing and getting you in tune with your real self.

When I left there that night I was on a trip. I was on an emotional trip. I had been into it—honesty and universal love—and I dug what was going on. My wife was much less impressed. By Saturday morning I was getting signals from my wife that she was beginning to think that this was basically white folks' bullshit.

We spent the day, first evaluating one other person in the group. Then the games. Eli gave us a large sheet of paper—there was this one large, double poster size sheet for the entire group—and each individual in the room was told that this is your paper, totally yours, and you can do anything you want with it, and they put out a box of crayons. Eli stressed that to me: "This is your paper, you have the rights to it." And he told that to everyone else, so that if someone was writing something you didn't like, you had every right to go in there and scratch their stuff off. We had been scribbling for a while when one guy picked up the black crayon and got busy in a corner, bordering off an area for himself in which he had some object, some very boxy-looking object, and he was busy building a wall around it to protect it. People became aware of it and began to attack it with their crayons, everyone writing into his area, and he was getting livid with rage. Eli wouldn't intervene. Maybe he would have said something if we had hit the guy or if he had hit us. Anyway, that was one game we played.

After that, people gave some idea of their problems. Now, sometimes you couldn't see what they had as problems. Like the tall, blond, buxom girl, pretty face, working downtown—free, white, twenty-one, looking like a mini-Mae West. I mean, she says she's got a poor self-image. Well, that seemed to me like a crock of shit. If you're black, living a black experience, you can't take these white folks' difficulties too seriously. They are the power structure, the power figures, the ones that have got. I looked at this big-busted girl and I thought, "Here you are, the white mystique of the sex symbol with a decent job downtown, and you're complaining." Maybe I was wrong, but I felt nobody could see where I was coming from. Still, people were getting into one another.

After lunch it was the drawing paper again, this time individually. Eli went around defining the meaning of the pictures. Actually, he would just find a wall or impediment to a free relationship in almost all of them, except with this one girl because she drew a butterfly. He was telling us we all had hangups. Looking back on it, I think there was a formula to the whole encounter, a standard bag, a rigid format that he had to go through. It didn't matter what you drew. If it was a field of flowers, he would still see it as a wall. He would find a way to imply that there was some impediment between you and totally communicating yourself, that you were hiding behind your role. Now, even then I thought, "So fucking what?" We all know we play roles. I don't think there was any true attempt to have a definition of what the real you was, except it was supposed to be a hell of a lot better than the you that drew the picture.

Now we're getting towards evening, and each one is giving their thing, what's on their mind. At this point I was really going off on just the vicarious delight of getting into other people's business. At one point in time we were told to get up and go to the person you most trusted in the room and tell them one of your inner things. I ego-tripped then because two people came to me and there was this hand-holding bag. I came away with another general impression about the encounter: It's a great place to get laid because you get these people with their defenses down with all this loving one another stuff.

After the dinner break things got heavier. Eli became the questioner, going to each one, digging down deep. People would go through these emotional upheavals, crying and getting it all out of them, and other people would console them. It was obvious that once you broke down, did your crying spiel and got off the hook, Eli was finished. By the time it got around to me I pretty well knew what to do. It was a tense situation. You can really get into other people's problems and get upset with them. You can also avoid getting into them which is what Brenda did. But I readily admit I was into the scene.

Eli stood in front of me; it was my turn to go through an emotional change. I did this confessing thing, admitting my lack of ability to express my love for my wife. Eli said, "Do you love her?" 'Yes, I love her." "Then go tell her." I prostrated myself before Brenda and just told her how much I loved her. She was rubbing my head, but she was making no comments. Then Eli says, "Do you believe that?" As I remember, looking up at her, there was doubt in her eyes, and I could hear her thinking, "Nigger, is you crazy, going through all this ridiculous shit?"

Brenda and I had one more session with Eli, the week after the encounter. This was the spiel that came down: "I'm not going to tell you not to get divorced or to stay together, but I feel that you have a lot going for you. What you should do about your sexual problems, one of the solutions to this, is to get a broader sexual experience. Have this within your marriage. Maintain your marriage and have these outside relationships, and if you're really strong and you've really got it together, you can do this and come back and share this with one another. This will strengthen your marriage."

Now, Eli knew that I was a straight arrow. Many people have this idea of what black dudes are into, but he knew I had been totally faithful, and I felt maybe I was unnatural to be this way. Brenda admitted that she had curiosities about others, which is only natural after her sexual experiences with me were not satisfying. So we listened to Eli and agreed that maybe he was right about this free sex thing. But I knew I wasn't going to volunteer. The guy who had recommended Eli was the guy she wound up in bed with. She told me about it one night, in detail, just like Eli had suggested, and I was off the wall. But I had agreed to it, so I couldn't do anything. For the first time in my life I became impotent. This went on for months. I finally called Eli and he met me in a restaurant. I told him that I was thinking maybe I'd never get it up. Eli looked at me and asked how long I had been impotent. I told him three months. He said, "That's nothing. When I first started living in an open relationship—with Audrey—I was impotent for eight months. I would hate it when I knew she was going out with another man for the weekend. We'd have to spend hours talking about the problem, taping our conversations and playing them back. Now I can just send her a note: 'I hate it, but it's okay.'"

Well, let me tell you, in my depressed state, that wasn't much comfort. I moved out of the house and took a small apartment. The divorce came through five months later. I never saw Eli again.

"I was on an emotional trip," said Ben Parks, remembering his experience with the group that first night. "I had been into it—honestness and universal love—and I dug what was going on." Encounter groups tend to create what Gustave LeBon once called "hallucinations."[5] Ben's hallucinations were typical of group euphoria during an encounter weekend. In numerous interviews with couples who have been to encounter groups, we find that there are no two people more enthusiastic than a man and wife still high on a marathon encounter, still drenched in an oceanic wave of love, caring, and sensual awareness. There are no two people more confused, lost, and finally disillusioned than a couple swept into an encounter experience, stripped of their defenses, then left desolate, with no coping tools or defenses for their exposed psyches.

Yet it is possible for couples to profit from shared experiences. How can a couple decide whether an encounter weekend will offer danger or support? We put this question to a man who has studied encounter groups more extensively and thoroughly than any person in the country—Morton A. Lieberman, PhD, professor of psychology at the University of Chicago and author with Irvin Yalom and Matthew Miles of *Encounter Groups: First Facts*.[6]

Lieberman recommends that any potential encounter group member examine his or her own motives. "Do you feel that an encounter group can 'save' you and change your life? If you expect salvation, major upheavals in your life and your personality, by all means avoid encounter groups," he says. "Your risk of serious psychological distress or damage from such participation is high."

Lieberman and an associate, Jill Gardner, compared the psychological profiles of 656 persons who went to five growth centers (which often sponsor encounter weekends) with profiles of 150 patients in private psychiatric clinical care. They found that three fourths of the people who went to growth centers resembled clinical patients in terms of motivation for seeking help and degree of psychological misery!

If you hope to benefit from an encounter weekend, you should bring to the experience four qualities: (1) a genuine desire to change, but *not* a desperate need to change; (2) a reasonable degree of skepticism; (3) a personal history of relating successfully to people and interacting productively with them; (4) a genuine liking for other humans.

Even if your personal motives are sound, an individual or couple shopping for an encounter weekend must carefully scrutinize the leader. "You are, despite the theoretical paraphernalia that packages him, buying the leader of the group," Lieberman cautions. "Unfortunately, professional degrees are not, per se, a guarantee of competent and constructive encounter leaders. In our own research we found that some highly trained professionals—psychiatrists and psychologists—proved to be destructive leaders at worst, inert at best."

To avoid such leaders, Lieberman recommends these precautions. "Your first problem is to find out as much as possible about the leader before joining his group. Perhaps you will be able to observe another group in session and thus sample the leader. If not (and sometimes this will not be possible), ask the leader to describe what he does and how he does it, so that you, the prospective participant, will have some idea of the type of activity you would be engaging in, and above all, what the leader actually does in the group setting. Talk to people who have been in groups. Question them about how the leader acted toward members of the group."

Then get a good sense of who and what the leader is. "Charismatic encounter leaders are dangerous," Lieberman says flat out. "If a leader is described to you as inspiring, believing totally in what he is doing, imposing, visionary, stimulating, dramatic with a sense of mission—in other words, *a very special person*—you are probably describing a charismatic leader to be avoided at all costs. If the leader has 'the answer,' a monothematic, one-idea approach to change and human development, he should be avoided like the plague."

Do encounter groups, with all their techniques and gimmicks, actually work? This is the question Morton Lieberman sought to answer in reviewing eighteen months of academic surveys of various kinds of encounter group therapy and self-help groups. In his article "Change Induction in Small Groups,"[7] two studies were particularly interesting to him.

Groups of people were told they were going to participate in a weekend designed to produce "changes" in them. Two of the groups became involved in structured and unstructured sensitivity training. Two other groups were exposed to recreational activities, nature walks, dancing in the evenings. All the groups reported that there had been a high degree of change. In fact, the nature walking-dancing group had even more positive things to say about how they felt about themselves than those in the groups that went through the whole rigamarole of encounter techniques.

If the results of encounter group experience are so questionable, why should a couple even consider the possibility? We put this question to Mike Halbert, a PhD psychologist in Philadelphia who spends most of his time in educational and sociological research. Mike does marriage counseling as an avocation, dealing mainly with what he calls "normal neurotics." He has led encounter groups for the Unitarian Church as well as for a local growth center. He sees the encounter group, when run by a responsible leader, as an experimental training ground, a relatively safe place for people to try out new feelings, to test or rehearse new ways of behaving and relating.

"What we tried to do is use the extreme artificiality of a group environment to help people become less artificial. It sounds paradoxical but it isn't. What we keep doing through a bunch of techniques is to encourage people that they will be liked for being honest rather than for being nice. At best, the encounter group is an environment where you can play with and practice emotional behaviors you can't elsewhere. You can be infantile, you can be regressive, you can be assertive, which in a normal social or family life is not an easy thing to do."

In his follow-ups with about 150 people, all of them highly educated, upper middle class members of the Unitarian Church, Halbert says he found that about one-third of them said the encounter experience had been one of the most significant experiences of their lives and that some of them even changed jobs, seeking a work environment which was more "humane." Another third reported that the encounter was an interesting experience, that they had shared some feelings, maybe cried, but in terms of lasting impact it had been "no big deal." Another third said that nothing much happened to them during the encounter and that they didn't feel it was particularly good. A very small percentage said it had been a miserable experience and that it had made them deeply unhappy.

Halbert has also led encounter groups for a growth center for prospective encounter group leaders. "I wouldn't let some of these people lead a sick dog or pussycat. They're crazy!" Many of them, Halbert said, were manipulative with no idea of the psychodynamics involved in groups, and they came on "like gangbusters" despite their total lack of awareness. "I suspect they do a lot of harm," says Halbert, who then dropped out of any association with that growth center.

Some of the things that may be done in the name of growth (including seven people sitting on a woman's back, breaking several of her ribs) are not growthful or therapeutic, but rather pure and simple manipulation. As noted family therapist Virginia Satir told us, "Just because a therapist puts himself or herself in the class of being 'humanistic' does not mean that they are more humanistic in their approach." Like the term "humanistic," the phrase "here and now" can hide a multitude of abuses. The therapeutic salesperson is tuned in to the consumer. He/she knows that we tend to value what is happening now over what has past. Those of us who are emotionally upset are looking for the human touch—not the coolness of a computer or the intellectualizing of a person who stands aloof and takes notes. We ourselves are part of the value shift that produced sensitivity training and the encounter movement; a shift away from intellect, the mind, and symbols toward concrete expressions, the body, and emotions.[8]

Encounter groups can be restorative by allowing us to escape from the prison of our minds and what one therapist calls our masturbational past. It's important to be able to cry rather than talking about sadness, to be able to embrace, rather than talking about caring. But the catharsis that comes of releasing all this pent-up emotion must finally be integrated.

Too many of the so-called humanistic, here-and-now therapies rely on feelings as the solution to problems—feelings which are yelled, shouted, screamed, cried, and sometimes aggressively acted out. Virginia Satir, who has seen too many encounter weekend "casualties," some with broken bones and many with bruised psyches, rejects this type of solution. "I have absolutely no faith whatsoever in catharsis, in the notion that all I have to do is get my feelings out and everything gets well from that. Unless my head gets integrated with it, my body gets integrated with it, and my feelings get integrated with it, I don't become a whole person. If that kind of integration takes place, you have a basic change. If it doesn't take place, it's like a barnacle fastened on."

Encounter weekends rarely provide the time or individual attention necessary to integrate the emotional release into a new or changed behavior pattern. Because of the many limitations and pitfalls of encounter groups, we tend to feel that couples with serious marital problems should steer clear of them unless the group weekend is part of a more personalized, ongoing counseling program.

What about behavior modification, bioenergetics, psychodrama, and transactional analysis—some of the significant approaches which have fed into the encounter movement and now are affecting all phases of therapy? It is hard to find any modern marriage counselor who does not make a spoken "contract" with a couple as to the changes they are seeking (behavior mod); or one who has not suggested to a warring couple that they beat a pillow or mattress to release their anger (bioenergetics); or one who does not suggest that husband and wife reverse roles or assume the role of an absent mother or father who is party to their problem (psychodrama); or one who does not talk of the psychological games couples play, the need to understand each other's "child" ego states, the importance of the "I'm O.K., You're O.K." outlook in married life (transactional analysis). Is your therapist using or misusing these concepts? To help you judge that for yourself, we've gleaned from a harvest of interviews, books, and papers some of the basic ideas behind these four new approaches to therapy.

BEHAVIOR MODIFICATION

The term "behavior modification" conjures up all kinds of scary images—and not without good reason.

Donald M. Baer, professor of human development at the University of Kansas, regards the idea of pain and punishment in therapy as an accounting problem. In an article in *Psychology Today* he gives the example of a man who had a twenty-year history of being a panty fetishist. The man bought, stole, wore, fondled, and masturbated with panties—a compulsion which pained him greatly. After fourteen weeks of electroshock treatments when he held or looked at pictures of women in panties, plus some other therapy and with the help of a considerate and patient girlfriend, the man overcame the painful anxieties he had about women and panties and went on to get married.

Baer, who himself refuses to use pain in his therapy and does not permit his students to do so, still asks society to look at the bottom line. "Which

punishment is tougher and lasts longer?'' he asks, comparing the panty compulsion to electroshock. ''Here we have a bookkeeping problem, not a moral
one.''[9]

Yet we are a moral society or at least a moralizing society. We view pain
as something bad, something evil. Those who would measure or apply pain
with seeming equanimity become in our eyes less than fully human, and
those who could calculate degrees of love have a similar taint.

We had this problem with the ideas of Edwin J. Thomas, professor of social work and professor of psychology at the University of Michigan, who is
also a marriage counselor in Ann Arbor. Thomas speaks in terms of categories, steps, inventories, computers, and assessments. For professor Thomas, the ways husband and wife interact can be treated like any other behavior and broken down in component parts, reinforced, or extinguished. What
is needed in marriage counseling, in Thomas' view, is not more kindness or
empathy but a special technology. Thomas has developed a new apparatus
for studying verbal behavior between couples called SAM (Signal System
for the Assessment and Modification of Behavior). SAM is a device for computing the couples' responses to the therapist's questions. It allows each
mate to indicate what he or she likes and dislikes about what the other says.
Each partner has a control panel. A wooden blind prevents one from seeing
the other. They listen and press a green light for a positive reaction (like,
agree, correct, keep talking), a red light for a negative reaction (dislike, disagree, etc.). The therapist sits and observes the couple and can modify their
conversation either by controlling the light signals the couple sees or verbally guiding the couple.

Why is SAM better than a mere human therapist? Thomas has found that
marriage counseling is too subjective. SAM—with its red lights and green
lights and its built-in tape recorder and computer—gives the therapist some
objective data.

New York psychiatrist and marriage counselor Robert Ravich has developed another way to objectify conflict between couples—the train game (Ravich Interpersonal Game Test). Each partner is given a toy train and two
strips of track—a short, direct route and a looping, longer alternative route.
If both choose the short, direct route they collide (electronically) and their
trains automatically stop until one player agrees to back up. Who will go
first? Will one always be forced to take the long route while the other goes
directly? How is the decision made—by shouting, by a previous discussion,
by calmly discussing the problem, or will the players, as one couple did, pick
up the toy trains and throw them at each other? As with the SAM apparatus,
the train game allows the tester to record the results.[10]

Both SAM and the train game are in experimental stages. They are expensive instruments. The portable SAM is $2,000, the train game costs $3,000—
making these instruments too costly for widespread private use. But who

ever thought tape recordings, television cameras, and videotape equipment would become a part of therapy? For all one's resistance to the eerie 1984 feel of marriage counseling technology, one has to admit that recordings of our behavior can help to bring buried conflicts out into the open. These instruments can be useful tools, as programmed learning machines have become useful tools for the teaching profession. But the teacher, we think, cannot be replaced. A therapist needs more than computers. He/she needs to process this data through the human instrument.

Clearly separating himself from those who quantify behavior is Israel Goldiamond, professor in the departments of psychology and psychiatry at the University of Chicago, who uses behavior modification techniques to help people change the behavior they wish to change.

"I can teach you to start getting out of life the things you want out of life," says Goldiamond, seated in his office near Chicago's Museum of Science and Industry. "If it turns out the things you want out of life, upon analyzing this, are impossible—given the kind of mate you have—and it is worth the problems, then you will get a divorce. I don't consider that necessarily a failure. I'm interested in having people learn what is the appropriate thing to do—in terms of what they are after."

A couple with a fourteen-year-old schizophrenic son came to Dr. Goldiamond as a court of last resort. Their son lay around the house, obese, naked, masturbating all day long. Authorities had told them there was no hope for him and that they would have to institutionalize him in a state mental hospital—something the parents refused to do on moral grounds. "Can you do something about our child?" they asked Goldiamond. "No," he said, "but I can do something about you. You are my clients, not that child. I will work with you and we'll develop a program. We'll contract with each other so that you'll get what you want." Goldiamond turned to the mother and asked, "What do you want?" "I want my son—" Goldiamond interrupted, saying, "No, that's your son's business. What do *you* want?"

The woman then said she wanted to return to her career in public relations. And the father wanted some time for just himself and his wife—away from the harrowing problems caused by the son.

Goldiamond agreed that those were reasonable grounds for a contract. "I will teach you how to change your behavior in such a way that when you interact with your son, your son will produce the kind of behavior that you will like. This will mean, then, that you don't scream at him. This means you have to learn how to read this child, how to start talking to him, so that the child gets from you what he wants."

With Goldiamond's help the couple did get what they wanted. The mother did go back to work, the father found some time away from the burden of the child. And the child improved greatly. "My contract with them was fulfilled," Goldiamond said.

Benjamin C. Belden calls himself a behaviorist. He claims to use the principles of B. F. Skinner and others in marital counseling at his Chicago Center for Behavior Modification.

Belden cited a rather memorable example of a contract negotiated between a couple he was treating:

It seemed that the husband was more interested in sex than his wife. The husband wanted to have fellatio. The wife's interests ran in the direction of having an ideally furnished apartment; French Provincial furniture was more to her taste. A contract was then negotiated whereby the husband got fellatio five times a week and the wife, well, she got her French Provincial furniture.

Some behaviorists object to a fellatio/French Provincial-type contract on the grounds that it fails to take into consideration the difference between interior decorating and interior psychodynamics.

The wife, in this case, might have had a moral as well as psychological aversion to oral sex. The behaviorist is not, or at least should not, be in the business of negotiating away people's moral beliefs. The man's insistence on fellatio five times a week might also have been subject to a contract modification, teaching and training him to gain satisfaction from sexual intercourse and other erotic activities which the wife could have viewed as more palatable. The contract is a negotiated concept, one which must be fully subscribed to by all the individuals involved *equally,* in a nonoppressive manner. To have a contract which oppresses and thus denies people freedom calls to mind the worst fears about behavior modification therapy.

Behaviorists like Goldiamond are very clear, very precise about the kinds of specific, agreed-upon "outcomes" or goals a couple and a therapist can set. Goldiamond asks each client several questions about what they want to occur as a result of therapy and how those results might be objectively measured.

Then he would want to know what areas in the client's life he or she wants to remain unchanged. A careful review of the client's past efforts to change his or her behavior followed by an inventory of the client's "assets"—strengths, skills, successful problem-solving incidents in the past—is some of the pertinent information which the behaviorist obtains.

The husband of a highly competent conference manager complained to Goldiamond that his wife never entertained at home, that since no one was invited to their house, they were never invited out. The wife said that her mother had never entertained at home so she never learned how. Goldiamond had the woman carefully list all the facets of her conference manager's job. He then stressed those tasks she had accomplished at work which were similar to tasks involved in throwing a dinner party, such as whom to invite, seating arrangements, meals, and so on. The woman was then able to transfer the same energy and thought into inviting people to her home.

Many therapists, regardless of their psychological persuasion, have adopted some behavior modification techniques. For example, marriage counselors around the country believe it's better for the client, as well as for the therapist, to get a clear, specific statement about the "problem" and about the desired "outcome."

Other therapists rely very heavily on a specific time frame for therapy. Almost all the legitimate therapists agree that a person or a couple should notice some relief from the *initial* pain which brought them to the office in from three to seven sessions; too many therapists are loath to make such a promise during the first visit.

This isn't to say that all the couple's mental pain will be gone in three to seven sessions or that in fifteen sessions there might not be even greater pain, but that there should be some movement, some progression.

Contracts often have a way of sifting out the real problem from the pseudoproblem.

Goldiamond gives the example of the successful sales executive in a department store whose wife left him. A marital problem? It would seem so on the surface. But it turned out that although the man was a very successful sales executive, he was very often working late into the night on his paperwork. He would arrive home close to midnight, exhausted, and fall quickly asleep, much to the wife's dismay. Did Goldiamond engage them in marital therapy? No. He treated the husband's "work" problem. Goldiamond taught the man how to stop frittering away the morning at the coffee machine being a hail-fellow-well-met, how to use the morning hours for sales meetings and the afternoons to do his paperwork so that he could come home at a reasonable hour and devote time to his wife. The marital problem disappeared.

Goldiamond receives no fee from patients; they are referred to him through The University of Chicago's psychiatry outpatient department which charges people based on their ability to pay. One of the nation's leading practitioners and theoreticians of behavior modification, Goldiamond is also one of its severest critics. "Nothing sickens me more than these little descriptions that behavior rises and decreases. That's Mickey Mouse—keeping little clocks on the number of behaviors. A scream is one set of conditions and not another. The issue is not how many times you scream. The issue is where do you scream, what causes the scream, and so forth."

He is also wary of unscrupulous practitioners. Before beginning therapy with a behavior modification therapist (or any therapist for that matter) Goldiamond recommends that the client ask for a curriculum vitae, a résumé of the therapist's education, professional experiences, professional societies, and other activities. The next step is to get on the telephone and check those credentials—call the hospitals, universities, other therapists, and associations listed. The therapeutic world is a small one and Goldiamond believes that it will take no more than five phone calls before someone who knows the therapist will be able to provide some pertinent information about how well qualified (or unqualified) the therapist is.

We need not be afraid of studying behavior and even modifying it in a scientific manner. What we have to fear is the use of modifying techniques by people who have lost touch with the total person. Just as we are more than the sum of our chemical parts, marriage is more than the sum of two people's behavorial components.

BIOENERGETICS

"There is no emotion without motion." Bioenergetic therapist Sarah Allison was addressing a group of marriage counselors gathered in St. Louis for the annual American Association of Marriage and Family Counselors convention, an opportunity for private, pastoral, and agency affiliated therapists from all over the country to exchange ideas and learn new techniques for dealing with marital ills.

Sarah Allison, PhD, with her husband, Harry, PhD, practices bioenergetic therapy at the Marriage and Family Growth Center in Tulsa, Oklahoma. Bioenergetics is a technique for releasing the so-called hidden energy in the body. Mrs. Allison gave an example of how a marriage counselor can use a common, ordinary bath towel to improve communications between spouses.

A woman is sitting in the therapist's office, telling her husband of her discontent.

"I am so sick of the fact that you never pick up your underwear. I am sick to death of picking it up off the bathroom floor."

But according to Mrs. Allison these are just words to the wife, words she's uttered so many, many times. So the therapist hands the wife a towel and tells her to get a good, firm grasp on one end of it while her husband holds the other end. Then the therapist tells the woman to voice her complaint once again, but this time, "I want your words to match the energy you have. I want it to be a consistent flow of energy. So the woman violently twists the towel and lets out with, "I am shit sick to death of having to pick up your underwear off the floor, year in and year out! I've mentioned it to you so many times and you never change!"

Then, for the first time in the husband's life, says Mrs. Allison, "he knows it's real; he's experiencing it." The husband realizes how strongly the wife feels about it, how her complaint is something much more than a whim, that it's important to her "on a gut level." And this realization, claims Mrs. Allison, will cause the husband to respond.

Mrs. Allison calls the towel "a bridge for tenderness," a means by which couples, out of contact with each another, can begin to relate. Mrs. Allison says the towel has certain "magical" qualities: It reveals the true feelings of one spouse to the other.

Many therapists have incorporated *some* bioenergetic techniques into their practice. It becomes especially useful in dealing with the rage one spouse may feel toward the other.

Larry never allowed himself to get angry at Ann. He never allowed himself to show any anger because he was afraid that his rage would become too threatening for his wife to deal with and understand. "Talking" just didn't work.

It happened that Larry and Ann had gone to a husband and wife marriage counseling team who were sensitive to Larry's dilemma. So instead of telling Larry he should allow himself some measure of anger, they showed him.

The therapist took a towel in his hand, took fifteen deep breaths, and whacked the towel down on a mattress as hard as he could. Then, without saying a word, the therapist looked his co-therapist wife directly in the eye. Then he repeated his actions, only this time he hit the mattress twice, grunting, yelling each time he struck the mattress, again finishing by looking his wife directly in the eye. Finally, the third time, he took his fifteen breaths and banged the towel on the mattress as hard as he could, twenty or twenty-five times without stopping—yelling, shouting, screaming, grunting with every beat. Then it was Larry's turn. Looking back on the experience, Larry described what it was like going through that "anger" session.

"All the symptoms of anger are there except that you're doing it in a non-destructive way so you won't hurt yourself and someone else won't get hurt. In any anger you have three basic things: you have noise, you have motion, and you have heavy breathing. It's very much like the process of having an orgasm. And afterward, like with an orgasm, you're physically exhausted, you're spent, you couldn't make a fist after that. You couldn't get angry at anybody. You've just spent your whole emotional being, as you do in orgasm, on that anger.

"Then, after, when you're finished, you and your wife come together and you say to her, 'Thank you for letting me show my anger and thank you for showing your anger in front of me. Thank you for being there. It helps.'"

Some of the basic tenets behind bioenergetics aren't all that new. It's "founder," Alexander Lowen, MD, believed that our bodies demonstrate what is troubling us. In 1901 Freud wrote that physical manifestations "can be traced back to incompletely suppressed psychical material, which, although pushed away by consciousness, has nevertheless not been robbed of all capacity for expressing itself."[11] Unlike Freudian analysis, bioenergetic techniques are concerned directly with physical actions. Release from suppressed psychic material comes through physical expression—not primarily through talk.

In an unusual case described by Mrs. Allison during the St. Louis AAMFC workshop, a young woman of twenty-two was brought in by her husband. She seemed to be schizophrenic and deteriorating rapidly. Her husband seemed to Mrs. Allison to have plenty of ego strength, certainly the stronger of the two.

The main complaint when she was brought in was she wouldn't get out of bed in the morning, and when her husband would come home at night she was still in bed—the breakfast dishes, the kids unattended to, and so forth. Harry worked with her bioenergetically and I was seeing her husband in just rather superficial counseling.

The question he continually presented to me, a very valid question, was "What's wrong with my wife? How can I help her? What can I do?" Well, it is a hell of a question. How do you convey to a guy that his wife is schizophrenic and it started so many years ago, and if he had ten courses at the neighboring university he'd maybe begin to understand schizophrenia?

In her bioenergetic sessions with Harry, this woman was working with her feelings about her father. Her father had sexually abused her, probably daily for many years, and she had done what the lovelorn columns advise that we do. "Girls, tell your mother this is happening." Well, I've found that often that doesn't work. What happened in her case was she told her mother. This was the straw that broke the camel's back as far as the mother was concerned. The mother checked out—this was cause for divorce—and left her, my patient, with the father. This just aided and abetted the extent to which she was always available for being sexually abused by her psychotic father.

So the four of us—the wife, the husband, Harry, and myself—went into a room where we have some equipment. The wife was given a tennis racket and a mattress and began hitting the mattress. She first started off bringing out all of her anger and fury at her father—"That son of a bitch!" And, of course, right under the fury is the terror, the terror of "There's not much I can do about this. I'm smaller, I'm subjected to his abuse," the terror that came out.

During this I was with her husband, who was standing off to the side. And then, as usually happens in bioenergetics following the anger and some awareness of the terror, came deep, deep sobs from the wife.

At this point it really got to the husband on a gut level. He went over, scooped her up like you would almost a little bird, and just held her. He knew and he responded. What happened therapeutically at that time was that he knew the words she was using to describe her father were some of the same words she had used with him when she got angry. Then he realized that he didn't always need to feel that her anger was all directed at him. He had an appreciation of her on an entirely different level.

You could take five years of psychoanalysis with this case before the wife could learn to trust a man. Through psychoanalysis she could have learned to trust the analyst and then hopefully this would have transferred to her trust for her husband.

But bioenergetic techniques concentrated that lengthy process into one intense experience. This was the first time in her life that this woman had experienced a man being comforting, warm, and tender, and not using it to his advantage sexually or using it destructively. His response to her was just sheer compassion, tenderness, and warmth.

These are the sorts of things that can happen in bioenergetic work. But a lot goes into it before you get to this moment. We're doing a lot of this with couples and also in our group work—having husbands and wives present during each other's therapy sessions and experiencing the beauty of a person working through their problems. We find it working very nicely.

Bioenergetic therapy isn't so much concerned with talking as it is with moving. It's not saying something but rather physically demonstrating it. Mrs. Allison described the way she handled her group therapy sessions.

"I have the group members pair up and fantasize something that is restrictive, constraining, that keeps you from experiencing your own body pleasure—some restriction that's been placed on you by parents, by a grad school program, an employer, someone that keeps you feeling bound up, tied up, and you're tired of it and you want to fight loose. You want to really get out of there and you're going to use your strength and energy. You have to really fight!"

And so there's a lot of huffing and puffing, grunting and groaning, yelling and screaming, and the people are, according to Mrs. Allison, "freeing themselves from some of the bonds they're in."

Other therapists, however, are less enthusiastic about bioenergetics. They point out that the psychological community has long been aware that the way people physically display themselves reveals something about their psychological state. "Body language"—the way you wear your hat, the way you sip your tea—provides clues which any sensitive therapist (or spouse) can detect.

Critics of bioenergetics are also troubled by some of the physical and verbal paraphernalia. They believe bioenergetics is basically an old idea wrapped up in a new package, complete with bioenergetic equipment (which can be purchased), a vocabulary of breathing, grounding, stretching (which can be learned), as well as a mystique which holds that bioenergetics is the one true mode by which people suffering the entire gamut of physical and mental problems can be helped. We trust Mrs. Allison with bioenergetic techniques because she has a strong clinical background, but we would caution couples who encounter a bioenergetic enthusiast to check his/her/their experience with other approaches. At best bioenergetic techniques represent a set of new tools—not a total psychodynamic program.

PSYCHODRAMA

Perhaps the first therapist to try to bring a social situation into the psychiatrist's office was Jacob Moreno, a contemporary of Freud and the founder of psychodrama. The theory of psychodrama concentrates on "tele," an individual's attraction to other people in a group, and "spontaneity," which is developed by acting out feelings and episodes so that problems can be more easily demonstrated to the psychiatrist. But the techniques of psychodrama, particularly different versions of role playing, are widely used in various forms of marital therapy.

The notion of having people act out their problems from different points of view was adapted by the late Fritz Perls in his use of the empty chair as a way of taking care of problems from the past. The deceased parent, the absent brother, the hospitalized mother—any person who had a bearing on the current emerging dialogue—could be imagined in the empty chair. In the purer forms of psychodrama, the different roles would be taken by different people in the group whom the patient (protagonist) assigned. As explained by Carl E. Hollander, president of the Colorado Center for Psychodrama, Sociometry and Sociatry and a student of the late Jacob Moreno, "The play is the patient's, but it is the therapist's responsibility to act as overseer." Psychodrama, in its stricter sense, has a *warm-up* in which the present problem or emotion is introduced, the *action* which shows through a number of scenes how the present problem is explained by the past, the *catharsis*, and the *integration* where the experience is put in context. During the *integration*, in Hollander's words, "we start putting the pieces together, taking time to say good-bye."

Fritz Perls used, as do today's Gestalt practitioners, briefer versions of the psychodrama technique, but the rationale is similar to Moreno's—taking care of material from the past that is crippling one's ability to relate in the present.

Robert O. Blood, Jr., and Margaret Blood, who do co-therapy with couples in Ann Arbor, Michigan, have adapted a Moreno psychodrama technique called "doubling" as a central part of their marital therapy. (Bob is also the author, with Donald Wolfe, of *Husbands and Wives,* an extensive study of marriage in 909 urban and rural families.[12])

A graduate of the Yale Divinity School, Bob Blood had been counseling on his own for twenty years. At the request of married students in the community of Swarthmore, Pennsylvania, Bob began working with his lively wife, Margaret, who held a masters degree in religious education from Yale and was gifted with warmth and empathy. The two had worked together briefly in a couples workshop, but in Swarthmore they began developing the techniques they use regularly now in Ann Arbor. Whereas Bob served as a problem solver for other people—what Margaret teasingly calls "a fountain of wisdom"—he learned, while working with Margaret, to structure the counseling situation so that the clients would be doing the problem solving. After training with David Mace, who later founded ACME (Association for Counseling and Marital Enrichment), Margaret began to feel that she didn't have to have solutions for other people's lives. "I could get them in touch with their feelings and help them to find a way of communicating so they could deal with their problems themselves."

When a couple comes to a session with the Bloods, they sit with the husband and wife facing each other and talking to each other, instead of the wife and husband facing the counselor (wiseman). Bob finds that this arrangement tends to shift the responsibility primarily onto the shoulders of the couple. Since the husband talks to the wife rather than about her to the counselor, she doesn't become as defensive toward him or as dependent on the counselor. Talking to each other is something the couple can do at home. The therapy session is taped and the couple is asked to listen to the tape together and then talk to each other about what they heard. The Bloods encourage couples to bring an agenda so that the actual counseling session can be used to negotiate a new response to an issue that has caused conflict.

The Bloods frequently use their "doubling" technique with those "who are more or less normal but are having trouble communicating and getting along."

"Doubling," explains Bob Blood, "means that one of us is speaking over the shoulder of one of the partners. I'm as apt to speak over the woman's shoulder as I am over the man's shoulder. We may use doubling to try to sharpen up something that's kind of buried in what the person is saying, bring the feelings more into focus. We have a hunch that there's something going on there under the surface, and we use doubling to help it emerge." If Bob Blood is standing behind the wife's shoulder, crouching near her like an alter ego, and he senses that she is complaining about her husband's television watching when she really means to ask if he's having an affair with another woman, then Bob may say, "What I need to know is, are you seeing another woman?" So doubling can be used to bring issues into the open that have merely been hinted at in the couple's dialogue. The technique can also be used to introduce new ideas which the therapists feel will help the relationship. As Margaret Blood explains, "We may get behind a person who has been very negative, very complaining, and make a clear statement—'I would like you to do this. This is what I want.'" Switching complaints to clear proposals, changing blaming "you" statements into "I" statements of personal feeling and desire, are some of the ways by which doubling, or talking for the client, can help to accelerate change in a couple's relationship.

Another psychodrama technique used frequently by the Bloods is role playing and reverse role playing. When a couple talks about something that went on, such as a big blowup, Margaret Blood may say, okay, instead of talking about this, role-play it as if it were happening now. "If it's a fight they had because the husband wasn't ready to come to the marriage counseling session this night and instead he was seeing somebody in the hospital, then they role play that episode. They say the things that they said then, as if it were in the present situation. And then sometimes we get them to play the opposite partner and act the way they wish he had acted. So they reverse roles and do the thing that they're asking their partner to do. They show their partner what they want, and at the same time they also find themselves; instead of being so ideal, they find themselves getting into their partner's shoes. They often realize in a new kind of way where their partner was at and why the partner was acting that way."

Reverse role playing is actually a dramatic way of seeing things through your spouse's eyes. In successful marriage counseling that kind of empathy becomes integrated into the relationship.

Psychodrama, which continues to be used at the Denver Institute and other places around the country, as a literal dramatic technique of role playing before an audience, has been adapted—perhaps diluted to the needs of marriage and family counseling. It can greatly accelerate the therapeutic process by introducing and integrating material from the past or bringing to the surface issues within a relationship that have always remained hidden.

TRANSACTIONAL ANALYSIS

There are now over 10,000 TA practitioners listed on the roster of the International Transactional Analysis Association. Millions of individuals mouth the terms "parent," "child," "adult," "strokes," terms first conceived by the late Dr. Eric Berne, founder of transactional analysis. Claude Steiner, Berne's student and collaborator, notes this popularization and homogenization of TA with dismay. Steiner, who charges a meager fee of $40 a month for weekly group therapy sessions, fears a takeover of TA by profit seekers in therapy and business who have no regard for the scientific integrity of Berne's original ideas.

In hopes of restoring the profound and radical aspects of Berne's thinking, Steiner reiterates three ideas which set TA apart from the mainstream of psychiatry:

1. People are born okay. Taking the position "I'm okay, you're okay" is the minimum requirement for good psychiatry and lasting emotional and social well-being.

2. People in emotional difficulties are nevertheless full, intelligent human beings. They are capable of understanding their troubles and the process

which liberates people from them. They must be involved in the healing process if they are to solve their difficulties.

3. All emotional difficulties are curable, given adequate knowledge and the proper approach. The difficulty psychiatrists are having with so-called schizophrenia, alcoholism, depressive psychosis, and so on, is the result of psychiatric ineptness or ignorance rather than incurability.[13]

Curability, involvement of the so-called patient in the therapy, and the assumption by the therapist that people are born okay are three ideas that run through all of Steiner's writings and group therapy work.

Beyond this new, democratic, and hopeful relationship of therapist and patient, transactional analysis brings a fresh perspective for looking at human interaction, an outlook we shall refer to as "the TA perspective."[14] Three of the major elements of this perspective are a new view of behavior as transactions between "parent or adult or child" ego states, the notion of "games," and the concept of the "script."

The TA therapist describes behavior in terms of three ego states: parent, adult, child. Parent ego states are those that resemble parental figures and involve nurturing and judging. Adult ego states involve objective appraisal of reality. Child ego states are remnants from childhood directed at creative and pleasurable, inquisitive or self-centered activities. Since a person can be in only one of these ego states at a given time, any relationship is a transaction between two people in two particular ego states. A wife comes up to the bedroom and notices her husband's socks on the floor and says, "Can't you ever pick up after yourself?" That's her judgmental, punitive parent talking to his child. He may respond as an adult, processing data objectively and arriving at a logical conclusion. "The socks are on the floor. I shall throw them down the chute." He might be contrite and respond as a frightened child. "I'm sorry, dear. I won't do it again." He might respond as a nurturing parent. "I can see you're tired. Why don't you lie down? I'll take care of the socks and start a bath for you." He might be an angry, judgmental parent. "How can you complain about socks when I've been out there beating my brains out so you could afford a washing machine and a dishwasher?" One can see the many possible transactions. The picture becomes even more complicated when one realizes that transactions are often crossed. She's talking to him as parent to child. He answers her as adult to adult. Or the transaction is masked or ulterior. She sounds like parent—pick up your socks—because she doesn't know how to let her child out. She really wants to make love.

If the series of transactions has a covert motive and a payoff, the TA therapist defines it as a game. "A game is the most common disturbance of observable behavior. . . . Games are the medium by which a person obtains strokes."[15] Going back to the socks on the floor episode, this couple may have a game which routinely precedes their lovemaking. The wife—into her punitive parent or "pig" parent, as Steiner calls it—discounts the husband for leaving his socks on the floor. The husband is contrite and acts like a frightened child. The wife rewards him with sex but still acts like the parent, this time a nurturing parent. "I'll let you have some fun because you said you were sorry." Why would she do this when she could send a clear message about wanting to make love? There may be a number of reasons related to her current marital relationship. But chances are some of the reasons go back to early adaptations of childhood, which brings us to the third major feature of transactional analysis—the script.

Let's assume the woman in the socks game lost her mother when she was very young. She never had an opportunity to behave as a child because she had to assume the parent role. So messages from her child ego state have to be masked as parental messages. It then becomes, "Pick up your socks," instead of "I'm in the mood for love." "The script is a consciously understood life plan, usually decided upon before the age of fourteen."[16]

People who have a destructive life script will tend to choose partners who engage with them in destructive games. Such was the case with Ralph and Dorothy. Ralph was an alcoholic who chose as his partner Dorothy, who also drank heavily. They both wanted to quit but played a "If you quit, I'll quit" number. Finally Ralph contacted Steiner. Steiner agreed to see Ralph but insisted on a "contract," in this case an agreement that he would not drink for one year. The contract, an integral part of TA treatment is a clear expression of what kind of cure or help is being requested and an equally clear and precise statement by the therapist of what help he can (or cannot) render.

As soon as Ralph agreed to pull out of the game, Dorothy followed with amazing speed. Like Ralph, Dorothy had wanted to stop drinking for some time, but it had seemed impossible. "Ralph and I had been having a lot of fights, especially after we were drinking, and the fights were getting more and more severe. I just felt there had to be something, yet I wasn't able to quit drinking by myself. When Ralph liked Claude I was very impressed because Ralph isn't easily impressed by people. I decided to go also. I went two weeks after Ralph started. I made a contract right away to quit drinking because all I needed was some help. I was convinced that I wanted to stay and I was going to try to stop drinking."

In the language of *Games Alcoholics Play*, there were three important reasons Ralph was able to keep his contract to stop drinking: (1) His therapist would not play Rescuer. (2) He no longer had a partner who would play Patsy. (3) He himself could no longer play either Persecutor or "It"—a nonperson, a lush.

Though Ralph and Dorothy's contracts only involved not drinking, they did a lot of work in their separate groups on their relationship. "I learned mainly that my transactions with Ralph were all screwed up. We weren't being really straight with each other. [They were either sending crossed messages or masked messages.] I discovered that once we became more straight with each other a lot of the fear and the tension in the relationship disappeared. Through the years I had felt very insecure with Ralph. There was always a fear that we would split up. After being in the group with Claude for three or four months, my whole outlook on the situation changed. It wasn't that I no longer felt we might split up. It was that if we did, I'd be able to handle it. The fear about what might happen left when we began talking straight to each other. Claude often talks about that, the whole mysticism of what's going to happen to you. When you bring it down and know exactly what it is, it isn't fearful anymore. I think that's one of the most important things that happened to me in terms of the way we relate to each other."

Dorothy's insecurity about herself and the relationship led her to swallow her anger. As the obese woman typically eats her anger, the alcoholic woman drinks it. She was encouraged in her group to express her fears and anger, and in his group Ralph was encouraged to understand what Dorothy's buried anger was about and how his chauvinism kept the alcoholic game going.

Ralph told us, "The thing that I've really been working on for the last four months has been male chauvinism. I found that a lot of the difficulty that I was creating in our relationship was my habit to power play, to overwhelm— to raise my voice and that was it. Dorothy had approached this subject in her group. At first I thought I could relate to it. Then it started bugging me—I couldn't be that bad; everything a man does can't be chauvinistic. And then I started working on it.

"I discovered the tie-in between chauvinism and the whole victim-rescuer-persecutor triangle involved with drinking. I figured that was part of our difficulty. As a drinker I was really into the victim role. In my relationship I would take on a persecutor's role, saying things to Dorothy like, 'You can't criticize me; you can't say things like that; what's wrong with you?'

"During one group session I suddenly started to cry. Claude told me, 'I want you to express your feelings, not your head trip, but what's coming out. Is it anger? Is it guilt? Is it fear?' I said, 'It's fear; I'm afraid. I'm afraid that I won't make it, that all this is for naught. I'm going to start drinking again.' What came out of me then was real fear, and the reassurance that I got was just out of sight. It was really good. It came out that I had tremendous fear as a result of a wartime episode; a grenade nearly killed me. I had been carrying around this fear ever since. I had to overcompensate for it by being a heavy, by being a dominant person and taking power positions. I knew at work I was power playing all the time, and I was obviously power playing in my relationship with Dorothy." This piece of awareness was a major step forward for Ralph.

While the stated goal of Ralph's contract was to quit drinking, the actual goal of the therapy was awareness, intimacy, spontaneity. Becoming aware of their crossed and masked communications, Dorothy and Ralph were able to start "talking straight" to each other. Becoming aware of their persecutor-victim-rescuer game, of their fears and not okay feelings, they were able to move toward a full, open expression and sharing of their identities, toward intimacy.

Ralph admits, "I was really narrow in my approach when I first went in. I went into the group solely to work on the problem with alcohol, nothing else, thinking my relationship with Dorothy was okay. It didn't take long—I would say three or four months—for me to see that alcohol isn't dissociated from the way you are otherwise. It was Claude's work and the work of the people with me in the group that called a lot of my behavior to my attention. It was then I decided I had to work on other things; drinking isn't just an isolated thing."

While Ralph was becoming aware of his life script, Dorothy was becoming aware of her complicity in the sexism and alcoholism. "I was aware of sexism," she says, "of my role in the relationship as a woman. Although I didn't like it, I didn't think it was really curable. I didn't think really that Ralph would change." Dorothy believed it was more important to have Ralph—to live with him, to have that security even though it meant an unfulfilling role for her. That was more important than risking change.

"I found out in therapy that it was really important for me to change because the relationship was not good for me. If I continued to be the way I was [victim or rescuer] I was not going to be happy; I was not going to feel good about things. It was hard to break the patterns, but a little bit at a time the patterns were broken. We haven't been just happy all the time we've been in therapy. We've had a lot of difficulty because we've been making a lot of changes. That's why it's nice to go back to group. You know if you have difficulties, you always have someplace to go. You know that Claude understands the whole situation, that he's aware of both sides of it. I don't feel guilty for telling things the way I see them because I know Claude is also going to see the way Ralph sees them."

Effective therapy has important carry-overs into a couple's daily life. During the therapeutic session the couple (1) become aware of crossed messages, games, and other routinized behavior, (2) develop hope that there are other ways to behave, (3) gain support for experimenting with other ways of behaving, (4) learn techniques that provide frequent opportunities to have new and more satisfactory transactions.

As Ralph puts it, "What therapy has done is really give us techniques to analyze what the hell we're doing and to try to get out of it and to solve the situation and not just let it slide. Right after Christmas I went into a real depressed state and it took me about two weeks to decide that I was really playing the victim role. Claude was able to give us techniques to deal with that."

One of the techniques that Claude and co-therapist Hogie Wyckoff taught Ralph and Dorothy was straight talking. When Ralph was playing victim, sulking around and in effect saying to Dorothy, "You're supposed to take care of me, to rescue me," Dorothy was to state clearly what she perceived.

"I had been dependent upon Ralph's emotions. If he felt good I would feel good and if he felt depressed I would feel depressed. I wasn't feeling anything that I wanted to feel. I learned in group, from Claude and from an absolutely marvelous woman, Hogie Wyckoff, how to take care of myself by making sure I did what I could do and then making sure I felt good. Hogie would say to me, 'You ask Ralph if there's anything you can do to help him with his depression. If he says no, then leave. You don't have to be around him when he is depressed. There's absolutely no reason for you to be there because if you can't help him then you're only hurting yourself and you're hurting your relationship by staying around.' I realized that it *is* hurting the relationship to always be trying to do something that is impossible to do; it made me feel bad and didn't make him feel any better."

Ralph believes this change in Dorothy, her refusal to play rescuer to his victim or victim to his persecutor, "showed the whole significance of the game trip." By making that decision to take care of herself, Dorothy told Ralph, "I'm not going to play your game." As Ralph put it, "I don't have anybody to play with anymore, so I snap out of the game rather than staying in it." Ralph admits that giving up the victim position, the you're-supposed-to-take-care-of-me attitude vis-à-vis women, was not easy. But he says, "It's really been good for me because it makes me more independent too. I'd better take care of myself." Without a rescuer, a victim simply has to become a person who takes care of himself.

"Take care of yourself" seems like a harmless phrase. There are those who use it as a form of farewell, like ciao or au revoir. But when a wife interprets "Take care of yourself" as an injunction to begin looking out for her own interests, when that simple phrase is applied to the bottom dog in the nuclear family, the results can range from revolution to dissolution.

As Claude Steiner sees it, "The classic relationship in family life demands a top dog." Marabel Morgan, in *The Total Woman,* is clear about perpetuating this top dog/bottom dog arrangement—though she uses the more attractive terms of king and queen.[17] Since that book was the biggest-selling piece of nonfiction in 1974, we can assume that many people find the notion of marriage as a democratic situation too utopian. Questioned more closely on their willingness to acquiesce to male dominance, many wives will say, "I'd like more freedom but my husband would never stand for it. Better to save the marriage than to free myself." Can married life be blissful with the husband at the helm?

"No matter how bad things are for both," Steiner, an acknowledged detractor of the nuclear family, told us in a lengthy interview, "top dog is more comfortable than bottom dog. As long as the man is the top dog, it's going to be the woman who cracks. He's sitting on her." In the past the woman has been the one to initiate marriage counseling. Now the situation is changing. Being a progressive community, Berkeley is one of the first places to feel this change profoundly.

"Here [in the Bay Area] many women are not allowing their old man to sit on them; they're fighting back and the men are beginning to crack. Women's liberation has indeed brought about a lot of problems for men that they didn't have before. The fact that men are cracking now shows that they were sitting pretty for a while. No matter how bad things are, if you can come home and have your old lady put on your slippers and let you get away with watching TV, let you get away with semi-raping her, you're going to be in better shape than she is. When she turns around and says to him, 'Fuck you. Go make your own dinner and masturbate with a paperback,' it's going to be hard on him. He's going to start looking for a therapist."

Of course, if the woman follows the "total woman" philosophy, she will never say or imply anything of this sort. She will always be ready for sex at her husband's bidding. Steiner understands that a change in this traditional setup will bring problems, but he'd prefer to see those problems than stick with the oppressive status quo.

"When it comes to sexual problems, man is simply accustomed to being in control. He can choreograph the sexual situation to his needs and to his moment of opportunity, which has made the woman in many cases unable to enjoy sex. Men manipulate so that they are ready to have an erection; they are ready to come. But when you're being manipulated that way you're not ready. This has gone on for years, centuries. Now women are saying, 'Wait, I'm not ready.' When she gets ready, he's not ready. Then he can't get it up and he begins to worry that maybe he's impotent, especially since the woman is coming on strong and making demands. So men are becoming impotent, having trouble coming, thinking if it's going to be that way maybe I'd better not do it. Things are really changing. Men are scared, around here anyway. Women are no longer just waiting for them to move in."

The single standard of sexuality, which Masters and Johnson have cheerfully advocated, is not easily accomplished in most marriages. Taking care of the "you," the "me," and the "us" in a relationship, which family therapist Virginia Satir sees as the blueprint for "peoplemaking," is a complicated process. People may be made that way, individuality may be enhanced, but marriages are not necessarily kept together. A single standard of sexuality means both people are entitled to sexual pleasure. It may also be interpreted to mean that affairs are not the exclusive province of males. In fact, recent studies cited by Linda Wolfe in her book on women and extramarital sex, *Playing Around,* indicate that the proportion of married women having affairs has increased rapidly.[18] Husband dumping is as common as wife dumping. The old commedia dell'arte character of the cuckold is more fashionable than ever. Women run away from home in even greater number than men. There is no denying that changing our views of sexuality and realigning power within marriage involve certain risks. In the case of Ralph and Dorothy, taking those risks paid off in their individual growth and freedom from alcohol, and it also improved their relationship. In other cases seen by Claude Steiner and Hogie Wyckoff, the payoffs were gained for the "you" and the "me" at the risk of the "us."

Sally, (thirty-three), and Sam, (thirty-eight), have three children, one of whom they describe as "a terror." They've been married for seven years. Sally calls Steiner with the complaint that her husband never listens to her, giving as an example her repeated interest in going to the mountains for a peaceful vacation and his disregard of that in favor of a noisy, bustling, action-filled holiday. This rather superficial conflict is, as often happens, the tip of the iceberg. When Sally's husband comes in, he complains that she won't have sex with him. As it turns out, she occasionally initiates sex, has no orgasm, and leaves him thinking, How long will it be until the next time? As therapy proceeds, with the two of them in separate groups, he admits to a number of affairs with different women. As Steiner describes it, "They have built a network of truths, half-truths, lies. There's no way you can have a good, feeling relationship if there are lies going on between two people. Not saying things that are true is a way of lying too. He lies to her, and that's one reason he won't listen to her, so as not to be confronted with lies."

This is one of those cases where you might say the therapy succeeded but the marriage failed. Steiner felt that he couldn't continue to see the two of them unless the husband told the wife of his affairs. When he told her, she was not surprised but she was hurt, indignant. She now knew how many times he'd lied. He felt better, honest, open. It became clear that they wanted totally different things from life. She wants home, family, peace, and quiet. He wanted action and couldn't abide monogamy. The child who was the terror is now behaving much better. The wife has learned to be more direct and open about what she wants. On Steiner's advice she has signed up for a sex therapy program, an all-women's group. As Steiner puts it, "I wouldn't presume to teach a woman how to have an orgasm."

Awareness does pave the way for intimacy and spontaneity but not necessarily with one's present spouse. Hogie Wyckoff saw this woman as a good candidate for a women's group. As Hogie explains it, "A woman who is really steeped in stereotypic sex role programming is coming from a place where it's hard to be powerful around men. It's good for her to be in a women's group, at least temporarily, until she feels she can take care of herself in a mixed group.'' In Hogie's view, the optimum condition for a woman who wants to break out of a female banal script which locks her into dependency, or overeating, or self-abnegation, or self-pity[19] is to be in a group with a woman facilitator who is a feminist.

By "feminist," Hogie means an advocate for women, not an advocate against men. The distinction is important. "The separatist feminist," as Hogie defines her, "believes that until men get their shit together we should stay away from them and protect ourselves. The feminist believes that men aren't going to get their shit together unless women give them feedback. My opinion is that men are hurting at least as much, if not more, than women, but men have more power. They're dangerous because they have power, but they've been mutilated. I can't see myself living in some Amazon community while the rest of the world is falling apart because of male dominance. It's crucial that there be total communication."

The woman in question went to such a group led by Hogie. She learned to express her fears and her needs. When her husband took up with someone else, she could identify what was happening to her, what was disturbing her. "One of the biggest things that changed about this woman," Hogie reports, "is her physical self. She was fifteen or twenty pounds heavier and in poor physical shape. Now she feels physically more powerful. She's lost the weight. She doesn't get colds all the time which colluded with the empty feelings she used to have. She's still with her husband, but now she has gone for her master's degree in social work so she can do therapeutic work herself. She has also established relationships with other men, outside the marriage, and is now more active sexually than her husband."

We can compare this outcome to that of the black couple who were instructed by their therapist to seek other sexual relationships. Here the decision came from the wife, and it came from a position of personal strength. Nevertheless, this open marriage outcome would still have been considered a failure by marriage counselors practicing in the fifties. And even today progressive marital therapists and others who have researched "affairs" indicate that divorce is far more likely when both partners cease to be monogamous.

According to Steiner, "It definitely complicates matters when people have other sexual relationships. We're told from the time we're born that it must be one man and one woman. When one of the two wants to love somebody else, it complicates things. But not to love somebody else complicates things too. Monogamy is the easy thing, in the short term. But strict monogamy can be very corrosive. I'm not talking about sex. It's emotional monogamy I'm talking about, the type that says you can't love a friend. Monogamy usually means you don't even love yourself, just that other, that spouse. Very often I'll tell someone who says they want out of a relationship that the first person I want them to consider now is themselves: Have a romance with your-self. You are somebody to love too. Your partner will have to share you, with you." To some partners this departure from strict emotional monoga-my will be viewed as infidelity. "The first form of infidelity," says Steiner, "is for the wife to say when the husband comes home, 'I'm taking care of me now. I need a walk.' It's very much resented. A man could be as jealous of her relationship with herself as with somebody else."

Although Steiner is not opposed to loosening the tight knot of monogamy, he certainly does not advocate a sexually open marriage as a panacea. To use his casual lingo, "Some people simply want to get it on with others out-side their marriage. If it's done in stages and at a similar pace, it's much less of a problem. But I respect the view of two people who feel they couldn't handle that complication."

The difference between Eli and Steiner is that Eli had one cure for every couple; Steiner is a contractual therapist. "I'm respectful of what other peo-ple want and believe." There is no way to keep the therapist's values from influencing therapy. Hogie Wyckoff believes that women, as well as men, should take care of themselves—with all the independence and personal power and responsibility that phrase connotes. Steiner supports people lov-ing each other. Those people can be married, divorced, living together, mo-nogamous, or into several relationships, as long as they are able to feel good about themselves and each other. One doesn't always know what kind of life-style a therapist or marriage counselor has chosen for themselves. But one can usually tell whether the therapist conveys that "I'm okay, you're okay" position—the conviction that "I respect where you're coming from and I won't need to discount or exploit you."

TA—DENVER STYLE

Warden and Carolyn Rimel treat people they say are "basically normal neurotics" with a TA approach as well as a smattering of Gestalt; an occa-sional dash of primal scream; a touch of psychodrama, spun through a blender of psychoanalytic training. The Rimels seem more comfortable with the structure of the nuclear family and marriage than are Steiner and Wyck-off. Politically and therapeutically, the Rimels are less radical but more rep-resentative of marriage counselors, just as their city, Denver, Colorado, is more representative of the American scene than Berkeley, California.

Denver is the city market researchers love for testing out new products. The old saw that "if it plays in Peoria" has been replaced by the fact that if it sells in Denver, the rest of the nation can't be far behind. Denver is a place with enormous appeal. One can play tennis outdoors, go for a swim, and then, a couple of hours later, while away the hours skiing down the slopes. For those reasons Denver has attracted many people from all over the country. There is a large, affluent, yet rootless population. Aspen is nearby, as are Vail and Colorado Springs, areas where people may contemplate the majesty of nature and avoid, perhaps, the vacuum within.

"We see a lot of people who are involved in what we call symbiotic relationships," Dr. Warden Rimel, a psychiatrist, says. "It's a parasitic relationship much like the one of Br'er Rabbit and Tarbaby, where you're stuck together and you can't function well at all together and you can't get apart. It's based on a 'I can't stand it' position where the parties switch from being a parent and adult to being somebody's child. They're just having a hell of a time.

"The case I had recently is a classic example. The husband got in a very symbiotic relationship with his wife. They have a two-year-old child and everything is up for grabs because everybody wants the child position. They're all fighting for it, but the two-year-old is entitled to it.

"The father's rerun that he is doing on the wife is that he wanted a sexual relationship with his mother, a very classical Oedipal thing. I got the father involved in a two-chair dialogue. He says, 'Mother, you never came through. You promised that you were going to have sex with me and you never did.' That's his whole premise. Women are disappointments, and that's what he's rerunning now. And his wife picked a man who was a rerun of her father. That's what I'm helping them become aware of—their unconscious contract."

Carolyn Rimel is seeing people who suffer from "stroke deficit,"[20] not enough positive, physical, emotional, or verbal support.

"What I've gotten people to do is to take a look at what kind of strokes they're getting—what kind of strokes do they want that they're not getting, to train them to ask for the kind of strokes that they want a hundred percent of the time. They may not always get it, but to ask for it and put it in a framework of what I call 'stroke strategy.' What kind of strokes do you feel a craving for? Excitement and/or response or what? We get large groups of people talking to one another and they list the percentage of strokes they get: what kind of strokes do I get out of my job? out of my home? where are the ones that I'm not getting that I want? what are the ones that I turn down that I really could accept? I get people to think about that and then start training them in how to ask for strokes."

The Rimels believe in the total demystification of therapy. People can read their own therapy records; they can read all about TA, because there are no "sacred books."

Warden has a rule of thumb for how long therapy should take before there is some definite change in the relationship. He tells couples that "if they aren't changing in the relationship or the relationship isn't changing and/or they aren't internally, themselves, making some changes within ten sessions, joint sessions, then the probability curve that X number of additional sessions is going to make any difference drops off pretty rapidly. I tell them that doesn't mean they may not need more than ten sessions, but that they may not need that many. I would bet that most of the couples I see specifically for couples problems come about five or six times."

Warden Rimel gave a case in point.

The husband's complaint was that she spent nearly all her time and energy focusing on the two teen-age boys. Her complaint was that he was gone from home too much of the time—and when he was home, she didn't get good feelings from him.

They learned about strokes and stroking. His complaint was she was sexually frigid. She told me in the individual session that wasn't true. She had discovered that she was a very sexy lady and could have orgasms galore with a young man she had had an affair with. And that had been possible because the affair hadn't been ruined by having to live with him.

In one session, it was about the fourth or fifth, we explored their sexual adjustment and found out that while they were both very well educated people, they were very ignorant about sex. She learned that he produces semen twenty-four hours a day and gets horny, in part, because it builds up a tension. She felt much more okay toward his sexual demands. He learned that her getting turned on sexually began in the morning when he was pleasant to her and showed some interest in her. Then she could reconcile the fact that at this point in his career he had to go out of town several times a month and that she could get strokes elsewhere.

He then decided it was okay for her to get those other strokes from the teen-age world her sons were in—football players and kids from the high school—that she wasn't going to have an affair with one of those teenagers. They both decided that it was okay to throw the visiting kids out by ten or eleven at night because they wanted some privacy.

They resolved a number of practical issues like that, got in one of our communications workshops for about six sessions. Then they came in and said, "What shall we talk about?" After they gave me a "Gee, you're wonderful, professor" kind of feedback, which I took and appreciated, I pointed out that they had done most of the work, and we decided that they could just see how it goes and call in when they think they're hung up or need some help.

The total cost of therapy was $555—$200 of which was covered by their insurance. For an investment of $355 this couple, who had been married sixteen years, with two children, resolved difficulties which in other circumstances might have caused them to wind up in divorce court—with all the attendant miseries.

Warden charges $35 for a forty-five-minute individual session, $45 for a one-hour session with a couple, and for the communications workshops, $20 a session. Carolyn charges $30 for an hour session.

The Rimels find one of the toughest types to treat is the "Great-American-Dream-Workaholic" a label which fits a number of doctors, lawyers, land developers, and businessmen. These are highly successful, hard-driving, ambitious, affluence-oriented men who are addicted to work. "That kind of personality," according to Warden Rimel, "plays havoc with the marriage relationship." Rimel reports that a good many of these men are coming to realize that the Great American Dream isn't making for happiness; that their hard work and ambition is actually wrecking their lives.

Fifteen years ago, when Warden Rimel first became a psychiatrist, he would have treated workaholics with failing marriages on an individual basis, seeing them two or three times a week over a period of two or three years. Now he sees them with their wives or in groups. These are men who are out of touch with their feelings. Rimel, and other psychiatrists and psychologists trained to do individual psychotherapy, have come to believe that getting in touch with feelings is more easily accomplished when a person is seen with their spouse or within the group context.

The wives of workaholics, as Warden Rimel describes them, "are either having affairs, are on their way to alcoholism, or are killing themselves." These women can hardly remain aloof from the problem, when they feel ignored or incidental to the unrelenting drive to realize the Great American Dream. They may be encouraging their husbands to continue with their destructive work fixation. If the husband is to change, the wife may have to help ease the pressure, give up the extra car, move to a more modest house. The husband may have to spend more time with the family, freeing his wife to pursue interests other than the acquisition of more possessions. Workaholism is not only an individual problem. We agree with the Rimels that the chances for treating it effectively are increased if workaholic and wife (or workaholic and husband) seek help together.

Many classically trained psychoanalysts and psychiatrists, realizing the limitations of individual therapy, are reeducating themselves, learning techniques from transactional analysis, Gestalt, and behavior modification, dispensing with the couch and using more confrontation, seeing couples and groups instead of only individuals. A therapist who has been trained in the older psychoanalytic methods of treating people individually but offers the option of other approaches can make the most responsible and responsive type of marriage counselor.

CLERGYMEN

Psychoanalysts, committed to protracted individual therapy, have become strange bedfellows with the clergy. As one minister-therapist told us, both groups are trained in a particular way that no longer fits what's happening in the world. Both psychoanalysts and clergymen have something helpful to give but their methods frequently prevent them from being effective. Few husbands or wives have $5,000 to $25,000 or 500 spare hours to spend for psychoanalysis. Couples shun the clergy as marriage counselors for other reasons. They fear the pastor will discourage change and simply support the status quo. Will the minister tell the oppressed wife that she must bear her husband's abuses as Jesus bore the cross? Will the rabbi urge the harassed husband to put up with his wife's continual nagging because she is a good mother to his children? Will the priest comfort the young wife pregnant with her third in three years while sternly warning against birth control? Some of these doubts and fears, according to nationally known marriage counselor Edward Rydman, are well founded.

Rydman is a humanistic psychologist whose experiences range from administrator of planned parenthood clinics where he dealt with low-income black, white, and Mexican-American families to a current marriage counseling practice in Dallas, Texas, with a considerable number of "superrich" Texans among his clientele. He trained with Fritz Perls for three years before Perls became a guru, and he served as executive director of the American Association of Marriage and Family Counselors for five years.

Rydman is concerned about many abuses in the therapy field—untrained sex therapists and fraudulent marriage counselors who have nothing more than brief training under the auspices of questionable organizations. But Rydman says, "I get most of my shivers from clergymen who are doing therapy and who have no training for what they are doing.

"They're hooked into a religious system where they are representatives of God or representatives of the church," says Rydman, but that system often gets in the way of satisfying the personal, psychological needs of couples who come to their ministers for marriage counseling or other forms of therapy. Fears of the hereafter, for example, can paralyze individuals with guilt and anxieties that get in the way of their marriage relationship.

A woman came to Rydman recently asking for help to overcome her terrible fear of flying. Her husband came to the session and mentioned to his wife, "I want to take you to Paris for a vacation." She replied, "I can't go to Paris unless we can go by boat." He said, "I can't take that much time off. We could fly and save a tremendous amount of time and have a delightful vacation." She said, "I just can't fly." As they spoke to Rydman and to each other, it turned out that the woman had been seeking counsel from her clergyman and she was very much involved in a conservative church. "I'm afraid if that plane crashes I'll be killed." "Well, what is your fear about being killed?" asked Rydman. She said, "It isn't the fear of being killed so much. I did something bad in college and I will probably go to hell for what I did that was bad."

The clergyman who counseled her about her behavior in school for which she was expelled had left the woman with this notion of going to hell. In twenty years she had not been able to extricate herself from this "fear network." In fact she had left her fundamentalist church because she still thought of herself as a bad, even doomed woman. Rydman notes that the clergyman who gave the woman hereafter counseling was not a trained counselor; "some are trained well in pastoral counseling."

Yet there need not be a conflict between religion and a modern marriage. A 1974 *Redbook* survey of 100,000 predominantly married readers—one of the most extensive reports on female sexual preferences since Kinsey's—found that women of all ages were more likely to report satisfaction with their sex lives when they described themselves as religious. And wives who categorized themselves as moderately religious were more likely to report satisfaction with their sex lives than women who described themselves as "not religious." While Kinsey had reported in 1953 no significant differences in female sexual satisfaction between the religiously devout, the moderate, and the nonreligious females, the *Redbook* survey suggests that religion has a positive effect on sexual satisfaction in marriage. Robert and Amy Levin, who conducted the survey, suggest this change could be due, in part, to a changed attitude of the clergy over the past twenty years.

"Moving away from the idea that sex is intended exclusively for procreation, increasing numbers of enlightened ministers, rabbis, and priests have been teaching that sexual pleasure is not only a legitimate expectation but also a necessary element in a good marriage. . . . A positive religious approach to sexual pleasure, which links sex with marital fulfillment, is likely to have considerable effect on women for whom religious authority still serves as a sanctioning force in life. It can relieve them of guilt and inhibition almost as effectively as it shackles them when the message from the pulpit links sex with sin and damnation."[21]

Dr. Lloyd Rediger, one of the new breed of clergymen, is in the unusual position of being a marriage counselor to ministers. Connected with the Wisconsin Council of Churches Office of Pastoral Services, Rediger draws heavily on a solid psychiatric background with special training in transactional analysis. He represents the progressive clergymen, who are recognizing and admitting their own flaws—in their marriages and in their frequent role as marriage counselors.

Rediger enumerates the advantages of seeking marriage counseling through your minister, rabbi, or priest. (1) A clergyman was attracted to and trained in a field that is oriented toward helping people. (2) He does not rely on a fee. (3) He's on call anytime. (4) He sees people in a great variety of situations, all of life's crises, many of which the typical therapist may not be exposed to. (5) He goes to where people are instead of expecting them to come where he is. (6) He possesses a theological framework that has been proven over centuries to be helpful to people. Whether or not these are good reasons in your mind will depend on how you feel about your church, synagogue, or temple and whether you and your partner will feel comfortable discussing various aspects of your relationship, including sex. To some of us, religious leaders call to mind guilt, sin, blame, castigation. But for those who find religion a source of acceptance, compassion, and understanding, pastoral counseling may be a wise choice.

If you should decide to seek advice from your minister or rabbi, keep in mind that he should meet certain standards. Did he have special training in dealing with couples? Some seminaries require as little as one semester of clinical experience; that experience could be in the ward of a state mental hospital, in a clinic for children with learning disabilities, or in an alcoholics' ward. The title of reverend or rabbi does not automatically mean the man is qualified to help you. Many people will find it difficult to ask direct questions of their religious leaders, but we feel the enormous variation in clergy background requires that you overcome these inhibitions and get things clarified immediately. A certain amount of mutual vulnerability is necessary in the therapeutic relationship, so find out whether your clergyman is the type that can admit his own human frailties.

Lloyd Rediger suggests that the person going to their pastor state: "Here is my problem. How does that look or sound to you? Do you feel you can give me any assistance, either personally or by referring me to someone, or is it simply out of the range of possibility for you? How would your theology relate to this problem? Do you have any special psychological perspectives on marital problems?"

Rediger realizes that the role mystique of the clergyman might prevent people from asking such questions directly. They can ask around the community. If there's a clergy association, ask the local chairman, or if it's in your denomination, call and find out what kind of record or reputation this person has. "That's what you do with a lawyer. You just don't walk to the guy with a shingle. You usually check him out with a couple of friends or another attorney or call the bar association. I think you've got the same right and responsibility to do that with the clergy."

One serious drawback to the pastor as marriage counselor is the traditional Judeo-Christian sex role divisions which may hamper many clergymen from relating to the wife who feels oppressed or curtailed by sexism in her marriage. Dr. Rediger, in counseling pastors and their wives, is combatting one particular version of sexism—the expectation that the wife become her husband's professional assistant, in this case, the assistant pastor. Rediger notes that the curve of case load for pastors' spouses has recently shot upward because the women have finally found a place to unload all the resentment that's been building up. They're expected to be with their husbands at meetings, to listen sympathetically as congregants unburden themselves over the phone, to answer problems, and set an example in dress, manners, and child rearing. In a conference he runs for clergy, Rediger states that, "The church doesn't get two for the price of one. The spouse has the same rights as anybody else to choose her life and career and may not choose to be related to the church." When counseling clergy couples, says Rediger, the wife may complain that her husband is available to everybody but his own family. The dutiful, passive woman who seems to fit the traditional demands of a clergyman's wife may be a boring sexual partner. He may want her to be more aggressive and stimulating instead of lying dutifully in bed.

Even when the complaints are clearly sexual, Rediger spends a great deal of time helping couples to establish better communication. One of his favorite techniques for improving couple communication is the "gripe-feedback" method which he has adapted from the TA book *Born to Win,* by Muriel James and Dorothy Jongeward, and hands out on small printed cards.

The gripe-feedback method [says Rediger] has to do with problem solving and conflict resolution. The ingredients are: First, you've got to start talking with each other before anything can happen. It's no fair to withdraw or to imagine what the other person is thinking. You've got to check it out. You've got to talk and make your verbal investment in each other. Second, you've got to give each other permission to be angry, hurt, demanding, accusing, and so on, without taking it personally, as though it were an attack on you. If you don't ventilate the emotional pressure it will contaminate everything else and make any rational, adult behavior impossible. Third, the person has to know they've been heard by their partner. Otherwise they're going to keep pounding their partner over the head. So we take time in the gripe-feedback session to have the one who has listened feed back the gripe. The partner doesn't go into the courtroom game of attacking or defending or adding "Yes, but" to the feedback, but simply repeats or summarizes what he or she heard his partner saying until the partner agrees, "Yes, that's what I'm feeling. That's what I'm trying to get across to you." Then we switch roles and it's the other person's turn, so there has to be equal time and attention. Fourth, given the fact that you're talking, that you've had a chance to ventilate pressure, that you know you're being heard by your partner, what would be your positive suggestion for change in this situation or for this decision? Positive suggestions are laid out on each side and fed back so each knows there's been an accurate hearing. Fifth, negotiations are the final step, but many adults don't know how to negotiate.

Rediger helps them to overcome the win-lose notion that if you get what you want, I don't get what I want. Whenever a couple comes to a session reporting something good that has happened, he says, "Okay, how did you make that happen?" and they identify what they did differently.

In short, Dr. Rediger does what good marriage counselors of all persuasions do. He helps couples to identify their resources, as well as their problems, so they can eventually feel independent—not conflict-free, but capable of dealing with conflicts as they come along. With such methods in hand a couple no longer feels helpless. They begin to know what to do, and with each conflict resolved they can say, "Hey, look what we did!" Marriage starts to feel good again.

3

Family Therapy

"You're not just marrying her, you're marrying her whole family." How many of us have heard a grandmother, aunt, or cousin repeat that old saw! What a ridiculous idea, that a couple who will be living in another city and only seeing their families on holidays, will be "marrying" that family. Perhaps this was true in the old days, when people lived in the same town or village from birth to death, when mothers, fathers, brothers, sisters, aunts, uncles continued to interact with a married couple and their children throughout a lifetime. But now, with that extended family tradition all but dead, how can her family and his family still be in the marriage?

Consider some of the ways the family is still in the marriage. First of all, the marriage itself may have been a reaction to the family of origin. Many marriages are overt, conscious escapes from home: *I married him to get away from my dad and mom fighting all the time. I married her so I wouldn't have to see Dad drunk another night.* Married people offer an amazing range of reasons to escape their original families. They wanted to get away from a family's coldness, from their repressive Victorian attitudes, or from their extreme protectiveness and smother-love. Many marriages start with the premise that the formation of a new family can allow one to achieve independence from the old family.

But the old family has a way of making itself felt in every phase of the marriage, from the sexual relations of husband and wife, to their patterns of relating, to their ways of parenting, to their concept of proper male and female roles.

Let's take the man who escaped from a repressive, Victorian home. Let's assume he was attracted to a woman who came from a warm, affectionate family whose attitudes were more liberal. She was attracted to the dignity, restraint, and refinement which were qualities her own family lacked. But in bed she finds her husband cold and unyielding. He reacts to some of her

67

suggestions about foreplay, oral sex, and fantasy with an attitude of disgust, an attitude that would have made his parents proud. When they are in public he cannot bear any display of affection such as hand holding or kissing. Highly dissatisfied, the wife hopes that children will add meaning to her life. But they find themselves clashing over styles of parenting—hers includes feeding and holding the child on demand, nursing instead of bottle feeding, even nursing in public. He finds this repulsive and threatening. After the child is two years old, during which time sexual relations of husband and wife have deteriorated, the wife decides to look for a job. A tremendous clash occurs over this issue, the husband insisting that she cannot leave the child with a stranger. She insists that her mother worked and it never harmed her. He argues that his mother never worked and if his wife took a job it would make his competitors believe business was bad. Couldn't she at least wait until they were better off financially? The problem is "solved" by having another child. Three years later the couple divorces—she in order to have a more satisfactory sex life and to pursue a career, he in order to find a woman who can accept the traditional responsibilities of a wife, a woman, well, more like Mother.

During the course of this six-year marriage, the couple has seen their families of origin only twice a year. Did he marry her family? Did she marry his?

Psychotherapy has always recognized the importance of the family: from Freud's shocking suggestion that one's whole psychosexual development is based on the early experiences with, and attraction for, mother or father, up to Eric Berne's concept of a "parent" ego state which one internalizes from childhood and carries around until death. Therapists have known that the family of origin is in the marriage, but only in the past twenty years have therapists attempted to treat the whole family.

Some of those who pioneered the family therapy approach, such as Nathan Ackerman in New York City and Don D. Jackson in Palo Alto, California, realized that they might work with an individual for years only to find that the patient would return to the old way of behaving once back with the family. The family was simply more powerful than the individual or the therapist. The family had a history. It had rules laid down and reiterated, often in subtle, indirect ways. Not just the obvious rules, such as "In this family we don't eat without saying grace," but the covert rules such as "In this family touching and hugging is considered vulgar" or "In this family no one can separate from Mother." The family had ways of communicating which might be open—smiling when happy, shouting when angry; or indirect—smiling when miserable, blaming when scared. How could a therapist, meeting for one or two hours a week with an individual child, mother, or father, hope to change a system—a set of rules, a method of communicating, a language, a way of interacting, a view of the world and of strangers?

Therapists began experimenting with seeing the whole family. The "craziness" of schizophrenics began to make sense when the family system came into focus. If mother says, "I will die if you grow up and leave me," the child faces an impossible situation. He can't help growing up, but he grows up as little as possible or in ways that continue dependency. His "craziness" is the only solution. The identified patient in these schizophrenogenic families often turned out to be the only one still striving for growth in whatever crazy manner, the only one who had not given up on life.

In less extreme situations, where a child was misbehaving in school, the therapist found that a marital problem was the source of the trouble. The child had reasoned this way. "I know Mom hates Dad, especially when he drinks, but she doesn't want me to know, so I'll try and not tell her because it would make her feel worse. And besides, maybe part of it is my fault." But the child's feeling came out anyway, in "bad behavior," because the child did want someone to know, someone to help. So the parents brought in the "bad" child so she could learn to behave better. When the therapist had them come to the session, it turned out that the child's misbehavior was only a symptom of the marital problems. Pretty soon therapists were refusing to see a child alone. They began insisting on having Mom and Dad there right from the beginning.

Family therapy has been a grass-roots movement, with clusters of practitioners around the nation innovating simultaneously. Dr. Nathan Ackerman and his group at the Family Institute in New York; James L. Framo, Salvador Minuchin, Ross Speck, Ivan Boszormenyi-Nagy, all in Pennsylvania; the late Don Jackson in Palo Alto, working with Virginia Satir and Jay Haley, who moved to Philadelphia; Satir then working in Palo Alto with Shirley Luthman and Martin Kirschenbaum and influencing thousands of others through workshops held across the country; a cluster in Chicago with Dr. Charles Kramer; a cluster in Atlanta around Carl Whitaker, and then a certain amount of cross-pollination as these people have discovered each other, interacted, and moved to other universities, other hospitals and clinics.

Family therapy, then, is a very diversified approach which has one basic assumption: The family is a dynamic system which affects all its members and is affected by each member. A change in one member of the family means a change in the others. Therefore you can't just treat the so-called "sick" member of the family. You must treat the entire system.

What does this mean for you as you grapple with marital problems? It means that if you see a family therapist, he/she/they will want to see you and your spouse. If there are children they will want to see the whole family at some point in the therapy. The family therapist will use various techniques to help you understand how your family system works—including family sculpting, family reconstruction, and even family of origin sessions which require at least one meeting with your own mother, father, sisters, and brothers.

Many of the families who see Philadelphia family therapist James Framo are already moving toward divorce. Framo cannot always arrest this movement. "Some people cannot be dissuaded from divorce," he told an audience of marriage counselors. "They feel their identity is at stake."[1] But at least they can find out whom they are really divorcing—their spouse or their parent. If one does not gain this information about the connection between marital problems and early family conflicts, then there is the danger of the same problem occurring again and again. One method which Framo uses in his family therapy is the family of origin session. Toward the end of the therapy program, when changes have occurred, Framo will urge the couple to bring in their mother, father, sisters, and brothers. He has had people coming to Philadelphia from California and Texas. The greatest problem in pulling together such a session is not the distance, but the fear and resistance of husband or wife. It is amazing how many grown people in their thirties, forties, and fifties are scared to death of spending two hours in the same room with their mother and father.

"Ask me to climb Mount Everest, ask me to swim the Atlantic, but don't ask me to bring in my mother." That was one man's plea to Framo. But Framo is often able to overcome the initial resistance of his clients. Usually the results justify the effort. One woman finally consented to a family of origin session after great resistance. The woman had been in individual therapy for eight years, much of it spent talking about her mother. She viewed her mother as a towering figure, "twenty-five feet tall." Next to such a giant, she was a helpless, tiny child. After the family of origin session,with her mother, father, and siblings present, this view was dramatically altered. "My mother kept getting shorter and shorter," she told Dr. Framo.

Most of us have a less distorted perspective of our parents, but distorted it usually is. As Framo notes, "Most people upgrade or downgrade their parents. They don't get to know their parents as people." Framo's family of origin sessions provide people with more realistic views of their parents. The mate is not present during the session, but receives a tape recording of what goes on, so that the process of bringing family issues into focus becomes an ongoing one, shared by both husband and wife.

"Due to family programming, most people are unable to make a genuine commitment to their mate. Their primary loyalty is to their family of origin rather than to the spouse, even when adults consider themselves liberated from their parents." These loyalties are particularly compelling when they are what Ivan Boszormenyi-Nagy calls in a book by that name "invisible loyalties,"[2] loyalties of which we are not aware. If we go back to our original couple with their Victorian/progressive, cold/warm, calculation/spontaneity conflicts, we can see how difficult change would be unless each spouse recognized his or her loyalties to the family of origin.

They came to the marriage hoping to escape from their families of origin and wound up replicating what they had experienced as children. They were both disappointed that marriage had not made right what had been amiss in their own families. Were the Victorian husband to accept the fact that he was still wedded to his family's system of restraint and repression, he might begin to move toward a new system which included a real commitment rather than an effort to stifle his wife.

The wife might go to her separate therapist, perhaps one who would reinforce her growing feminist consciousness or one who would help her accept the "flaws" in her original family. But as Framo points out, "When someone goes through individual therapy while they are involved in a marital conflict, what happens is another marriage is formed." The outcome may look favorable for one of the individuals—in this case the wife at least would be free to pursue her career and perhaps find a more suitable mate. But the outcome for the family as a whole would not be promising. Even after a divorce she might continue to hate her husband, withholding the children from him, arguing over money. As Framo notes, "As long as one's ex-mate is considered the enemy, one is not free because hate is a relationship." As for the divorced husband, he may feel he is subsidizing the wife's promiscuity. He is thrust into a strange, unfamiliar surrounding, deprived of his children. He will either repeat his mistakes with another woman or live a life of bitterness and resentment perhaps reinforced by his mother or at least by her ghost, or he may become depressed or suicidal.

In this scenario, family therapy will not necessarily prevent a divorce from occurring, but at the very least it will help the couple to disengage with dignity and with less damage to the children. At best it could help this pair to bring their invisible loyalties to light and in so doing, help them form a new, more vital family system.

THE FAMILY AS A SYSTEM

The word "system" may not be one you are accustomed to using in connection with the family. It has the ring of things mechanical and inhuman—IBM system, missile system. But to the family therapist a "system" is a pattern of actions, reactions, and interactions within a given family. The health of the family depends on how the system functions. Is the family system open and flexible enough to allow each member to grow and change, or is it closed and repressive, making change difficult or impossible?

As Virginia Satir notes in her readable yet substantial book *Peoplemaking,* closed systems evolve from a certain set of beliefs which include the following:

- Man is basically evil and has to continually be controlled to be good.
- Relationships have to be regulated by force.
- There is one right way, and the one with most power has it.
- There is always someone who knows what is best for you.

Closed systems tend to subordinate self-worth to power and performance. Closed systems have bosses; closed systems resist change. In an open system, self-worth is primary and "change is welcomed and considered normal and desirable."[3]

In closed systems, communications tend to be indirect. The opposite of the truth is often communicated—anger for hurt, blame for fear, indifference for love. Understandably this mixed-up form of communication can have a confusing, if not devastating, effect on children.

Claire and Mike Ridker, who do conjoint couple and family therapy out of their home in Evanston, Illinois, and are also founding fellows of the Gestalt Institute of Chicago, worked with a family who had just such a distorted pattern of communicating. A mother had been referred to the Ridkers. Her fifteen-year-old daughter had been in a residential treatment center but the center had asked that the girl be removed because of her disruptive behavior. The mother was looking for another place to put the girl, since mother and daughter constantly squabbled. The woman was a widow who had found another man but was afraid to bring the man into the house. The daughter had started acting obstreperous after her father had died. The mother was afraid of what might happen if another man came on the scene. She showed this fear by shouting at the girl. On her side, the girl was terrified that her mother would abandon her, as her father had when he died. The daughter showed her deathly fear of desertion by constantly making demands, blackmailing the mother with the implied threat, "I'll go crazy if you don't do as I say." It was the only way she could think of to keep her mother from leaving her.

The Ridkers quickly perceived that these messages were *incongruent,* the communication not in tune with the intent. Using skills acquired during 400 hours of training with Virginia Satir, in addition to their formal training in psychology and social work and their special training in the Gestalt approach, this therapy team decided to concentrate on the family's incongruent, stressful pattern of communications. They could see that everyone in that family—there was a son and another daughter in addition to the mother, her secret lover, and the "identified patient"—everyone was concealing fear and weakness inspired by threats. Were the threats *real*? The daughter believed her mother would leave her. The mother believed the daughter would get crazier or kill herself if she married the man she loved. The Ridkers had to teach these people that they could express what they were feeling without anyone dropping dead.

Claire and Mike explained and modeled some direct ways of communicating, or "leveling," as Satir calls it,[4] in which their voices and facial expressions and body positions matched the message. They taught them that "blaming" is a way of making someone else regard you as strong, a message that inspires fear. They explained to the seventeen-year-old son, who had smashed up several cars during a quasi-delinquent period, that distracting behavior—be it restless gestures like humming, jingling change, tapping, scratching, nose picking or even misbehavior in school—could be a way of ignoring the trouble in the family. They explained that "placating"—behavior by which one avoids the issue in an effort to prevent the other from getting angry—can actually have the effect of evoking guilt. Even the cool, distant, "computing" behavior exhibited by the healthy daughter at times was a way of pretending that the family problems were harmless, a behavior that often inspired envy. Finally the Ridkers helped the family to level with one another—to show anger if they felt it, but to show it clearly without undermining someone else's self-esteem. The mother was angry when she came home from work and found the house in a state of chaos, the pets unfed, the plants unwatered, and everyone's clothes strewn about the living room. These would have been the times when she blamed and threatened the fifteen-year-old. She learned, instead, to make clear demands. The daughter began to take responsibility for her pets and plants. She began touching her mother during the group sessions, and several times she and her mother cried and embraced each other.

Slowly they realized that their fears had been partially in the realm of fantasy. The mother loved her daughter and would not abandon her. The daughter could handle her mother's clear demands when she knew she was safe, so she didn't have to blackmail her mother any longer. The son, who had chosen to remain aloof or get in trouble, became more involved and began to express concern. His mother didn't have to placate him. He didn't have to feel guilty. Finally, for the last of the four family sessions, the mother brought her lover, now her fiancé, into the family meeting. They had decided to marry, and the children were preparing to have him move into the house. The daughter would live at home. There was no more talk of putting her in a treatment center. She still had occasional arguments, still forgot at times to care for her belongings, but she no longer needed to do these things to capture mother's love, so she did them less and less frequently. The family had learned to level with each other.

If an individual is caught in a closed system which allows for only one boss, then a change in the sick or subordinate spouse can be disastrous to the "boss." Here is a tragic case in point from the files of a former psychoanalyst who became a family therapist after treating this individual.

A married woman had been coming to a psychiatrist for some time because she felt continually depressed and frequently wanted to commit suicide. For four months the psychiatrist had seen the depressed woman by

herself, never with her husband. Gradually the woman progressed from suicidal inclinations to relative stability. The psychiatrist was pleased with her
progress and had decided to raise the possibility of terminating treatment.
As soon as the woman came in for what he had thought might be her last session, the psychiatrist realized she was deeply troubled. Before he could say
anything the woman announced, "My husband has killed himself."

Charles Kramer, head of the Family Institute of Chicago, used this tragic
case, which actually happened to one of his colleagues, to illustrate the limitations of individual therapy, the need to understand the family as a system—not just a collection of individuals totally in control of their destiny.

The system in this suicidal relationship required one strong, healthy partner and one weak and depressed. It is this sort of neurotic dependency that
holds many marriages together. This tacit agreement that one be, or appear
to be, strong and the other weak is violated when the weak one makes a
change on her own.

SCAPEGOATING

Just as some marriages depend upon the sickness, weakness, or depression of husband or wife, some families depend upon the sickness, misbehavior, or problems of their children as a means of avoiding the resolution of
their marital problems. Therapists sometimes refer to this process as scapegoating. In a case related by Dr. Michael Solomon of Denver, Colorado,
seven-year-old Ruth was the scapegoat.

Ruth was hospitalized at the National Jewish Hospital in Denver for serious asthma when she was seven. Instead of evaluating the girl individually,
Dr. Solomon asked to see the whole family together, suspecting that Ruth's
asthma might have to do with her inability to separate from her mother.

The history of the family confirmed Dr. Solomon's suspicions. The child
had first developed asthma within a week after her mother took her off the
breast. When the mother separated the child from the breast, the father at
the same time got another job. He had been working together with his wife;
the husband and wife had never been separated. This was a family in which
separation was so difficult that for the father to leave the house in the morning for work was a trauma to the mother. She broke down just at that much
of a separation. She could handle the father leaving if the child had asthma
because then the child couldn't leave.

Part of the treatment at the National Jewish Hospital is parentectomy—
involving a one-year separation for the parents while the child is treated at
the hospital. Unbeknownst to the hospital staff, Ruth's parents moved to
Denver from Boston when she was accepted for treatment. The mother
would go to the school Ruth attended every day to look at her through the
fence and talk to her. As Dr. Solomon perceived it, "The mother couldn't
give this child up to treatment." Every time Dr. Solomon got close to some

of the real problems in the family, the child would play her part by getting sick and threatening to die. After working with the family for nearly a year, focusing on the parents' relationship to the child, Ruth said, "I think that I should be sick for the rest of my life." The mother said, "Why in the world would you say something like that?" This seven-year-old child answered, "I've figured out that when I'm sick, the two of you know what to do, and when I'm not, the two of you don't know what to do. If I'm sick, you don't fight. If I'm not sick, you fight."

A year after the treatment began, Ruth was discharged from the National Jewish Hospital. Once Ruth was removed as the vehicle for the family problems, Dr. Solomon proceeded to concentrate on the marital problems.

Did Ruth's parents wind up with the "all-American," together marriage that so many of us hope for? No. As it turns out, this dream marriage is enjoyed by no couple all of the time and only some of the couples some of the time. What therapy did for Ruth's family was to change their system from a rigid, closed one which kept Ruth asthmatic, to a more opened process which allowed Ruth to escape from sickness and helped her parents not to an ideal marriage, but to a better, more satisfying relationship. Ruth has not been hospitalized or even been seriously ill for three years.

Men and women have a much easier time admitting they they are having trouble with their child, that their child is "sick," misbehaving, having problems, than admitting that they are having trouble with their marriage.

THE KID'S SICK; WE'RE FINE

A mother and father bring in their sixteen-year-old daughter, claiming she is having severe problems. During the first interview the child says, "Fuck all of you. I'm not coming back here if my life depends on it." During the next interview the parents show up by themselves. They tell the therapist that the real reason they asked for treatment was that the father had punched the mother three weeks before over a package of chocolate-covered marshmallow cookies. The mother was supposed to be losing weight and, like an alcoholic hiding his whiskey, she had stashed away these great marshmallow cookies. Her husband caught her devouring them, became furious, and punched her in the nose.

According to Dr. Solomon, who supervised this case, the parents of this sixteen-year-old had gone from being children to being parents without ever learning how to live together as man and wife.

"This is a man who married his wife from home. He lived with his mother and then took on his wife. As it happened, his wife had lost one of her parents early in her life. The two of them really, at that point in time, were not adults who were marriageable but children who needed parenting. They got married and lived in his mother's house and had no sexual contact with each other whatsoever for the first two years of the marriage, but stayed married.

They moved away from his mother's home and began to try sex. He had some problems with impotence, which didn't bother her because she wasn't thrilled about the whole thing in the first place. They had two children and put the children in between them. She became a mother and gave up being a wife, and that was terribly comfortable for her.''

We've heard many versions of this avoidance syndrome as we listened to different couples around the country. Couples can avoid dealing with many things quite well, especially when they have children. But when those children—who stood between the pain and helped them avoid looking at each other—try to move out from center stage into their own lives, then watch out. The parents are going to resist with all their might, as if their lives depended on keeping that child in the middle. Without her they face a life with a stranger—their mate.

So with the couple who brought in their "bad" teen-age daughter, it turned out that the sixteen-year-old, far from not doing well in adjusting to adulthood, was doing too well. She was about to leave them, and the two of them, once and for all, were going to be left alone, and that was the one thing they couldn't deal with.

Unfinished business is what many couples have to deal with. Sometimes the business is seventeen years old. With this couple it turned out that the teen-age daughter had an older sister who had died as an infant. The mother and father had never mourned for that lost baby. With the help of the therapist the mother began to grieve over the loss of this baby. "If you were to hear it," said Dr. Solomon, "you would have thought the baby died five minutes before she started talking. That's the amount of feeling she had about it.''

People can carry with them an unbelievable amount of psychological pain. Letting it all hang out is not always necessary or desirable. One need not relive every insult, every disappointment, in order to function in the present. While it is seldom necessary to relive one's past, an effective marriage counselor can help a couple deal with losses that have crippled their emotional life. The parents who had never mourned for their dead baby were able to do so, seventeen years later. Gradually they were able to communicate. She would put a note on the refrigerator door that said, "I need love and attention." He came in the house, saw it, and wrote at the bottom, "So do I. See you in therapy.''

They were too frightened in the beginning even to discuss these needs with each other until they came to see the therapist. But the mourning over past losses freed them so that within twelve sessions they were beginning to relate to each other as adult to adult, husband to wife.

According to Dr. Solomon, parents who can relinquish their adolescents have attended to work of earlier stages much more appropriately. But he adds that any family separating from an adolescent is in crisis. Those without any basic, long-term, chronic problems in their relationship may simply need what Dr. Solomon calls a "push over the hill." One such family came for treatment with their two teen-age boys. The mother expressed beautifully the normal sense of loss that a family feels when the children grow up. "What I wish for is to say good-bye to my children with a smile on my face and a tear in my eye," she told Dr. Solomon. "I want them to grow up and to be happy people in their own right. But I'm sad about what I'm giving up. If you're giving up something that's good, that has a lot of meaning to you, you have a right to be sad. You don't have a right to hold onto it, but you do have a right to be sad."

When the children heard their mother say these words, they were much more cooperative. This family was able to negotiate a satisfactory separation from their children and, at the same time, deal with their husband-wife relationship which had coasted for twenty-five years.

For example, the wife had received a portfolio of her inheritance when her father died. But she had never wanted to deal with the fact that she was competent and could be independent if she wanted to. So she had handed the portfolio over to her husband and never asked how much she had inherited. During the family interviews—after twenty-five years of marriage—the husband admitted that her income per year was almost double what he was earning. He had left home at the age of thirteen. She didn't leave home for a long time and continued to think of herself as a dependent person. Dr. Solomon says you find these two kinds of people gravitating toward each other. Their affinity had resulted in a good match, but the separation from their adolescent sons meant they would have to alter their relationship. Their family system of dependent wife/independent husband would need a reassessment. After twenty-five years, that's not surprising.

If we compare the parents of the asthmatic young Ruth, who had a history of chronic emotional problems, to this couple, who underwent what therapists call a "stage specific crisis," we can see the prognosis for the latter family is more favorable. Both went to the same therapist; both had family therapy. But a therapist is no magician. A marriage can grow and improve as the people are willing and able to grow and improve.

As pioneer family therapist, Carl Whitaker (now professor of psychiatry at the University of Wisconsin in Madison), expresses it, a therapist is like a piano teacher. "Some folks will come in and just bang on the piano and leave. Some will keep working and developing. Some will even wind up playing Beethoven." It's a matter of where you're at and where you want to go that will influence your choice of a therapist and the amount of change that actually takes place.

THE AFFAIR AS A SYMPTOM

Leila and Bruce wanted to go far. They wanted to play Beethoven, as Dr. Whitaker would put it. Bruce was studying to be a therapist himself. His wife had a degree in sociology and was active in campus affairs, spending a good deal of time counseling women who wished to return to work or school after time off for raising children. They had read many books on psychology and were quite sophisticated about therapeutic techniques. Doctor, heal thyself, one might have suggested. But of course this doesn't work in medicine or therapy. Ironically those who have the greatest familiarity with psychiatry—including the psychiatrists themselves—often don't seem to be able to master their own marital and child-rearing problems. You can't perform an operation on yourself, no matter how skilled you are. And as Carl Whitaker has said, "Therapy is like a surgical operation. I know there's going to be pain. The relationship [of therapist to client] is what makes the pain bearable. The anesthetic is our relationship."5

Bruce and Leila had been married ten years and had two daughters. During the last year of their marriage Bruce had become involved with another woman. He didn't know whether to leave his wife and children or break up the affair and try to work on changing the marriage. Family therapy helped them change their family system. Bruce and Leila give a highly articulate account of their experience with Carl Whitaker.

> BRUCE: It was either leave or find a way of satisfying myself within the marriage. And my model as far as my own parents go was to find satisfaction within the marriage. My parents were very devoted to each other, and so for me to split would have been very uncomfortable. I didn't see any reason why I couldn't be as happy in my marriage as I felt like I would be out of my marriage with this other woman. I knew the only way I was going to work that out was with a therapist.
>
> LEILA: At the time Bruce suggested therapy I was enraged; I was just beside myself I was so angry. Bruce's parents were exactly the opposite of me. He came from a together background. My father left when I was very, very young, and was in and out of the home. Mother and Father were divorced twice. In my case, I was living out a self-fulfilling prophecy. My father abandoned my mother and so Bruce would abandon me. I wasn't only mad at Bruce; I was mad at what had happened to me as a child, and I was carrying my mother's anger on my back. I went to that session because part of me was okay. And one of the early things Carl said was, "I'm not saving your marriage. I'm interested in you, Leila, and you, Bruce." And one of the things I learned first was that we weren't there to fix us. We were there to take care of ourselves.
>
> During that first session I was beside myself. I had the whole thing in front of me. It was like tunnel vision. I couldn't see out at all. Bruce is going to leave; I am going to be stuck with these children; I am going to have to do just as my mother did. I felt the way people must feel when they're going to be executed. By that I mean it had a feeling of inevita-

bility. Nothing will stop it. The juggernaut is going along, and I'm in front of it, and I'm going to get it. I felt helpless and angry. I can remember the first thing that Carl did, too, which for me was really important. He said, "Cry," and he really meant it. It's the wonderful thing about him. He said, "You are really in a lot of pain. I can hear it, and I can accept it and know that you are in pain." Which all of a sudden took me off the hook because I didn't have to convince him that everything was terrible.

BRUCE: I went to Carl feeling unsure about what the hell to do. I didn't know if I was going to keep living in the house or leave for the Coast. I was hoping that Carl would say, "I think you ought to stay here and work this out," or, "I think that leaving would be a bad idea right now." So at the end of the first hour, after Leila had cried and I had laid out my dilemma, Leila said, "I want to know what Bruce is going to do." And I said, "I don't know what I'm going to do. What do you think, Carl?" And he said, "Call me when you make up your mind."

I felt like I'd just been strung up by my teeth. Because here we'd come to the great man. He was going to sort all this shit out for us but he leaves me up in the air. "Call me when you make up your mind." Hell, I thought we'd just made a deal that he was going to sort it all out for us. Still, we wound up calling for another appointment, even though I hadn't made up my mind. At the second session I remember saying, "I don't know what to do. Would it be a terrible mistake?" He said, "If you follow your affect, you'll have to deal with the results later." What he means is right now your feelings say that you want to go; you want to be rid of problems. You can go and feel really good, but you'll probably have trouble with it, regret it later.

LEILA: He seemed to be saying you have to deal with things. If you flee from them, you turn around and marry the very same woman all over again. How many women go out and marry Fred or Larry and do it all over again because they never dealt with the craziness that messed up their first marriage. Essentially Carl was saying, "You're liable to take it with you in your little sack. You might not regret it, but you might have to relive the same problem later on."

Carl asked Leila and Bruce to bring their two daughters, ages six and three, to the next session. Like many couples who have been living with serious marital problems, Leila and Bruce were afraid to bring their children into the therapy sessions. They thought they could protect them from their marital problems. But family therapists believe that the children know when Mommy and Daddy are not getting along. Whitaker goes so far as to state that they know as much about the upset as the parents do. When the family admits the upset openly, the children are freed from the fears and burdens they have been carrying concerning their parents. As Carl Whitaker put it to another family who were reluctant to discuss problems in front of their child:

> I trust children's intuition and their understanding to be very deep in these very early years. I don't think they need to be in every time . . . but I think each time they come they contribute, and I think each time they come they get something from it. They get something from it because they have a sense of their family trying to do something about itself. And I think this keeps them from being panicked, in their bed at night by themselves, or being panicked at what they overhear, or what they think they overhear, or what they're afraid is going on. . . . I think the real facts are never as dangerous or as frightening as the fantasies and dreams that children can have about this, particularly when it involves Mommy and Daddy.[6]

LEILA: I had a three-year-old in the office who had her foot in the sugar bowl and one foot in Carl's groin, while Carl chewed on a piece of paper balled up in his mouth.

BRUCE: He's just enormously engaging and he loves kids. Janie got on the table with her legs up in the air and offered to feed him paper and he ate it. I don't know how he got rid of it. They had sugar all over the office.

LEILA: He told Janie he was a carrot. If the kids were older he would have talked with them about us, but being younger, we just let them do what they wanted to do. If we would have been tight and uncomfortable, I think he would have taken that up with us, but we weren't.

BRUCE: Carl will often take the youngest child who's capable of dealing with questions and say, "What's going on with Mom and Dad?" Rather than have the kids sitting there while the parents thrash something out, he gets the kids in right away and gets their view of it, because kids tell the truth. They may talk about painful things, and from that he can build up a notion about how the family operates. The kids will tell a lot of really important things about how they see Mother and Dad, or Mother and oldest daughter.

LEILA: But it's frightening for you as a parent. I was afraid that Janie was going to say something. I was really afraid that she was going to open her mouth. "You should see what they did last Friday night!" I had an awful feeling about it. We talked about it with Carl later, and he knows that parents get frightened, but he'll say, "Got any stories to tell about Dad?" And the six-year-old will say, "Yeah." And you know that she knows. You're hoping like crazy that she can't verbalize it too well.

BRUCE: But he would talk more about how the family related to one another. There's very little discussion about hassles, more about, What's the relationship like? How is Mother like Older Daughter? How does Mother get Older Daughter to bug Dad or not bug Dad? It's the system in the family where most of the dealing is.

LEILA: She asked our oldest, Kimberly, "Don't you think your daddy trusted your mom to take care of you?" Automatically Kim would know just exactly what he was talking about. She'd say, "Yeah." He'd say, "Are there a lot of times when you feel Daddy doesn't really trust Mother?"

BRUCE: But Carl is different because he feels his way into things. He says, "If you've got to ask what it is, you ain't never going to know." He might do something crazy, something that seems fantastic, and yet it makes sense later. He once asked me, "Do you have a kind of sense of a peaceful life?" And I bridled, because I was thinking, What's he after now? I said, "Yeah, sure; but not too peaceful." "Hm," he said, "going to tempt God, huh?" And I said, "Yeah, I'm going to tempt God, every once in a while." He sighed and said, "God might not like that." I mulled this over and realized, for the first time truly understood, that I could do anything, but I had to be willing to put up with the consequences. God was a metaphor. He says a lot of enigmatic and paradoxical things.

LEILA: I'm kind of explosive and Bruce is very even-keeled—especially before we went into therapy, that's how we were. Carl once asked Bruce what he did with all his anger at me. Bruce admitted it was hard for him to deal with, and he usually didn't express it. Carl told him, "You're going to cheat her of all those feelings." That gave Bruce permission to let out his anger. But Carl didn't manipulate us. He became so sensitized to our problem, he became part of it.

BRUCE: He does like to stir up trouble. With us, after about five sessions—he had seen us; he had seen the kids—I'm sure he had an idea of what we were like and where he wanted to go. He said, "I'm going to be a father for the two of you, and from now on, Leila, when I'm talking to you, I don't want you, Bruce, to interrupt. And, Leila, when I'm talking to Bruce, I don't want *you* to interrupt. Because the two of you spend so much time taking care of each other that you don't have any time for yourselves."

LEILA: And if I could say the biggest thing that happened to Bruce and me, I would say it would be our individuation. We separated and at that point we began to grow, really.

BRUCE: We were busy catering to our view of the other person's weaknesses, and each was taking care of the other so that neither would fall apart. He once told us an interesting little poem, and it went,

"If I am I because you are you, and you are you because I am I, then I cannot be I and you cannot be you. But if I am I because I am I, and you are you because you are you, then I can be I and you can be you. And just maybe we'll be able to get together." I didn't understand what he was saying at the time, but he held up his hands with the fingers interlocked and said, "Yeah, you're just like this."

LEILA: We had thought we were so marvelous together, but now it was a tremendous relief not to take care of the other, not to worry, not to hurt for him.

BRUCE: It's not letting the other person have the pain that is naturally part of life. It's like taking too good care of a child. We know so much about our spouses. We know those things in life that hurt them, the things that are difficult for them. And we set out to protect them from themselves, in the way you protect a child. But it's not a child; it's an adult.

LEILA: There was another thing going on while Bruce was having his affair. I had a sort of affair too, although it was not a consummated affair. I mean it was not sexually consummated. It was a friend of ours. He and his wife were having a great deal of difficulty. And we became very attached to each other. It came to the point where a decision had to be made about what we were going to do about it. That was going on at about the same time that Bruce's thing was going on. Bruce and I were scratching each other to make something happen—either to make it right or to separate. The affairs made us deal with—are we going to live with each other dispassionately for the rest of our lives or are we going to live with each other passionately? I mean not only sexual passion, but, the way Carl put it, are we going to live together or back to back, refusing to engage with each other?

BRUCE: I really started to feel hopeful when Carl gave me permission to say to him whatever I wanted to, as if Leila were not there. I wanted her to hear about my thoughts, but I didn't want to take responsibility if they would hurt her or make her fall apart.

LEILA: But Carl was very careful not to make any alliances. After about the third session I called him, sobbing and carrying on. He listened, and he said to me, "I feel you're in a lot of pain. I want you to bring your feeling in. By the way, does Bruce know you've called me?" And I said, "No (boohoo). What difference does it make?" He said, "Is this the way you treat your husband?" I was beside myself. Here I am bleeding to death and he's scolding me. He said, "If this is the way you treat him, sneaking around his back, calling me up on the phone, you deserve him to leave you. If you've got something to say to me, you bring it in." I knew right away that I couldn't have a special pact with him.

BRUCE: Shortly after that Carl brought in a co-therapist, his wife,

Muriel. We said, "What's she doing here?" He said, "I don't know. I guess I brought Muriel in to be with Leila." He acts on intuition a lot, but his reasons always turn out to be very solid reasons. See, I had never come out and said, "I need someone to take care of Leila so I can have permission to talk," but he knew it, and then he brought in the co-therapist. Leila told me that day in the car, "I can't understand why he brought Muriel in. All I felt when she came in was relief." Then I knew that Carl knew. I felt a shudder right down to my toenails. He was telling me, "Okay. If you're afraid to talk, here's somebody to take care of her."

LEILA: With the co-therapist, we could switch back and forth.

BRUCE: For us the most important thing he did—and bringing in the co-therapist was an extension of it—was to split us up so that each one of us could be responsible for just ourselves for a while. It gave me a lot of permission to be myself. It let me be angry, take risks. It gave me permission not to be so safe, so orderly and neat, to risk bad feelings. For me that automatically made the marriage better.

LEILA: I had been very quiet through therapy until Carl's wife came in as co-therapist. My anger was something that I feared greatly, especially in connection with Bruce. I didn't know how to get angry at a man because if I got angry at a man I'd be punished. I would get left or I wouldn't be loved. [That's what had happened with Leila's father.] Muriel is not a trained therapist, but she was her own woman in the sessions, even though Carl is so strong. One time Muriel looked at me funny and she said, "Leila, can you talk to Bruce without asking him to help you?" And that absolutely gave me goose bumps. It absolutely blew my mind. We had some real lulus with Muriel and Carl, the first fights we'd ever had where they were finished. They weren't repeated. And then we began to realize that we were surviving this anger. We could fight and not end the argument with nice, rounded corners, and it was okay.

BRUCE: It's not that all our problems went away then. There wasn't anything magical like that. Maybe we just began to feel more like struggling with them without any extra help.

LEILA: Finally I began to feel I was finished with therapy. I wanted to see Carl and Muriel socially, but that was it. I was through. I wanted to do things on my own. I guess I had come to the point in my life where I felt I could live and be me with or without Bruce. I had come to the point in my life where I felt I could love him and fight with him and raise the children and live my life. I had finally gotten hold of myself. I was really legitimized.

To Carl Whitaker the family is a unit which is greater than any one of its parts. "I don't think the mother and father are in charge of the family," says

Whitaker. "I think the family is in charge of the family. The world's greatest lie is, 'I didn't marry her blankety-blank family.' You *do* marry her family and she *does* marry your family. Covertly, manipulatively, they're always in it."

Whitaker's particular brand of family therapy emerges from ten years of working in the Atlanta ghetto hospital, from teaching, learning, and doing therapy with the faculty of Emory University in Atlanta where he was chairman of the department of psychiatry, and from pioneering new forms of therapy with schizophrenic patients.

"One of the big differences between family therapy and individual therapy," according to Whitaker, "is that in individual therapy you have to be concerned about whether you're going to be dangerous: the old medical thing—at least don't do any harm. I don't think that's true in family therapy. I think in family therapy the only real issue is whether you have enough power to make a change. In family therapy in contrast to individual therapy, you don't get far by just listening."

In an earlier interview published in *Techniques of Family Therapy,* Whitaker told Jay Haley and Lynn Hoffman, "I've learned that you can go on holding a family together and staying with it without changing it. I'm not willing to do that anymore. I want to get in with enough power so that I'm going to be able to get out. I don't want to stay the rest of my life with my finger stuck in the dike."[7]

While the traditional Freudian analyst avoids confrontation or even eye contact with the patient on the couch, Carl Whitaker sees himself as an "invader." "I want to get into the middle," he told us recently in his office at the University of Wisconsin. "I'll be her boyfriend and his boyfriend and his mother and her father and the devil's advocate." As one colleague describes it, "Carl reaches down into his crazy bag and pulls out something which is absolutely right at the time." We saw how important his comment about tempting God was for Bruce, how his little poem, "If I am I because you are you . . ." led to a sudden awareness of the problem, a revelation, an epiphany. He can eat paper that a child feeds to him, tell a homosexual that he's a bit envious of those who have had the experience of lovingness toward men. He can talk "schizophrenese" with a schizophrenic or fall asleep in the middle of a session if nothing is happening. Within the agenda of *change,* he can be as playful and free as a child. Though his words and actions could be mistaken at first for the irresponsible statements of an egocentric seeking to show off to the people who have come to him for help, it turns out his surprising behavior, his poetry and paradox, is based on a deep commitment to each family he treats, a commitment to help them change. He is more creative than most therapists. And whether or not one believes with him that "we are all schizophrenic in the middle of the night," it is clear that the revelatory experience of therapy or even conversation with Carl Whitaker is more conducive to change than hours of rational talk.

Another important element of Whitaker's approach is the establishment of himself as a trusted authority, somebody who has enough power so the family can relax their previous compromising arrangements. He conveys the sense that he will protect the family. "They don't have to be in terror about Father admitting that he feels homicidal about his wife. They don't have to fear that I'll condemn him or let her die in panic. That's the kind of strength I feel from the beginning."

When Carl Whitaker comes to that first family session, he has a definite strategy in mind. He has already insisted that both the husband and wife should come. Ninety percent of the time, according to Whitaker, the wife or husband who has phoned will not object to bringing the other, as well as the children. He claims this was even true years ago when he first came from Atlanta to Madison, Wisconsin, where family therapy was brand new. Whitaker's experience, and that of other family therapists, suggests that men are able and willing to be in therapy if their presence is requested or demanded. And in recent years the men themselves may be the first to call, as Bruce was the one to initiate therapy.

"I spend the first hour taking over, getting data, capturing Father," says Whitaker. "I think of him as the first thing to do. It's very much like chess. The king is very important. Of course, he's impotent as hell and he's hidden behind the children and a castle so nobody can get to him. But he's very important in a symbolic sense. The queen, the mother, I leave very carefully alone until I've gotten myself established as a loving, caring, powerful person. Just as in chess, you'd better save the queen for midgame. If you lose her you've had it." (This works because Whitaker is, in fact, a loving, caring, powerful person—which keeps the therapy from becoming mere manipulation.)

During the second session Whitaker is likely to flip the problems back to the family. He does not want to make them into mere chess pieces, despite his analogy. So he could say, "Where do we go?" They reply, "We thought you were going to handle it." He says, "No, I can't help you." They answer, "What should we talk about?" He says, "I don't care. Whatever you want." Finally they may tell him about the fight last night. Thus the family is led to initiate something themselves.

"I do this flip regularly," says Whitaker. "I establish myself as the rule-setter. But it's very clear in my head that they're the ones that have to carry this ball. I'm the coach. I can't carry the ball and I don't intend to. I'm very clear in my head that I work for them."

In addition to doing these flips, as he calls them, Carl Whitaker deflects some of his enormous power by never making a regular appointment so that the family must decide after each visit if they want to call.

One family told us, "Carl figures at the end of each session that people are in a sense rehiring him. But you always feel he's available. He tells you when you decide to stop, 'I'm always available to anybody who has ever seen me. They can always come in again. Whether it's in two weeks or two months or ten years.' He's committed to you.''

NETWORK THERAPY

At sixty-four Whitaker is one of the senior family therapists, but he continues to be on the "growing edge" of change in his field. He has already participated in one of the latest innovations in the family therapy field, an approach called "kin network therapy."[8] Network therapists hold that the system needing change is not just the immediate family but the larger network of grandparents, relatives, and close friends who shape our behavior. In a recent network session, Whitaker joined Philadelphia-based Ross Speck. Speck had gathered together thirty people—the "sick" man, his wife, their four children, the sick man's brothers and sisters, the wife's brothers, sisters, and mother. As Carl Whitaker described the network concept, "If you get two ounces of anxiety in each of thirty people, you've got a man-sized dose. They begin to cook. And once they're started cooking, *they* do all the work." In Whitaker's opinion, a system—be it a family system or the large system of friends and relatives which approximates the community—is not going to change unless there is anxiety. Anxiety, in Whitaker's view, is the motor that makes therapy move. A smug family, a smug community, will not be open to change. But few families today are smug; most are anxious and some feel desperate. Family therapy, and even the extended approach of network therapy which is strikingly close to community action, represent an attempt to build supports into a social system which has left the American family bereft and isolated, feeling sick when it is trying to change and healthy when it remains static.

RIGHT YOU ARE IF YOU THINK YOU ARE

Another daring innovation which Carl has tried from time to time and which has now developed into the treatment of choice for certain therapists is called "paradoxical intention," known to some of us as "logical extreme" or "reverse" psychology.

Whitaker calls paradoxical intention the "leaning tower" theory. If we look at the family as off-balance, skewed in a certain direction, threatening to collapse, then we can see it as a leaning tower of Pisa. Instead of trying to straighten the tower, rectify the imbalance by pushing or coaxing it back into an upright position, the paradoxical approach is to have the therapist lean with the family until the old, off-kilter structure falls over. Only then can a new structure be built.

To us this sounded more like a game or a joke than a serious approach to change. Then Carl gave an example of a young man who had been in and out of mental hospitals, who told his therapist that his problem was sitting in front of the TV all day. He had no desire to move, to go out and work, even though his father was a hardworking laborer who was dismayed over his son's inactivity. Instead of trying to convince the young man to go out and work, the therapist suggested that as long as he was just sitting in the living room, he might as well make himself decorative. He suggested that the man hold a bunch of flowers while he watched TV. He did. His father came home from work, exploded at the sight of his son in front of the TV with a bouquet of roses, and the structure crumbled. The situation had reached an absurd extreme. The young man said every time he thinks of staying home and watching TV, he remembers himself with the roses and he gets out of the house.

To find out how this unusual approach works with families, we interviewed the founders of the Brief Therapy Center, part of the Mental Health Institute in Palo Alto, California. They believe paradoxical intention is the most effective way to change family systems. Here are a few examples described by Dr. Richard Fisch and Dr. Paul Watzlawick, some of them based on cases they shared with colleague John H. Weakland.

A couple came to the Brief Therapy Center, so named because therapy is limited there to no more than ten sessions. They complained about their in-laws. The husband's mother and father were treating the couple like children. The son had never succeeded in establishing his independence, and when he married, his parents continued to run the show. They bought a home for the couple, furnished it to their own elaborate taste, and visited the pair four times a year, staying for three weeks each time. During these visits the mother would ban the young wife from the kitchen, insist on preparing all the meals, buying all the groceries, and washing all the dishes and clothes. The father would take over the repairs in the house without consulting the son. He would tinker with the two cars and do the gardening. When the wife tried to pay for groceries the mother-in-law would refuse. When the son would try to pay a restaurant bill, the father would grab the check and leave a huge tip. When the in-laws left, the wife looked for a rare and expensive gift which she promptly mailed with profuse thanks for the parents' generosity. A more expensive gift would follow the next week, courtesy of his parents.

"What specific goal would you want out of therapy?" asked the therapist. After some discussion the young man said he would like his father to say, of his own accord, "You are now grown up. The two of you have to take care of yourselves and must not expect that Mother and I are going to pamper you indefinitely." With this as the agreed-upon goal, the therapist suggested the following strategy. Before the next visit by the in-laws the wife was to stop cleaning the house. She was not to do any laundry or wash any dishes, pots, or pans. She was to leave the refrigerator and freezer empty. The husband was to leave any faulty appliances or auto defects unattended. When the parents came there was to be no arguing when they paid for grocery and restaurant bills. In fact, the young couple were to select the most expensive items. The wife was to let all the dirty dishes accumulate. She was not to assist her mother-in-law in the dishwashing. When the father was repairing the cars or doing the gardening, the son was to occasionally check by saying, "Hi, how's it going, Dad?" And then he was to go back to reading or snoozing. The young couple was to accept everything from the parents as if it were their due and to be as perfunctory as possible in their thanks.

The couple carried out most of the therapist's instructions. Two weeks later they reported to the therapist that the husband's parents had cut short their visit. Just before leaving, the father told the son in no uncertain terms that he was spoiled, that he had been treated like a child far too long. It was damn well time for him to start acting like the grown man he was.[9]

This was one of the milder cases that have turned up at the Brief Therapy Center, according to Dr. Watzlawick, who has a private therapeutic practice and is clinical assistant professor at the Stanford school of medicine. "Most of the people who come here see themselves as hopeless. They've been pushed around from one specialist to another, so they see themselves as wastebasket cases." Charging no less than $1.00 and no more than $35.00 per session, the brief therapy team has seen an immense range of cases in eight years—"Anything that could ever wander into any outpatient clinic from chronic schizophrenia to alcoholism to bed-wetting, marriage problems, teen-age problems, family oriented kinds of problems, weird, atypical problems such as 'My-big-toe-will-not-go-down!' We actually had this one case—the big toe stuck up. He'd been to doctors. Nothing wrong with his toes, so he was finally referred to us to get his big toe down." They did get that toe down in ten sessions, and it stayed down according to the follow-up report routinely carried out by the center three months after every case is concluded.

One such wastebasket case came in through a probation officer. A twelve-year-old boy had been brought to the probation officer by his parents. He had driven the family car. Even though he had returned the car without a scratch, the parents insisted that they would have nothing to do with the boy. "You just have to keep him," they told the officer. Out of desperation the officer called the Brief Therapy Center and the family agreed to come in. Psychiatrist Dick Fisch describes the case in his Brooklyn, street-savvy, hard-nosed style, with the suave, urbane European Watzlawick injecting comments.

FISCH: These rather uptight, very conventional parents bring in two young teen-age children who have been difficult to manage, partly because they'd been diagnosed many years before as having mental brain damage. They'd been on medications for that, the kids themselves not really pulling anything very bad, just the parents too appalled by even minor kinds of things. "We told him to brush his teeth at ten and it wasn't until ten fifteen that he got around to doing it''—literally! Not bad people or anything like that, just very, very uptight people with rather narrow views of the world. Things were brought to a head that night the twelve-year-old took the family car out for a spin, handled it rather well, parked safely. But this to the parents meant, "My God! Nothing can stop him now."

WATZLAWICK: This was a constant fear, the fear that they were out of control. The fact that this little boy who could hardly look up over the steering wheel drove this huge station wagon without producing a scratch, drove for half an hour, came back and parked the car—that simply proved to the parents that the situation was absolutely critical. Had he crashed, that would have been different.

FISCH: Yeah, then at least he would have had the fear of God, and that would have slowed him down, which was the phrase that the father used. The parents brought the kids to juvenile hall claiming, "We cannot control these kids." They were going to leave the one who drove the car with the probation officer, but the officer was able to persuade them to come here, out of desperation—typical of our cases. These people were quite pessimistic about anything good ever really happening with this kid. Many therapists would have challenged that pessimism. But Paul Watzlawick adopted the strategy—in our view of things quite correctly—of being very pessimistic himself. [One leans with the tower of Pisa.] The tactic was one of more pessimism than the parents: "There's very little we can do for him in ten sessions so don't count on us to do very much."

WATZLAWICK: We told the parents that in order to do something in the short time available, we had to see them at their worst. Consequently they were to take them off medication because this only blurs the picture.

FISCH: "Take them off all medications. Do not give any parental guidance this week. We have to see how rotten and evil and ugly the ulcer is." Now, this is said in front of the children, and the children—who were rather obedient in all the sessions they attended, just occasionally nudging each other—were told, "Now, children, as you've heard me say, for the purposes I mentioned that we need to see just how bad things are. You are not to try to restrain yourselves in any way. Just be yourselves and you won't be getting in any trouble with your parents because I've just told them to expect that this week you were going to be very bad."

The parents came in the next time and said, "Well, you know, we took them off the medications and it wasn't bad at all." So this started to defuse the situation. Evidently these kids didn't need medication. The drab diagnosis of brain damage might not have been that appropriate anymore or relevant.

Paul [Watzlawick] then went on vacation. We all volunteer our services here. I took over then. I'd been watching every session. We all watch each other work through a one-way screen. I still was looking for a deeper change, the tip of the iceberg that could change the substructure for the better. It came out almost by accident. The mother—this unimaginative, gray woman—suddenly pipes up, saying, "This week I know that Philip is in perfect control of himself." I said, "How do you know that?"—because all we'd been hearing was, "He's on the verge of loss of control." She said, "Oh, I have an intuition that can tell me even if he's ten miles away. If I don't have that sense of impending doom, then I know Philip is in control. When I have that sense of impending doom, which I have most of the time, I know he's on the verge of being out of control." I made a tactical error by challenging that and said, "What in the world are you talking about, lady, with this mind-reading crap?"—because I was worried that if she goes on with this mindreading business, then it doesn't matter what the hell the kid does. She's going to be bringing about a self-fulfilling prophecy. She stuck to her guns and said with no doubts, "Whenever I've trusted my intuition I've been right." Well, I realized I was batting my head against a brick wall.

Meanwhile, I'm getting telephone calls in from John Weakland over the intercom phone. "Dick, you'd better get off that kick," he said. "You're hitting your head against a brick wall and you'd better make a U-turn." Then something occurred to me. Here's a woman who has been saying, "These kids have the power I don't," but as far as her intuition goes, she's saying, "That's the one power I can trust. That I have." So I did some quick thinking as to how to redefine that intuition as a power, but a power that you have to use in a way that gets you to shut your mouth because that was a big part of the problem.

WATZLAWICK: The theme from the very beginning was if this mother would only shut up and stop this minute observation in all detail, and prediction and self-fulfilling prophesies about what they're going to do next and so on, things would be all right, so that a way had to be found to make her shut up, and this is what Dick hit upon.

FISCH: Essentially, instead of trying to knock down and eliminate what she was bringing up—this intuition business—I decided, "Okay, I'm batting my brains against a brick wall. Let me see if I can use it." So I made a U-turn by saying, "All right. I know I've been challenging it. I've been giving you a hard time. Now let me tell you the real reason for that. I do believe that people can have this intuitive power. I just wanted to test out your confidence in it. Now that I know you're really confident in it, let's get on with the business." I said, "Since you do have this power, could you see if you could change, since it seems to function as a receiving set?" And I started calling it radar. "Okay, you can pick up ten miles away what your kid's doing. But since you've got this power, there is a possibility that if you really put your mind to it you might turn also into a sending set and you could get him to behave essentially through the same radar mechanism. It doesn't sound likely, I know, and it's far-fetched," I told the mother, "but go ahead. See what you can do with it."

One of the ways I thought they might test it out was in this business of sending the kid to the store. Usually they gave him these terribly condescending, involved, directions, including what streets to cross when he came back from the store.

WATZLAWICK: Including a prediction of all the possible temptations that might arise on this corner and on that corner.

FISCH: So essentially I said, "Okay, in testing it out you don't know whether you can do it, but if you can, obviously you will need to keep your speech, your directions, to a minimum. If you make your instructions too detailed, as detailed as you've been making them, you won't know if your kid behaves whether it's because of your instructions or your radar. So give him a minimum of instructions, something as inadequate as 'Here's five bucks. Go to the store and bring back a dozen eggs and a carton of milk.' Just that little. I mean that's not enough, really, to go on. Then use your radar when he leaves. 'Come right back.' Guide him."

Well, she tried it. "I could see him in the store looking up at the clock, debating whether to wander off like he always does, and I concentrated real hard." This was the older son, Jim. " 'Come back,' I thought. 'Come right back with the eggs and the milk.' He came right back! And then I had another opportunity to use it. I got a call from the school that Philip was hanging around the bike racks and was five minutes late getting back into class," which indicates the surveillance system she'd set up where she had gotten the teachers to call up when the kid was late getting back into class! "So I thanked the teacher and I sat down, and I concentrated real hard. 'Philip, go back into class. Philip, go back.' And I got a call a few minutes later. Philip was back in class! I don't know whether it was coincidence." I said, "Well, it may be coincidence, but the timing is sure something." Now she had the power; she had the power to direct her kids just by thinking and giving the most minimum of directions.

I had also told her a story beforehand about an article, a true article as a matter of fact, by Marie Bonaparte, who is a French psychoanalyst. She had written a theoretical article that essentially, in the early dawn of man, before there was social organization, humans used to communicate by mental telepathy and that because of the necessities of social organization and the introduction of speech and later writing, this became atrophied in human beings, so I told her this is one of the reasons why I think some people still have that ability of intuition. "The more you talk," I explained, "the more it weakens your powers." So she shut her mouth. She gave the kids quite adequate instructions because that's all they needed—"Go to the store, come on back when you get the stuff." And it was one of these nice cases where things worked out fine.

WATZLAWICK: Two things need to be mentioned. First of all it's a nice illustration of Milton Erickson's principle, which is to take what the patient is bringing you. She brought this. Dick used it. He didn't say, "Look, this is weird. Nobody has this mental power."

FISCH: That's what I started to do.

WATZLAWICK: Yeah, but then he made the change. Our second goal of treatment was, we asked ourselves, "What is the evidence that this family has indeed changed?" One, of course, was that the boys were not getting into trouble anymore. But there was a second aspect that affected the parents' married life. As a result of this behavior, this "uncontrollable" behavior on the part of the kids, these parents hadn't been out, hadn't had any social life.

FISCH: Since the birth of the younger boy, twelve years before, they had had no social life.

WATZLAWICK: They had never been anywhere.

FISCH: They regarded these children as potentially kegs of dynamite that were about to go off in all kinds of destructive and embarrassing ways.

WATZLAWICK: Burn down the house.

FISCH: These are uptight people. Therefore they assumed, "We can't risk the embarrassment of bringing people into the home." And if you don't invite people into the home, you don't get invited out. "We can't afford to risk a usual baby-sitter to handle these kegs of dynamite. A young girl is not up to it and an old lady is too old." They'd never been anywhere without these kids. If they went to a movie, they had to take the kids along. So one of the goals of treatment was for these parents to go out to a movie without the kids—just once.

WATZLAWICK: We didn't tell them that.

FISCH: We alluded to it.

WATZLAWICK: But it was our criterion. If, in the follow-up interview, we found out that these parents had now some semblance, some little bit of a social life on an adult level, that would be further indication that the therapy was successful.

FISCH: We were willing to settle for just their going to a movie once without the kids because we figured if they did it once we'd be certain they'd come back, the walls would still be standing, and everything would be fine because these kids were not that bad. But if you do something like that once, then why not twice? Well, they did better than that. They'd been to a movie once and it went well, and they were feeling more and more relaxed. So by the time of the follow-up, they were about to go up to the seashore for a weekend without the kids. They had also invited a couple in for dinner. They were being invited out. So it was a real nice case.

There were many other cases described to us—a favorite being the couple who felt their marriage was growing stale and were trying hard to have fun, without success. Their attempted solution at planned spontaneity, their serious efforts at fun, simply perpetuated the problem. So Dr. Fisch told them to work at experiencing "nofun." "They were to sit without talking and think of nothing but dreary, somber thoughts. As they were sitting, trying to experience what nofun feels like, one of them started feeling silly and ridiculous. One giggle led to another and they just started having an uproarious time laughing about how idiotic nofun is. For the first time in a long time they wound up in the sack."

Since the trip to the Brief Therapy Center in 1975 we have heard of other therapists in other places—family service associations and private groups—who have been using this paradoxical approach successfully. Some report the approach works best with families who have a strong resistance to therapy. The more rigid the family system the more resistant the family would be to the standard talk and professional insight approach.

Thus, the main skill one looks for in a family therapist is the ability (developed through talent and training) to evaluate a given family system, to use the appropriate techniques to suit the family problem and to assess how much a given family is willing and able to change.

The Landers family is staid and conventional. George and Cynthia Landers have been married for twenty-three years. They are both in their fifties, both are professionals—he a dentist who also teaches and she a legal secretary. Both have conservative moral and political views. Their first son was a football hero in high school. Their third son is a straight-A student. When their middle son, Brad, was thirteen, he began taking a deep interest in the activities of student radicals. As a protest gesture during the Kent State killings he set a fire in his school playground. George and Cynthia Landers, intelligent and reasonable parents, were totally at a loss when this outburst occurred. The school counselor recommended Charles and Jan Kramer who work as a co-therapy team and head the Family Institute of Chicago, a division of Northwestern University's department of psychiatry.

Charles Kramer is dour and bearded, inspiring trust along with just a touch of severity. Alone Dr. Kramer might seem too forbidding. But he works almost exclusively now with his wife, Jan, a bright, cheerful, and outgoing woman who softens the gruff edges, much as Virginia Johnson renders her partner William Masters more reachable.

While the paradoxical approach of Watzlawick and Fisch or the playfulness and innovation of Carl Whitaker might have frightened or offended the Landers family, the Kramers, who have an air of safety and substance about them, were a good match for this family.

The Landers family went back to the Kramers a second time when their son, at sixteen, was chased by the police for speeding and wound up totalling the family car. Even a year after this episode, Brad's father could hardly bring himself to mention what he considered a shameful event and a sign of his personal failure as a parent.

GEORGE: The first time we went to the Kramers we went for a period of from three to four months. We had begun to communicate better, to be a little more open with the kids; there was more give and take. The Kramers sort of pushed us out of the nest. They said try it; we're always here. The second time we went was a year ago. That lasted almost a year. It was more or less a sudden episode. We thought we were pretty smart, but with Brad frustrations were building and the thing sneaked up on us.

BRAD: I had problems with the police, which ticked it off.

GEORGE: That's totally out of character for Brad, even more so than for the other two kids. That made the situation even more painful because in our minds it was something even more serious. It was longer before I was able to see the light. I was hurt, hurt in myself, guilty and angry with myself because I felt things weren't the way I had thought they were. I had missed the boat.

I felt I was being more accepting of other people's points of view after the first group of sessions. I had begun to be more open—let the family hear my problems and I would hear theirs. I had begun to see that everybody doesn't have to have the same goals in the same family, that one is not right and one wrong, and I began to accept the differences. I had always been the book drag, trying for the honors. But my oldest son didn't care about getting the A; C was good enough as long as he could play football. Well, that stopped bugging me. And with Brad in junior high becoming an activist—I couldn't see it then, but I began to realize Brad could wear dark glasses and have his own political views, but that had taken a long time.

BRAD: In junior high I was a fantasizer, picked up on Vietnam, the "Conspiracy Eight" trial, Kent State. I felt for the students. At fourteen, I felt helpless but wanted things to change. I started arguing in class, carrying signs at school. All this kind of peaked and I got in trouble at school. I set a fire on the playground at school, I guess as a form of protest. I was standing on a corner at the time and looking at the fire. I questioned it, saying, "Is the world that bad that this is going to help it?" A custodian came and put it out. I felt like a student on a campus, having a cop come over and put a student down. I became angry again. I could just feel for the students. I had friends who helped me with things like the fire, but I didn't have any backers really. My parents thought the students who protested were a bunch of hippies, freaks; you know, radicals. I kind of got angry at that. I thought they were lumping the whole group together as freaks. We got into some arguments at home about it too. The student protests did hit home.

The second time we went to the Kramers I didn't feel too good about it. It was twenty-four hours after the accident and I was still—I got into a chase and then there was this accident—excited, wrought up. I got there and I felt like I was being picked at and people were trying to pry out of me what happened and I just didn't feel like talking. After the second time I was able to open up. The first time the Kramers seemed like a couple of doctors trying to pry into everything. The second time they were friends. They were open.

CYNTHIA: I think you felt free to call them if you needed them.

BRAD: I did call them when I felt really uptight.

CYNTHIA: Both times unhappy incidents took us there. I knew we had to do something. I wanted some help and yet I didn't want to go. More often than not it was painful for me because we were trying to seek answers to problems. Often it was frustrating.

BRAD: With the accident I think the Kramers made it easier to take; they tried to cool the big thing. I don't think I took their teasing as badly as Dad took it. I took it as an easy kind of joking comment about it.

GEORGE: When I have a problem I don't want to be bugged by levity about it. I can't stand anyone being happier than I at that point. If I'm miserable other people who look less miserable bother me. I often felt, in general, that the Kramers were champions of the kids. We came off the heavies. They were highly critical of us because we didn't see a lot of reason for telling everybody, even other members of the family, about this thing. They kept suggesting that we were too secretive about the accident. It used to bother me when Dr. Kramer would kid Brad about the accident. It was nothing to kid about. After all, it was traumatic for me.

CYNTHIA: I don't think it bothered Brad.

GEORGE: Everyone in the family didn't see that incident the same way. There were times when it seemed to me Brad wasn't hurting nearly as much as I was. It took a while to realize Brad was hurting too, but it wasn't showing. Maybe mine was showing, but I didn't have to show it to myself. I knew I was hurt. So there were times we would get a little upset with the Kramers.

CYNTHIA: I thought of us as fairly permissive parents, but we realized there must be something wrong if this much tension was building up in Brad and we weren't aware of it.

BRAD: Part of what I got angry about was my parents' feeling, "It has to be us. Where have we gone wrong?" I kept saying, "It's a problem I have. I have the hangups and I have to figure it out." The Kramers took the position that I had to learn to cope with the tension. Going to the Kramers pushed me into opening up; it helped.

CYNTHIA: I think perhaps the children weren't telling us their feelings, but with the Kramers we reached a point where they could open up and say things that maybe otherwise they might have thought would hurt us. But they felt more free to say it there. "Keep off the pressure, Mom and Dad." So it was highly beneficial.

They did talk about who feels left out, who's like who. We also got into family history, which was interesting, back to our own grandparents, which brought out interesting things. "Were there members of the family you didn't care for? Were there difficulties between parents? Divorces? Fights?"

GEORGE: Some of those things I never accepted. We didn't accept everything.

CYNTHIA: Sometimes they tried to fit us into slots.

GEORGE: I thought they missed the boat several times.

CYNTHIA: You told them, "That makes me mad as hell!"

GEORGE: For example, one of Cynthia's sisters has been a major problem in their family. The Kramers questioned, did we really have to have a scapegoat in the family? As if the sister were the scapegoat! Now, that was uncalled for. I told them so, as if we had just come saying, "Hey, help Brad." I was angry about it. There were other times they listened to some things more than others because that fit their idea.

CYNTHIA: I didn't feel guilty about the way I had raised the children; I didn't feel good either.

GEORGE: If anything, I felt I had missed the boat. I should have known earlier in the game. There was no interblame between Cynthia and myself. In fact, the Kramers thought we were abnormal. We just don't fight very much. But we have loosened up more. Cynthia used to be concerned about the kids using dirty words, that sort of thing. She's tossed that out.

But I think our family has become more a family of people rather than parents here, kids there. I think there is more of a feeling of working together, supporting one another. There's a feeling of intersupport. These sessions helped us realize that kids aren't something you always have to control. If you let up on the control maybe you'll get along just as well. If they louse up, it isn't a reflection that, gee, you really did something bad.

As we've loosened up about the kids, I think we've started having more fun—our walks and things. It's more you and me again than it is you and me and all the diapers. And we realize that we still have the right to have some fun, just the two of us.

I think I've been able to talk more about my problems. Kids can understand that just because you're fifty, not all your problems are solved. I feel now I have an understanding audience to bring things to that may be bugging me, like at work. One of the major things I got out of it was the idea that there need be no hesitation in saying, "I feel lousy today." It's so easy for a man to say to himself, "I feel bad, but to talk about it is going to sound silly."

BRAD: Prior to going to the Kramers I pictured Dad as a pillar of iron, real strong. He'd come home, have dinner, go to work. After going to the Kramers, well, he kind of seems like a person, a human being, which is kind of nice.

Brad needed a change in the family to facilitate a change in himself. Realizing that his dad was human and vulnerable allowed him to abandon his flirtation with delinquency and to proceed with the business of growing up. Brad's father went from being the boss of a closed system to the participant in an open system. Therapy helped him to become less rigid, to loosen his iron grip on his family and on his own emotions.

The Kramers are not miracle workers, but they do facilitate minor feats of transformation—the stuff good therapy is made of.

VIRGINIA SATIR: BUILDING OPEN FAMILY SYSTEMS

Building an open system when one is surrounded by closed systems, at work and in the community, is often a very difficult task. With this in mind, Virginia Satir began seven years ago taking groups of families into the Sierras for two-week sessions of multiple family therapy and enrichment. Virginia brought to this experiment a masters degree in psychiatric social work from the University of Chicago and fifteen years of experience as a therapist and teacher of family therapy. Working with the late Don D. Jackson, MD, at the Mental Research Institute in Palo Alto, California, Virginia Satir developed ideas and techniques which have become basic to family therapy, many of which are included in her 1964 classic, *Conjoint Family Therapy*.[10]

A tall blond woman who radiates warmth, strength, and support, Virginia Satir handles large groups of people as a great conductor works with a symphony orchestra—making each individual feel necessary and important, yet always aware of the total harmony.

On the multiple family retreats she usually takes eighty to 100 people representing fifteen to eighteen families. The family members have ranged in age from nine months to eighty-three years. There are customarily three or four assistants—professionals in the process of being trained as family therapists. The total cost for the two-week session is $700 per family.

When the families troop up into the mountains they are faced with the problem of establishing a new community. They have to get their tents ready, cook the food, set boundaries, establish fire and safety rules. These are the types of survival tasks that have traditionally cemented communities, tasks which few families in urban or suburban America face today. Virginia reinforces the communal spirit by encouraging full communication among the participants. She gives everyone a "second family." The children get a second set of parents; the husbands get a second wife (with no conjugal privileges, however). So the once-isolated nuclear unit has a natural family, a second family, and adding to this Virginia develops a "conclave"—three families which act together as a support system at regular town meetings during which people can express any gripes or worries.

During the second week Virginia works with the individual families but she does this while other families are present so as to produce what she calls "maximum payoff." If there's more to be done Virginia makes a referral to another therapist, since her time is now devoted to multiple family retreats and intensive teaching workshops. Even within the two-week sessions the results Virginia Satir achieves are sometimes surprising.

"One year," she told us, "there was a little boy that came. I think he was about ten years old—and he looked a little sullen. He got treated like everybody else. In two weeks he became the star of the place. His mother told me later that she'd heard about the Sierra trips when her boy was in a psychiatric hospital in Massachusetts. He'd been there for four years. The doctor warned that the Sierra trip would ruin the boy. But as it turned out he never had to see the inside of a psychiatric hospital again because of the tremendous kind of things that happen. There's such openness and trust and validation and support that all kinds of changes get completely made. And that kid became, in therapeutic jargon, completely 'well.' "

Virginia Satir radiates a boundless faith in people's capacity to grow and change. Miraculous changes are not common in therapy, and they usually require much more than two weeks of even the most intensive therapy. If one is skeptical about Satir's high hopes for the human race, at least there is no doubting her personal belief in human potential.

"Carl Whitaker and I have something very much in common," she noted when we sandwiched a three-hour interview into her tight schedule of lectures and training sessions. "First of all we absolutely, completely, care about people—both of us. We would never hurt anybody. We would never be destructive to them. Secondly we really absolutely, completely believe that people can grow. We absolutely believe it. We'd put our lives on the table for that. And the third thing we absolutely believe is that anything a person needs to do for growth, he can learn.

"We as individuals feel free to do whatever the situation demands in whatever dimension is appropriate: to be humorous, to set up a game. I am not stuck in any kind of therapeutic box. If somebody goes through a catatonic episode, I can lie with them for eight hours with my body and breathe life back into them." (In Atlanta, Whitaker bottle fed several schizophrenic patients, rocked them, and fed them, allowing them to regress back to infancy and grow again—the process taking as long as three years.) "Carl Whitaker and I both believe in the creative use of oneself—the freedom to innovate on the spot, to understand the relationship of things so well that one sees how and where the system is operating. With me trust is developed so that people feel free to let themselves take risks and I'm free to invite them to do it."

The Rooney family—Bob and Betty, a couple in their forties with six children ranging from twelve to twenty-two—attended a multiple family session with Virginia Satir in the summer of 1972. They decided to take the trip in the hope of resolving some rather typical problems. Betty needed to accept aspects of her personality which she had disliked—her assertiveness, her "bitchiness" as she calls it. Bob was prone to depressive moments and felt dissatisfied with his job. "I didn't feel that I wanted to be where I was," he says. "I felt kind of stuck." The older children needed to separate from the family, and communications with the teen-agers needed improvement. In short, the Rooney family was a normal family, which is to say a family with problems.

BOB: It was a beautiful setting high up in the Sierras, seven thousand feet above sea level. We camped around a lake. Everybody hiked in, some of the supplies were packed on horses, and if we wanted any more, we carried it on our backs. It was an inaccessible place, very private. We camped wherever we chose, everybody in their own tents, but there were many together times, shared meals, shared meetings. There were nine families and fourteen professionals, fifty-five people altogether. With six kids, ours was the biggest family.

You know, this multiple family thing is something that Virginia pioneered. And part of the way that it came across was that you were kind of an intimate witness of some other families going through their thing and being part of that and making connections with yourself as an observer.

Secondly we were doing our own family, our own personal things, so there was an opportunity for personal therapy. We also had the opportunity to be students, to learn from Virginia. There were some times I remember as painful, mainly when I was talking about my relationship with my kids and how it had been difficult to get close to them.

BETTY: The whole group of fifty-five met with her every morning in the meadow, until twelve thirty. Then, after a two-hour lunch break, there was an afternoon session followed by a communal dinner. At night she sometimes saw people individually. The "family-stress ballet" was one of the first things on Virginia's agenda. The aim was to get the family or a member of the family to describe what the postures are in their family—the blaming and the placating and the being superreasonable, how everybody stood and where they stood in relationship to the other family members. Virginia got us to portray physically what was happening emotionally.

That's one of the exciting things about working with her. She gets you to physically do it, and it takes away all the garbage of words, and you get the feel of it really fast. She showed us the different postures and demonstrated how to structure them. If you're blaming, you pout and look angry, if your placating you might cower and clasp your hands in supplication. If you are "computing" you stand apart from the others. If you are trying to distract the group from the problem you might jump, dance, physically show that you are trying to divert their attention. Afterward we volunteered to do our family-stress ballet. Within three days there was a tremendous amount of trust built. There was trust right away with Virginia. Bob had wanted to have a relationship with the kids and Virginia had me go around and give each child permission to have a relationship with Bob. That's something we had been working on in our family for a while. I hugged each of the children and I cried. She noticed immediately that Stuart, our youngest, was upset, and she asked, "What's that about?" That's the way she operated. Boy, she picks up, she listens, and she watches the things that are happening in the family, and she works on that. So Stuart and I told each other how we felt, and it was a very beautiful meeting of the two of us. This sort of little vignette happened all the time.

BOB: I had the problem with my sons of not talking straight. Virginia took the role of my son John when I came home from work at night. I played myself. A couple of scenes evolved about what it's like when I walk into the house after work. Sometimes they were funny, sometimes very meaningful. It pointed up what it must have looked like from John's point of view, how little direct communication there was between John and me—not much more than a "hello." I had time there, up in the mountains, to go off with the boys and come back and talk. As a result of the whole adventure I did have a better connection with my sons, the older sons especially, and it was a lot easier to talk to them.

BETTY: And you're also able to let them "own" their own problems and not feel that you have to play rescue with them.

BOB: Right. I had felt I needed to help them somehow or I wasn't being a good father. It turned out that Michael didn't want help with his motorcycle, for example. He just wanted a little consulting on it, a little sympathy. But he didn't really want me to help him. That he would have resented. He wanted to do it himself, and he did wind up taking the whole thing apart and putting it together by himself. One of the things I had hoped for was better rapport with my sons, and that's one of the things I got.

BETTY: Our main objective was, as parents and people, to resolve things with our kids. The other agenda which I had was to get in touch with my bitchy side, and I did just that.

I wanted to feel good about standing up for myself. I had had a very difficult time with a neighbor of mine, and I think she epitomized for me a lot of the nuns who had figured prominently in my past life. My great need was to be able to stand up for myself with people who acted very authoritarian. I had what is called a "parts party." A parts party is something which Virginia has put together, a role-playing type of thing to help people get in touch with parts of themselves they have rejected or felt uncomfortable with. For me this was my inability to speak up for myself. The host or hostess selects five or six characteristics that they like about themselves in terms of five or six people. They could be Jack Kennedy for charm or Queen Elizabeth to represent their dignity, usually figures that are known. So you end up with five or six characters from history or public life that you'd like to have at your party, each representing one of the traits you like about yourself. Then you name about three characters you would not like to have at your party under any circumstances. They're frequently Nixon or Hitler, and they usually represent things like negative power, evil, hatefulness, fear, jealousy—usually parts of people that they deny or reject. "Oh, I don't have that part," or, "I don't like that in me. I want to get rid of it." Virginia notes down the adjectives you have selected for these unwanted people. And then, with volunteers chosen to play each part, good or bad, she has them intermix. The host watches and Virginia directs, sometimes heightening the conflict that the parts have with each other.

With over fifty people to choose from, there was a marvelous selection. I had nine parts in my party. I had to ask various people, "Would you be willing to be my warmth? Would you be willing to be my wisdom? Would you be willing to be my bitch?" The three parts that I didn't want to have were negative power, bitch—my manipulativeness, or what I call my sleaziness who came in the person of Frank Sinatra—and tragedy, personified by George C. Scott. These things evolved into my ability to feel pain and my ability to manage.

BOB: The point is that you need everything you've got, and you don't want to perform any psychic surgery and get rid of a piece of you. But you may want to evolve parts into something more useful to you. The party allows you to watch your parts interact, to see what happens when you, they, are under stress. The party becomes bedlam.

BETTY: Virginia asks the parts to try and take over the party. So sexuality

starts to try to lie on the floor or screw somebody. Power gets on a chair
and starts to make a speech. Warmth tries to hug everybody. And tragedy starts berating everybody, telling them how awful everything is.

BOB: And every once in a while she'll cut it, freeze the party, and go
around, and you can observe which of your parts are getting together.

BETTY: Who's fighting with whom.

BOB: Which of your parts are cooperating, which of your parts are in
stress, and does that have meaning to you.

BETTY: And who is trying to leave the party. Some of your parts are head-
ing for the door. They can't handle it.

BOB: It's a neat exercise. Various parts start to compete with each other,
and eventually they have to find some ways to cooperate and work
together toward an integrated party. A lot can happen in a couple of
hours.

BETTY: I finally saw those parts of me that I hadn't wanted as okay. They
can be useful to me. They're not something I need to throw away. I
came to a place where I can accept my manipulativeness, my tragedy,
my negative power. I felt very whole afterwards—instead of saying
something is good or bad, saying that's all me. Finally I could accept
them, you see, as part of me that I no longer had to push away or pretend were no good. That's really one of the objectives of all of therapy,
to say, "Hey, can you accept yourself as a whole person?"

BOB: What Jung would call "individuation," and a lot of people would call
"integration," and some would call "getting your shit together," Virginia Satir did by means of drama, this little gimmick, this parts
party.

There was another technique that Virginia used which also employed
role playing, something called "family reconstruction." It allowed me
to get in touch with my own family of origin in a much more realistic
way than I had before. Virginia tries to make you aware of how you got
where you are, what background you carried to where you are, and how
you can come to know your parents as real people instead of roles. In
my family reconstruction other people took the parts of my parents, my
brothers and sisters, and other important people in my life. Using my
memory and imagination, I reconstructed the story of my parents—as
young teen-agers, as young lovers, when they were married, their marriage ceremony, what their life was like when I was born, my being
born, how they reacted to my birth, and what life was like during those
early years in my relationship with my mother and my father, ending up
with some direct communication with my mother and father, using the
persons playing those roles. The whole experience of getting in connection with roots happened for me the first time during that multifamily
session with Virginia. So Betty, through the "parts party," and myself,
through family reconstruction, came away with a feeling of wholeness

and strength as individuals. We began seeing all kinds of strength in our kids. They really blossomed. When we finished we felt neat about ourselves as a family.

It was also the beginning of a long hassle about our relationship, which is still going on. But the part of it I remember is Betty's feeling of emerging independence, and her feeling of rejection by me because I was threatening to leave my job which was her security and my feeling of a lot of pressure of—"Don't do that." I think things were just starting to bubble to the surface at that stage of the game.

BETTY: We shared a lot. We would have a thermos of coffee that I would fill at night, and we'd have it in our tent in the morning and talk for a couple of hours. So we shared a great deal of what was going on with ourselves.

BOB: My depressions—I would have depressions from time to time— seemed to be worse for Betty than they were for me. There was a lot of dependency in our relationship. It was very difficult for me to relate to other women. So those two weeks gave me the opportunity. I don't mean I was fucking around, but I was able to make other connections. I remember giving a massage and getting one from a gal, I can't remember her name. I saw it happening all around. Our kids made a lot of connections, not only with kids but with adults.

BETTY: Yeah, I made connections with people up there, but I also realized you can't be close to everyone.

BOB: Of the fifty-five people that went up there, we still see about a dozen, and our children have remained close with some of the families

BETTY: I don't think anybody up there was what you would call "sick." I think the people were a pretty normal cross-section of people, some with real problems, but I don't think that any of them were terribly neurotic.

BOB: I think that all of us had real problems, and that's normal.

The parts party, the family-stress ballet, the town meeting—these are some of the techniques Virginia Satir developed to facilitate change. Other therapists rely heavily on videotaping of interaction between husband and wife in order to catalyze change in the family system.

IAN ALGER AND VIDEOTAPE

New York therapist Ian Alger, visiting associate professor of psychiatry at Albert Einstein College of Medicine, works primarily with couples groups and other groups. Dr. Alger finds videotape helps couples to understand how they work together to perpetuate their hostility. Seeing themselves somewhat as the therapist sees them often allows them to alter the relationship.

"If you look at fifteen minutes of a couple coming in and talking, how they move, how they arrange themselves, how they seat themselves, how their gestures cue each other in, you'll see that they're acting as a team, that they're putting on kind of a performance. You can quickly help them then grasp that they are both in something together.

"Even if they're fighting, even if they feel antagonistic, nevertheless they come in, to use the idea of sociologist Erving Goffman, as a little acting troupe putting on an act, cuing each other, expressing one thing verbally and another message nonverbally. If you can move couples through video to a new understanding of this process they're caught in, it can quickly undermine a lot of the back-and-forth acceleration of bickering and fighting that goes on. The video is very useful for that."

The family is similar to the family portrayed in Pirandello's play, *Six Characters in Search of an Author.* They have a particular scene to play, and if the therapist does not intervene in some way with a technique that helps them alter the scene, they will continue to exchange the same lines and actions.

"The crucial intervention that video allows is that you can both look at it together," continues Alger. "It tends to break the idea that there is a hierarchy where the therapist at the top will be able to look down at your behavior, knowing it and interpreting it better than you can. Video is a kind of equalizing or egalitarian method that tends to democratize therapy.

There's one couple I've been seeing, for example, and I used it a couple of sessions with them after we'd been meeting for about three months. The man was struck by the frozenness of his expression. He had never had any awareness of just how frozen-faced he was. He has changed since those two sessions increasingly, and he has told me he could never get the appearance of that face out of his mind after he saw it and talked to his wife about it. And he felt very differently than he looked. He was telling us together the other day that someone had asked him what he'd gotten from therapy, and he said he was almost embarrassed to tell him that the most important thing he got was that look on his face that he saw. But it is astounding that since that time—that's about two months ago—there is a difference in his behavior in the sessions. His face is absolutely more animated, which seems like a miracle, but it really is more animated. But I don't think it was just from seeing it and trying to make it more animated. I think he realized he was not communicating what he felt, and he became very aware of that and very interested in it. He thought a lot about it, worked on it, and he *is* communicating now in a different way. So that's exciting. That's just a simple little use of it, but a very important one because it changed the way his wife feels about their communicating entirely.

The importance of expressing visually what is going on psychologically led to a technique called "family sculpting," in which a family member is encouraged to create their version, their tableau, of family relationships.

FAMILY SCULPTING

Peggy Papp of the Nathan W. Ackerman Family Institute in New York has refined the family sculpting technique into a very effective tool for cutting to the core of family relationships. "The Chinese have a phrase for it: A picture is worth a thousand words. When you talk you forget what you said yesterday. You forget what you said an hour ago, five minutes ago. But a picture is almost emblazoned on your mind and you never forget it."

Instead of having families tell her what is going wrong, she will ask the husband, wife, or child to *show* her. Thus she has more than a physical diagram of the family dynamics, she has a moving picture. Videotape can only record what is happening in the therapist's office. Family sculpting brings in material from the home which may accelerate the process of change. As Mrs. Papp points out, "My whole emphasis in therapy is change. I like to be as economical as possible because I feel that years and years and years are spent with ineffective therapy where people just sit and talk and talk, and nothing happens, and they never change their behavior. They ruminate, they reflect, they analyze, and they go out and do exactly the same thing. A great deal of therapy is ineffective."

Family sculpting requires an effective therapist to make it work. If the therapist is too intrusive the family will show what they think the therapist wants to see. If the therapist is too laid back, the family will not put the technique to any effective use. Here's a sample of some of the guiding questions Mrs. Papp asks during family sculpting:

"When you are depressed, show me how depressed. How far down would you go? Would you go any further than that? How do you get up? Who helps you up? Does anybody help you up? Where are the members of your family when that happens?" Mrs. Papp tries to let the family lead the way so that it's their picture. She does ask them to change it, but she asks them to change in their way.

If a child is sculpting her family and has them all tangled together, Mrs. Papp might ask her to concentrate on certain basic triangles within the family. What is it like just between you and Mother and Dad?

As she points out, emotional relationships tend to form into triangles. "Whenever you have an intense emotional relationship between two people, under stress they will bring in a third person to try to resolve that. The easiest example is between a husband and wife. When they can't resolve a quarrel, they bring in a child, either as a scapegoat or as an ally. That's the most common, and we all do it. Or one of the parties brings in a mother-in-law or they bring in a mother or somebody at work. In families these triangles form all the time."

Another method Mrs. Papp uses to condense therapy is the "reversal."

"A wife complained that her husband never gave her any praise, that he was not sympathetic toward her, and was always critical of her. Everybody always puts themselves in the victim position in their family. So I asked her what would happen if she went home and when her husband walked in the door, instead of waiting for his praise and attention, she went over and lavished it on him?" When we laughed at her example, she noted, "Your reaction is exactly the same as everybody's; they immediately laugh. A reversal always gets a laugh. Every time I suggest one, a person bursts out laughing. First of all, it gets them out of that role of the victim, and secondly, there is something fun about doing a reversal. I always think therapy should be fun. And also, it works!"

Mrs. Papp is flexible on many points but she firmly adheres to one rule set down by the late Dr. Nathan Ackerman, founder of the Family Institute and a pioneer in family therapy. The rule is that both partners in the marriage be involved in the therapy, not just one. She remembers how Dr. Ackerman used to joke at staff meetings, asking the most inexperienced therapist, "Do you think that couple should break up?" If the therapist said yes, then he would say, "Well, send them both to individual therapists. The best way to break up a couple is to send one of them to an individual therapist or each of them to separate therapists."

Ackerman's insight that the couple is less likely to remain united if they see separate therapists has been confirmed by a number of therapists. The trouble is that some couples wait until their problems are so severe, their arguments so vicious, that they have to be seen separately for a period of time.

YOU'RE NOT SICK—YOU'RE JUST GROWING

Shirley Luthman is co-director with Martin Kirschenbaum of the Family Therapy Institute of Marin in San Rafael, California, where the first doctoral program in family therapy is getting under way. She is one of the strongest advocates we've encountered of putting the family in charge of its destiny.

The whole process of family therapy, as Shirley sees it, is one of teaching people to "take their own executive. When someone goes to a doctor, very often he or she will turn the whole thing over to the doctor, and the doctor makes the diagnosis, and tells them what they should do. Well, I don't believe in operating that way. If I go to a doctor and he tells me to do something, then I check it with my intuition. And if that fits for me, I'll do it. If it doesn't, I'll go someplace else. See, I retain the executive, and that's what I teach people. Never give away the executive, the final authority, to anyone. Never put somebody else's head higher than your own."

Such thoughts would have been regarded as heresy as few years ago. Even as late as 1974 an international congress of child psychiatrists would not recognize family therapy as part of the mainstream. It was considered a stepchild, worthy of attention, but not equal to the other Freudian heirs.

The basic difference between many of the newer therapies (including family therapy) and classical psychoanalysis is the difference between the medical model and the growth model. The medical model requires a patient and a doctor, symptoms and pathology or sickness, which only the doctor or authority could diagnose. The medical model has an air of respectability, and Freud may have adopted it to lend legitimacy to ideas which were regarded during his time with great suspicion.

But Virginia Satir and Shirley Luthman (who studied with Virginia) and many other family therapists use a growth model. Virginia told us recently that, "The only way anything can proceed is if hope is established." The medical model has less room for hope because one comes in with something missing or lacking or defective. The growth model has no doctor and no patient and no sickness. The possibilities for change and progress are already there in the persons that come to the therapist. They are already growing, but the therapist helps them to accelerate or modify the process. Is this *too* optimistic? Shirley Luthman and an increasing number of other therapists say no.

"There is no such thing as sickness or health," says Luthman, crediting her mentor, Virginia Satir. "There is only growth." Symptoms, in her view, are only barriers to growth which can be overcome; they are not indications of sickness. "All the parts are there. Nothing is missing, so that the process then becomes one of teaching a person how to assert who they are in a way that is clear and congruent and spontaneous, how to assert who they are with another person so that there is no loss to either one."

This means that the things which bring a family in for help are signs that growth is trying to take place, but some barrier is making that growth difficult. The child who cuts up his mother's slips, pours perfume over her clothes, sets fires in the washroom, throws up, develops asthma or migraine headaches, is sexually promiscuous, gets into dope or is starting to do a little shoplifting—is not sick! At least not according to Luthman's growth index.

Is it possible that there is no sickness, no health, no right and wrong ways of behaving, only different ways? This is very difficult for so-called "well" people to swallow, and it is even more difficult for doctors treating so-called "crazy" people to accept. Perhaps it is a leap of faith which only few of us can make. But the fact is that therapists who have great faith in the potential of every person to grow—and who also have years of experience and supervision—seem to be highly effective.

As Virginia Satir explained, it stands to reason that if you've been doing the same thing and there hasn't been any change, it's hard to believe there could be any hope. But if someone makes it possible for you to see that there is something different that can happen, then you can take a step, and another step.

Following the example of the late Dr. Don Jackson, who trained Virginia

Satir and influenced Fisch, Watzlawick, Jay Haley, and numerous others—Shirley Luthman is trying to have a multiplier effect by training other family therapists. Working with Martin Kirschenbaum, she tries to instill in her trainees the principle that the tendency of all families is toward growth, that therapy simply speeds up the process. She puts great stress on the responsibility and possibilities of each family.

"The whole process of therapy is to teach people that they are responsible for what happens to them without their judging themselves, criticizing themselves, depreciating themselves, stopping themselves, putting themselves down, or rationalizing; to teach them to take responsibility for everything that happens to them without using that information to hurt themselves; to handle their self-knowledge in a constructive way.

"The minute you and I begin to really feel powerful, we don't need to hurt anybody. We hurt, steal, destroy, only when we feel powerless. A sense of personal power is the open sesame to the universe."

But how does a person achieve a sense of personal power when their own family and the community seems to tell them, "You're no good and you're not getting any better"? This is the problem for the poor family, the slum family, families that could never dream of spending $700 for a two-week family seminar. Families who are lucky to have $75 a week for all their needs could never afford that fee for weekly therapy sessions.

Joseph and Grace Giordano know such families well. Grace Giordano, now assistant head of nursing at St. Luke's Hospital in New York, spent her childhood on welfare and much of her career bucking bureaucracy to gain advantages for the poor and powerless, even risking her nursing career to demonstrate for patients' rights. Joe Giordano, now head of the National Project on Ethnicity and Mental Health for the American Jewish Committee, is a man who understands better than most therapists in the country that ethnic and racial differences influence not only styles of cooking but styles of neuroses. The Giordanos frequently leave New York's Upper West Side on weekends to run multiple family therapy groups at their informal country home in upper New York State. Families who come to these weekends are referred by other therapists, hospitals, and frequently by the enthusiastic comments of those who have participated in group sessions. The majority of the Giordanos' patients are from lower-middle-class neighborhoods. Many of them are living on the edge of poverty and many have been in and out of mental hospitals.

The Giordanos told us that when you stay in the clinical setting you tend to look at people as patients, but when you come out of that clinical setting,

you suddenly open up a whole different world. We'd have twenty-five people including our own kids, and they would provide an extended family for each other. A kid who could not work on something with his old man could do it with another father. The identified patient in the family is a person who has been in a hospital from six months to a year. Rather than emphasizing a lot of the pathology, we are building a healthy place, trying to create a kind of new communal feeling for families whose kids had been diagnosed as schizophrenic, to give them an experience of what a healthy family can be like. People's health was focused on. Out in the country they began to feel capable. They could suddenly chop wood. This girl who was afraid to walk without a cane could go into the woods and chop a big bunch of wood with an ax. In the city she was afraid to walk without somebody holding onto her. Out in the country she gave away her cane and she chopped the wood. Even people confined to a wheelchair express some of the creative stuff in them. Out here they sing; they go fishing.

Not too long ago we had a guy who had been hospitalized constantly— really one of the most frightened men in the world. He'd been through the mill of shock treatments and thousands of medications. For the first time in his life he played pool, caught trout, and stayed up the whole night singing Spanish love songs and reciting poetry. He came down the next morning and said, "This was the best night's sleep I've ever had."

Joe Giordano is particularly sensitive to differences in ethnic values when he sees families. Even the food the Giordanos prepare on family weekends reflects this sensitivity—rice and beans for Puerto Rican families, borscht and sour cream for those of Jewish background. Their training and experience, plus the fact that Grace is Puerto Rican and Italian and Joe is Jewish and Italian, gives them an unusual range of culinary and cultural awareness.

The Giordanos don't believe in pressing people for money. They might charge $5, $15, or $40 for a multiple family session. They might charge nothing. Both Grace and Joe have worked in clinics, Grace at a mental health clinic on the multiethnic Upper West Side of New York. They have realized that different family roles are related to one's ethnic background. Grace is a strong and independent woman who sympathizes with many feminist aims, but many of the women she sees come from cultures where women are encouraged to be passive. "I treat a lot of Puerto Rican women. In their houses, if you answer back to your husband, you get a rap in the mouth. We're not going to reject these women or these men. We can help them feel better about themselves within the context of their culture, allowing the man to keep his macho trip. If he needs that trip, he's entitled to have it, but Joe, being very gentle, offers such a man another kind of role model."

The Giordanos believe the role of the mama and papa, the relationship of the mama and the son, the nonverbal communication, all these aspects of family life differ in different cultures. A Jewish family and a Puerto Rican family have different expectations for men and women, and an Italian family will have still other special cues and characteristics that a family therapist should be sensitive to.

"One of the problems in multifamily therapy," says Joe, "is that so much is going on. You really need two people. With six families, siblings and all, you really need co-therapists to pick up on everything. It also allows us to be symbolically Mama and Papa, a real family, rather than authorities speaking down to a patient. We try to play down our power of authority. It's never equal. They know you're the therapist, but with a group of families the collective group is very powerful too.

The Giordanos have developed a professional-personal life-style which allows them to be therapists and advocates for the lower-middle-class blacks, Puerto Ricans, West Indians, and other minority groups. Joe and Grace explained the special problems and satisfactions of working with these groups.

These happen to be people who have buckled under stress. They've been labeled sick because the internal and external troubles have become too much for them. They've got marital problems, yes, but they've also got health problems, school problems, problems with the courts, with alcohol and drugs. By taking them with our family, with other families, away from the urban tensions, they begin to say, "Hey, there's health." They begin to play on their own positives, that they're not shit, because if you're poor, especially, society says you're shit, and you get pushed around. But with this new atmosphere thay say, "Hey, I'm something; there's something good about me."

When people come into our life space, we feel a responsibility for them. I will not get involved unless I'm ready to go all the way. And that's the commitment we both make.

We have people who are handicapped, who live with men who beat them, and who don't know where the next dollar is coming from. Their kids aren't doing well in school. But you don't concentrate on the pathology or you get totally overwhelmed. You stop and say, "What's good about you?" That's what I ask people. "What's good about you?" And they stop and say, "Nothing." And I say, "No, no. That's a copout." And then they start to look at you, and they're telling you. Sometimes I even make them write it down. With a couple, even a common-law relationship fraught with all kinds of insanity, I say, "What's good about her?" "Well, she's kind of understanding when I'm really flipping out." "And how is he good to you?" If you start on that, then you can start focusing on the well family. Because that is really your goal.

One couple in the Giordanos' multiple family group had been married for twenty-five years. They had never gone on a vacation. One of their children had been sick for a long time, a daughter who seemed to them to become more disturbed when she went into the hospital for treatment. The daughter was twenty. The husband was uptight and frightened, the wife sad and depressed though their other two children were fairly healthy. There came a time in the course of the family sessions that they had a chance to go to Europe. "Oh, we can't go because what will happen to the child if we leave?" The child was twenty years old, but they felt she wouldn't be able to survive if they left. Grace explained:

What Joe and I did was, after the big multiple family session we said, "Let's go and have some coffee," and we took them to an Italian pastry shop in the Village, a famous one where a guy plays the mandolin and serenades you at the table. Joe and I had just come back, a year before, from Italy, and we were trying to tell this couple, "Look, you have a right to go away and to enjoy," but how do you say that?

So as we ate the Italian ice cream and drank the Italian coffee, I told them, "It'll be like this. Somebody will come and serenade you at the table, and you'll have a chance to be fairly relaxed and free, something to enjoy. Why do you have to continue beating yourselves and *hoking* yourselves all the time?" I think it was that night that they decided. We had gotten them away from the office, with everybody moaning and groaning and focusing on how sick they were, to this simple little place.

The couple went away, and then she sent postcards. This woman who had been so sad and depressed, who didn't open her mouth for weeks in the office, she blossomed. She wrote me, "You have no idea all the places we've seen, the marketplaces, the food." They went away and they really had a joyous time.

The process of the group, and the two of us, allowed this family to separate. When the parents went away to Europe the daughter came to the group. She could not succeed in keeping them home with her. She was angry, but the group accepted it. They said, "You're pissed because Mama and Daddy went away, but it's okay. We're all here. You're not going to be alone." And they had her over for dinner, and everybody took her in for a time. She would yell and scream, but that whole process allowed her to push away, to make the transition, to make it on her own.

Values are changing in this country toward family, toward neighborhood. We can't go back to the old ethnic neighborhoods because in most cases they're breaking down. So how do people create community? What was the business in the sixties of the whole communal search? It's a returning to a family, a new kind of family. The whole feminist movement means different kinds of constellations. But we'll still have to find some way where people together feel this kind of helping from other people around them, a closeness, a security.

What I like about multiple family work is that it provides a larger community for people, a new network.

Access to a new network is what many American families are looking for. It's a sad commentary on our fragmented society that people seeking communal support have been forced to see themselves as sick before they can find help in facing even the most ordinary family problems.

Well-family clinics, as suggested by Peggy Papp, the many marriage-encounter and family-enrichment programs now getting under way, may provide the access to advice and assistance most families want and need.

Our political and social institutions, our churches and synagogues, are finally beginning to notice that the American family—cut off from relatives and familiar neighbors, adrift on a sea of possibilities—needs new ways of navigating. Sirens beckon with seductive cadences: freedom, career, sexual fulfillment, women's rights, children's rights. And the family members from their drab, leaky boat can only counter with weak and questioning voices—"sacrifice? security? predictability?"

While policymakers decide if and when to finally take action on behalf of the family, family therapists are helping to shore up the boats and provide new compasses. They strengthen the family by revealing its resilience, its flexibility, its hidden resources to meet the crises which change has wrought. They remind us that "The ancient trinity of father, mother, and child has survived more vicissitudes than any other human relationship."[11]

4

Sex Clinics

It is the best of times and the worst of times for people with sexual problems. Never before have there been so many places where a man who has never achieved an erection or a woman who has never experienced an orgasm can be helped. Never before have there been so many quacks and charlatans vying for sexual therapy business, with little more than a leer to recommend them.

Now that we are finally able to recognize sex as a natural birthright of every man and woman, we have to guard that birthright from those who would exploit us. The healthy openness about sexuality which allows a husband and wife to admit, at least to their therapist, that they are not able to pleasure each other, the growing equality which tells a wife she doesn't have to fake an orgasm anymore—all this has led to a boon and a blight called the sex clinic.

One kind of sex clinic is the type described by Sharon and Dave Carlyle—a place where help is available from competent and concerned therapists, a place where a relationship can be rebuilt.

SEX THERAPY: A SUCCESS STORY

"He would rape me once a month." This is the way Sharon Carlyle described her sexual relations with husband Dave. They had been married six years. She was thirty; he was twenty-six. During the last two years of their marriage Sharon had been suffering from severe depression for which she was hospitalized periodically and continued to see a psychiatrist until she heard of a nearby sexual dysfunction clinic connected to a suburban hospital.

The pattern in the Carlyle marriage was this: Capable young woman who has been brought up to regard sex as something "done to" a woman marries

113

masculine young man who has learned to "do it" to a woman without asking questions as to her satisfaction. The young man also happens to be, psychologically, an adolescent.

The couple leave their families and move to a suburb near a large city where he finds a demanding job which barely pays the mortgage on their small bi-level; she stays home to raise the family, closeted with the children during their pre-school years. Little stimulation is offered in this bedroom community where the husbands are gone from seven to seven. The attraction which they originally felt for each other, instead of being fanned, has died down to a few embers. Sex becomes infrequent, a desperate escape for him from continual masturbation. For her it is a repulsive burden—as one minister told her, a cross you just have to bear.

This could have been the classic background for a divorce or the beginning of a loveless arrangement where sexual satisfaction would be sought, at least for the husband, outside the marriage.

Instead, it is the preface to the story of a second chance through sexual discovery guided by two capable therapists.

SHARON: When we moved here a year ago last January I wound up at the community hospital with a depression that lasted up until about a month or two ago. I kept seeing a psychiatrist every week, then every two weeks, and I just kind of never came out of it. He kept asking "How's your sex life?" but he was the kind of person that I just didn't relate to. So I more or less told him, "None of your business." I had been going to that psychiatrist every week for a year, spending thirty-five dollars for each twenty-minute session. Finally he recommended the Forest Hospital Sexual Dysfunction Clinic. When we found out it would cost eleven hundred dollars we started to say no. But finally we borrowed the money. We figured, well, it's cheaper than a divorce.

I came here from a small town in Washington state, near Seattle. I was very lonely, very depressed, and I didn't want to come at all. I hated it here. I wasn't wild about Dave's family. We've been here fourteen months and I just met my fourth neighbor Saturday, the fourth neighbor since I've been here!

DAVE: Back in Washington, near Seattle where we came from, the neighbors were always there. We'd have winter get-togethers; we'd go out to eat. Somebody would watch the house if we were going away. But here it's a bedroom community.

SHARON: People stop in their houses to eat, sleep, and then they leave. They get out early and the women go back to bed. A lady came to read the water meter the other day and she says, "There's nobody awake on this street yet," and it was ten thirty. It's different. My children had nothing to do here either. They didn't know anybody. Everybody was just sort of closeted here. The whole family just sat in this room.

[The room is a small one, sparsely and poorly furnished. The Carlyles have three children, twin girls who will be six and a boy three years of age.]

I was taking quite a bit of medication. I just realized the other day how much I was taking because I was taking four pills a day, and I took one the other night to go to sleep and I was out for a couple of days, just groggy. After about the sixth session at the Forest Clinic I started decreasing my medication and I haven't taken any for a couple of months.

DAVE: She's a completely different person. She isn't someone who is nodding at eight in the evening or unable to say good-bye in the morning because she is literally doped up. It's made a big difference in her personality and how we both feel.

SHARON: It's hard to remember how it was. We were so far apart that I knew it was either do something or I was just going to pack up and go back to Washington. I was already planning what I was going to take because it was too far gone.

I think one of the happiest times I had was when he came home one night and said he'd met another girl. All they'd done was have coffee or something, but I thought, "Oh, good. Finally I can get out without my church condemning me." It was really bad.

DAVE: I think we just decided that, "Hey, look. There was something there in the beginning, and we have the children, and if there is help available, even though it is expensive and money is a very important thing, let's see what happens. Let's give it a shot." I think there was still a little bit of fire left. The embers were still there. I can't remember exactly how we came about the decision.

SHARON: I'm pretty sure it was my decision. You would have done anything then just to get me out of the depression. I just figured that we couldn't get any lower.

DAVE: The last gasp at retaining our marriage. I was optimistic about it, though, to a certain degree, because in the back of my mind I thought, "Well, finally it's going to prove out that it's her problem and not my problem." And as we got into therapy more and more, it became very, very difficult for me, especially the first several meetings. As I look back on it now, I can see it developing that it wasn't her problem—it was my problem. I was bringing the patient in, but in reality I was the patient.

SHARON: I kind of resent that now, because everybody—both of our families and everybody that knows me—thinks I'm the one that was in the funny farm, and I was the one with all the problems. Actually I did have problems but Dave caused many of them.

DAVE: Before we were able to go in for the clinic program we had to borrow the money. And the only place that we could go was to my father and mother. My wife asked my father.

My father and I, we used to live in Wisconsin. We used to live on a dairy farm up there. I worked with my father day in and day out, and yet he and I were as far apart as we are now from Seattle, Washington, so to speak. We functioned together, but there wasn't anything there. My father's a very cold—I guess that's the term—not very responsive individual, not the kind of guy that would sit down and put his arm around you and say, "Hey, I really love you." You know that type of individual—a very *masculine* type, I guess is what he would be called. I couldn't ask him for the money for therapy. There was just no way. As much as I wanted to, I could see no way that he wouldn't say, "Hey, you dumb kid." Sharon said to me, "We've got to have the money," and I said, "That's right, but I can't ask my father for it."

SHARON: But finally I asked his father for the money. It was horrible. It was about the hardest thing I've ever done, I think. I told him, "I have problems." I said, "We sleep in the same bed, but that's it." I just really told him exactly what was happening. I asked him for the whole thousand dollars and he said he'd go five hundred. So we coughed up the other six hundred from Dave's life insurance. That was a hard thing to do.

DAVE: We went first of all for one whole day of testing.

SHARON: No, in the very beginning before we went, I made several appointments and you kept saying, "Oh, we can't make it." So then they told me, "You let him call and make the appointment and then he'll keep it." So he did, finally.

DAVE: I was reluctant. I don't know; maybe underneath in the subconscious I was afraid somebody would come along and say, "It's your fault."

Before we were married my mother took care of everything. I could take my clothes off and throw them in a heap and they would be picked up and the bed made and the dresser drawers closed. Somewhere along the line it became a very bad habit, and after a while I was unable to make any decision. I never changed my room, never put up a poster or painted the walls.

SHARON: He never bought a pair of pants. He didn't buy a shirt. I had to teach him everything. It was like teaching a child—taking him to school. And I still have to fight it constantly—not to do his work, not to take responsibility for him. I still have to keep working not to slip back into the old pattern.

DAVE: After we started going to Forest I began to realize that I was going through a rapid adolescent change in a four-month period; going from someone who was unable to make a decision to now, finally, getting on the bandwagon, taking some risks, finding out that if I made a mistake, so what. Everyone makes mistakes.

Anyway, that's probably why I couldn't make those appointments. But once the decision was made, I wanted to go there. Maybe, underneath, I could sense that there was a bigger problem than just our relationship. Something caused it other than, again, the patient, my wife, having to see a psychiatrist and being at the nuthouse.

SHARON: First we went through an initial interview and then five hours of testing.

DAVE: Answering five hundred and seventy-six true and false questions and writing an essay about your goals in life and drawing pictures.

SHARON: The next step after the initial interview and the testing was when we were separated. Dave was with the male therapist, Leo, and I was with Jean, the woman. She asked all kinds of personal questions. She asked me to draw a picture of a man—nude. This is something that was interesting. When we came back together they told us to turn in the pictures. Dave had been asked to draw a nude woman. Dave's came out a little tiny thing, almost a stick figure with nothing showing. And mine was very explicit, very detailed. Well, the whole thing came out as— Dave had all this sexual experience before we were married and I had none, and he was very inhibited and I was very *un*inhibited, which was just the opposite of what any of us thought it was going to be in the beginning.

[Basing themselves on the original Masters & Johnson model, many dysfunction clinics offer a male-female therapy team. In this case the team was composed of Leo Jacobs, a psychiatrist, and Jean Warnack, a registered nurse with a year of special, supervised training in marital therapy.]

They're a good team. They complement each other. If Leo would use psychiatric terminology, Jean would explain, "Now this is what he means."

DAVE: Leo would have a tendency to get very technical and Jean could sense this. That helped. And it helped to have a female—for myself—in there, a woman who is married, and older than ourselves, who says, "This is the way it is. We've talked to a lot of people. It isn't just what Leo is saying." But yet we respected Leo. He never ceased to amaze me. No expression would change on his face, yet he was like a Book of Knowledge talking to you. I just couldn't believe someone could read another person in that short a time.

SHARON: What got me is Leo would just out and out insult Dave and I used to expect that Dave would get up and punch him in the nose, and he could do it. But Leo told him, "You sit down. I'm in charge here."

DAVE: Yeah. I said something half serious and half funny to Leo, something about, "Look, I'm paying for this meeting," and he said, "I'm in charge here." And it kind of ruffled my feathers for that meeting, but later on I respected him for it. I think he was trying to give us as much as he possibly could in the time allotted. Maybe he felt I was wasting time, and now that I look back on it maybe I was trying to tread water for a little bit.

SHARON: I cried mostly. I was carrying around a lot of guilt because I wasn't taking care of my husband and I wasn't functioning right. I had the whole thing. I really felt bad about everything, and that's how that first session went. I was very shocked when Jean said to me, "What are *you* coming here for? What do *you* want out of it?" and I said, "I just want to show my husband that I love him and I want to be a good wife." And they said, "What about you? Don't you want anything for yourself?" I'd never thought of that before.

DAVE: They didn't hit me with the idea that it was my problem until the second meeting.

SHARON: At the initial interview it was my problem. He was sitting in more or less.

DAVE: Right, but at the second meeting they said, "We feel we can help you." And for some reason I believed them. I really believed that they could help us. I think, going back to the partner concept, it was having Leo explain a little bit what he was doing, not that he was showing off, and Jean explaining what Leo was doing, what he had accomplished, very briefly but to the point, that gave you confidence you weren't sitting with a quack. And Leo explained that Jean wasn't just a trainee in there getting her feet wet, someone who was going to stand around in the dark trying to pull things out. You felt you were in good hands.

SHARON: I did, immediately.

DAVE: After the first meeting the focus began shifting away from Sharon.

SHARON: They got real technical. Exactly what does he do and exactly what do I do, and what doesn't he do and what do I want him to do? Things like he doesn't hold my hand and I want him to hold my hand. Very basic.

DAVE: For a while I couldn't understand it. *She* was the abnormal one and *she* was the unresponsive one. I was doing everything correctly, and "Let's get on with the program and get *her* cured."

And later on, they did go back more into my past history, my relationship with my parents, my parents' relationship to each other. In fact we wound up spending only twenty percent of the time on the sexual dysfunction. Eighty percent of the time we talked about our families, our feelings, why we couldn't talk to each other. Most of it wound up being about me. I felt as though I was getting double help, not only for the sexual problem I was having but for the immaturity, decision-making, this entire thing.

It was probably the fourth or fifth meeting before I finally realized that Leo was shooting the straight dope and not beating around the bush. I finally had to admit—and believe me, this bursts your male ego to pieces—"Look, big strong six-foot four-inch, two-hundred-and-twenty-pound individual. You ain't doing it right!"

SHARON: In the beginning I couldn't understand. I wondered when they were going to get to my problem. I was a wreck. I was a nervous wreck. I couldn't sleep. It was just horrible because I knew that as soon as we got in there they were going to get on him again and I just couldn't bear it. I wanted the guilt. All this time I'd been taking the guilt. I'd been wanting it because I didn't want him to have it.

DAVE: Right. One of the big things they brought out was when they said, "Let Dave go. Let him do these things. Let him make the decision. If it doesn't get done, let him be the one that's going to catch it. Don't be pampering him. Don't be making excuses for him."

SHARON: We weren't making love at all; well . . . maybe I was raped once a month. But that was about it.

DAVE: Right, that was about it.

SHARON: I'd be okay if we'd had sex within the last few days or even a week, but after that it got so I'd be thinking, "God, he might ask me tonight and what am I going to do?" So I had to get a good book and go to bed early or else I'd wait until he went to sleep—I dreaded it—or I'd pick fights, anything.

It was horrible. It had been like that for about three or four years, since just after the honeymoon. I came from one of those homes, very religious, you know, Lutheran. You turned on on your wedding day and that was it. Up until that time sex was out, and I lived by that code. And I just didn't turn on that day.

DAVE: In her home they looked at it as being taboo.

SHARON: It wasn't so much my home. I really felt that way. But I wasn't exactly cold to the idea. You see, I came from a home where my father is affectionate almost to a fault. Sometimes you just wanted to say, "Leave me alone." And our whole family is like that. We didn't close the bathroom door. Dad would be in there taking baths. It was just a very open, warm household. Dave never saw his father kiss his mother.

DAVE: If you ever walked around our house in your underwear, even walking from your bedroom to the john, my father would say, "What kind of an indecent so-and-so are you anyway?"

SHARON: When I got married I figured things would be the way they had been in my home. It was going to be warm. But it just wasn't. It's not that Dave didn't want to be warm, he just didn't know how.

When I had the twins he was going to drop me off at the hospital on his way to work. Very unfeeling, just left me out in the cold. And I was from a family that was so warm, and I'd just tell him, "Why can't you hold my hand or something in a movie? Nobody is really going to see you." But he wouldn't—absolutely not. In fact he admitted it one time. He said, "I don't believe in showing affection outside the bedroom."

DAVE: But I was the experienced one. I knew all these different techniques, and I had practiced them with other girls. I knew my wife hadn't done that type of thing. It had to be *her* problem. In no way could it have been my fault.

I fought it at the beginning. At first I thought, "I'm not going to let Leo burst my ego." But finally I sat back and listened a little bit. That bubble, that ego, just started to shrink more and more. And I didn't feel as though it was something harmful that was happening that my ego was shrinking. It was just getting down to a size where it could be tamed and worked with.

Leo would go back to my father. He would try to show how I was attempting to identify with my father. Dad is six feet five inches, weighs two forty, a big man. He's got big arms. He was a very masculine individual—jet-black hair—and I think an attractive individual, but yet very, very cold. And I think what Leo was saying, what he was pointing out, was "Look. All these things are good. But there has to be something else there besides this physical being. There has to be affection. Like sending flowers, bringing something home, greeting your wife at the door, hugging her, kissing her, holding her hand in public—that's as much being a male as being physically a male."

[Following the format that Masters and Johnson set forth in *Human Sexual Inadequacy,* most sex therapists make use of sensory exercises which take the emphasis off performance and seek to forge between the couple what Masters and Johnson have called in their latest book by that name, "the pleasure bond."]

Those exercises—boy! That just wasn't the male ego trip for me. They brought out first of all a dishpan of warm water, and they said, "Remove your socks and shoes." I had to do it to Shar first. "Now I want you to caress your wife's feet."

SHARON: It was hard for him. It really was hard.

DAVE: I was to sit there, and they said to be as emotional as possible. I think I felt a mixture of anger and laughter. "That isn't the area to work on," I was thinking. "You work on the genitals immediately. If you want to get a reaction you don't start at the feet."

SHARON: About two months later we finally got beyond the feet.

DAVE: The first three or four times with the foot caress it was just, you know, we've got to do this because we have to fill out that little piece of paper that says, "What was the activity and when did you do it?" and, "What feelings and emotions came out of it?" My answers were one-liners.

They said, "No. This won't do. You just don't get away with giving us one line. You can say a lot more than that. We want every type of feeling you've got, whether it's how stupid this is or my wife's feet are dirty or something. Anything that comes into your mind at that time." Although I never did get into long explanations, after a while I think I could sense that we were going to be able to get some help out of this, and I was literally hurting myself by not giving them more information.

SHARON: They were just exercises, and when we would have bad weeks where Dave was real low or where he'd had a bad session with Dr. Jacobs, our exercises were total failures, and at times we had to go back and start over again. I don't think the exercises did that much, except they made you touch each other.

DAVE: But it was like homework; we had to get it done—often at the last minute, like Sunday and Monday before our Tuesday meeting. We probably hurt ourselves by treating it as a mechanical thing. And this is the one thing that was still very, very difficult for me to do because Leo was controlling my sexual activities by saying, "Look. The only thing you do now is you have the foot caress, and that's it, big boy!"

SHARON: And Jean would look right at him and say, "And don't you touch any other part of her." After that—I think at the third session—I was so shocked; they showed a film, *The Male Caressing the Female.* They showed that and they said not to do the genital area but to do the rest, and I don't know how many weeks went by before we got to the genitals. Then they showed us *another one!* I'd never seen anything like that in my life, but when I realized nobody was watching me, then I could watch it.

[The films referred to show slow sensual massage and fondling, playful use of the vibrator by male and female, oral sex, mutual masturbation, and intercourse with the female in the superior position.] When we first started to fill out those little sheets that we give back every week, I thought we were really going to get into something I couldn't handle. And I'd write in there, "Please, no oral sex." And there was none, not one thing. We weren't supposed to have intercourse until the last week. But there was no wild stuff, nothing we had to do.

DAVE: Nothing outlandish.

SHARON: There was no push toward anything. We had four exercises, one of which we just couldn't master. After the foot caress, then the body caress without the genitals, then caress of the genitals. And then we were supposed to do penetration [penetration meaning the insertion of the penis with no attempt at coitus]; we couldn't do that. And then intercourse. So there wasn't any embarrassment. I figured we'd have to go through some very distasteful things at the beginning.

DAVE: They put our minds at ease: "You're not going to have to perform in front of us," they told us. "We're not going to sit here with lights on and movie camera and take it back and say, 'Hey, you did this wrong, dummy. You see what you're doing there? That's wrong.'" They reassured us that there would be no pressure, no observation.

SHARON: Well, how would I have ever gotten you there without being sick myself? Never.

DAVE: Probably not.

SHARON: I don't think it would have ever happened if I hadn't had that breakdown.

DAVE: It probably wouldn't.

SHARON: I don't know. I mean, it took a real shock. I was going to live with it. I got to feeling, if I killed myself I'd go to hell, but I honestly felt that I'd rather be in hell than be here. That had to be the very lowest I ever was and probably the lowest one can get. You see, we were kind of addicted to each other. If something was bothering him I would immediately get depressed to take the burden off him or take his attention away from his problem and put it on myself. Yes, we were addicted to each other, like a person would be to alcohol or narcotics or something. We had to learn to be two individual people before we could function as two different people.

DAVE: I think Shar hit it. We were living off each other.

SHARON: And getting all the bad parts from each other.

DAVE: We just were not individuals. We couldn't talk to each other. We'd kind of roll over things. I couldn't say, "God! Why don't you do something with your hair? You look ugly." And Shar, on the other hand, couldn't say, "Why the hell don't you pick up your clothes, you slob, rather than letting them lay here?" And I think these things would irritate us, drive a wedge between us, until we were further and further apart.

SHARON: And yet we were really very dependent on each other. For a time, when I was probably at my worst, I demanded that he come home for lunch every day, which took an hour and a half out of his day, and he was home for maybe twenty minutes. I had to have him come home. I wouldn't go to the store without him. And now, shoot! I'd go on vacation by myself. Not that I don't love Dave, but I feel like a person by myself. I feel like I did before we got married. I like myself again.

DAVE: When I first met Sharon I saw her as a very accomplished person. That's what attracted me to her. I thought, "Hey, there's a partner that's levelheaded, that can make the decisions, and I can just keep on going my merry way," at least what I thought was my merry way. "When it comes time to get the insurance, she'll call the insurance man and take care of that. All I have to do—I'm the male—is work the eight-hour day and come home, like my daddy does, put my feet up, and turn the boob tube on, and get back up the next day." For some reason I had this built up in my mind as the way life should be.

I never thought much about what would happen after the wedding. I guess I expected it to come automatically. You sign the certificate. You slip the bands on. You walk out of the church and that's it. Like you've slipped a program into your backbone somewhere that says, "Boom! You're married. This is what you do." Only her program isn't the same as yours, but she doesn't tell you. Like Leo and Jean said, the wedding day happens and the wedding night is there. The male with his superego is not going to admit that he doesn't know how to make love to this stranger, his wife now, and the wife isn't about to burst his ego by saying, "Hey, you're doing that wrong," or, "I'm getting no reaction out of that." If we'd just admit to each other that we don't know.

Leo and Jean asked me right out once, "Dave, do you love your wife or are you just living with her?" "No, I don't love her," I told them. That's a pretty cold fact. Suddenly out of nowhere they pulled a chart out showing a curve, I guess you'd call it. In the beginning, when couples first meet, it's love—puppy love, whatever you want to call it. It builds.

SHARON: Then it builds way up, when you first meet—on the chart it's a line going straight up like a steep mountain. Then you get married and the line falls off, clear down to the bottom. You're completely out of love, and that lasts for quite a while.

DAVE: Right. Then it's a matter of rebuilding up again to establish what I would call the actual relationship. It can happen very quickly or, as in our case, it can take years.

SHARON: It didn't even start to happen for me until my first orgasm. That was the turning point. That was the big thing for me. It really was. Dave had been away for a week. While he was gone I took care of myself very well. Everything went just perfectly without him.

DAVE: Which surprised me because I called her up numerous times and she was just bubbling all over the phone.

SHARON: We had had eleven sessions. And there were a couple of weeks where I decided nothing is going to help. I thought, "I'll go through with it, but I don't know." I figured, "Shoot. If I haven't had an orgasm yet, I never will." That seemed like such an accomplishment.

DAVE: As I remember, you laughed. It all of a sudden came together— an accumulation of all the talk, and Shar getting off the medication and my being away. All of a sudden, bang! It happened.

SHARON: I finally realized I'm normal, just like everybody else. I hadn't really believed it before.

DAVE: If only people would admit that something just hasn't clicked. As

Leo and Jean pointed out, if you don't feel good, normally, do you wait around? If you have a strange pain in your stomach for weeks or years on end are you afraid to go to the doctor? No. You've got a toothache that's just killing you. Do you sit at home and pop aspirins for six weeks until your face becomes distorted from an infected tooth? No, you go to a dentist and you get it taken care of. If you've got an infected toe that bothers you and you can't walk, you go to a doctor who takes care of it. If you have appendicitis, you're not content to sit and worry and hope it goes away. You go to a doctor and have an operation and get it taken care of. If people would just realize that you don't have to be wierd to go to a shrink.

SHARON: They are expensive though. You can go to a physician for ten dollars, but you don't get in a psychiatrist's door for ten dollars. Still, I see people trying to gather things to make themselves happy—furniture, houses. That doesn't usually work. I say if you're not happy, do something about it. If you have to change husbands or move or drop the whole works, do it.

DAVE: For us, going to the clinic was worth every nickel and dime we had to put out.

SHARON: And if we develop a problem again, I think we'll go back to the same place or do the same thing over again because there is no guarantee we won't fall back into the same old pattern.

Sex therapy, then, is not just a course in intercourse, but a program of learning to respond to a separate adult human being, someone you may have lived with for years but have never known, someone who may have become a mother or father or child to you, someone who has ceased to be a live partner, a lover, and is now entangled with you in a sick, decaying dependency.

In a relatively short, concentrated period of therapy, husband and wife can learn to flourish; they can experience an amazing, accelerated growth—as Dave described his transition from adolescence to maturity in a period of four months. They can establish a new relationship which doesn't require one of the partners to be sick or guilty or hurt all the time, as the Carlyles' bond required Sharon to be sick and guilty so that Dave wouldn't have to take on responsibility.

A sex clinic can be much more than a place where a woman learns to achieve an orgasm and a man learns to delay ejaculation long enough to pleasure his wife. It can be a place where a man learns to experience potency not because of mere mechanical manipulation or technique, but through a new sense of self-esteem. It can be a place where marriages are rejuvenated, where people are given permission to pleasure themselves and each other, where women learn to ask for satisfaction and men learn to tenderly nurture.

But just as sexual therapy may hold the key to a new relationship, it can also be bungled so badly that men and women become convinced they are sexual and psychological failures.

THE NEW SEXPLOITERS

The dangers here have been exposed just recently by the first and foremost sex therapist, Dr. William Masters.

"The current field of sexual therapy is dominated by an astounding assortment of incompetents, cultists, mystics, well-meaning dabblers and outright charlatans."

His professional and marital partner, Virginia Johnson, in a rare moment of anger, told us there's so much exploitation in the field now that it's disgusting.

Continuing his revelation in *Today's Health* magazine of "medicine's newest nightmare," Dr. Masters claims that in the five years since *Human Sexual Inadequacy* was published, approximately 3,500 to 5,000 new clinics and treatment centers devoted to sex problems have been established in the United States. "Of these," says Dr. Masters, "the most charitable estimate cites perhaps one hundred that are legitimate. Our instinct says that fifty would be a better guess."

Quackery in sex therapy is nearly impossible to prosecute because there is no legal definition of what is and isn't a legitimate sex therapist.

"No state, to my knowledge," continues Dr. Masters, "has any law requiring that a self-styled sex therapist be licensed, that he conform to any minimum standards of education or experience, or that he observe any special code of professional ethics. The states license and regulate various professional titles, such as 'psychiatrist' or 'psychologist.' If you go into practice and call yourself a psychiatrist, you must be one and prove it."[1]

Five states now have laws requiring marriage counselors to meet certain licensing standards. These states are California, Michigan, New Jersey, Utah, and Nevada. But even in these states a sex therapist may escape the restrictions which apply to a marriage counselor. (California has introduced legislation to close this loophole in the law. She complained of a serious pain in her neck, as well as an unhappy marriage. Thus, the person who calls himself/herself a "sex therapist" can operate in most states, as Dr. Masters puts it, "with no restrictions beyond those that would apply to a candy store proprietor or any other business person. As long as you behave yourself, pay your taxes, don't perpetrate provable fraud, and avoid the trap of practicing medicine without a license—avoid prescribing medicines, for example, or giving advice about a patient's kidney functions—then you can probably count on a peaceful and profitable career."[2]

One such quack, who ran a therapeutic "community" where members were encouraged to break ties with their families and homes in order to become "trainees," was making $84,000 a year, according to testimony during the 1972 hearings on abuses by unregulated therapists conducted in New York State. New York Attorney General Louis Lefkowitz admitted that there is no way to protect the public from fraudulent therapists who are careful. "They are within the law," said Lefkowitz, "or more accurately—the nonlaw."[3]

The testimony of some individuals during these hearings suggests that a number of people seem to want to be taken, seduced, and defrauded, such as the woman who continued seeing her therapist after he masturbated her during a thorough examination. She wound up losing the pain in the neck, and also losing thousands of dollars plus a houseful of furnishings. "He told me that all the material things I had accumulated were not bringing me happiness." The therapist in question avoided the use of drugs. "He believed that all you needed to do was to relax your body." And he was careful to place the responsibility for their sexual relationship on his patient's shoulders. "He said that if we were to become intimate that it would be my responsibility to take the first step of undoing his pants."[4]

But a couple going to a sex therapist can be harmed, even when they are less gullible and compliant than the lady with the neck pain. Since this field of therapy is only a few years old, couples are confused about what to expect, what is legitimate, and what is unethical. Many people have confused the research conducted by Masters and Johnson with their program of therapy.

Here is one source of the confusion. The first book written by Dr. William Masters and Mrs. Virginia Johnson (now Mrs. Masters) was called *Human Sexual Response*.[5] The material in the book was based on direct observations by Masters and Johnson of the physiological responses of approximately 600 men and women ranging in age from eighteen to eighty-nine during more than 2,500 cycles of sexual responses. In order to make these observations, Masters and Johnson employed such devices as the camera-equipped plastic penis, performance of intercourse in mirrored videotaped rooms, and the use of sexual volunteers. Such techniques were necessary to make a scientific study of sexual response. Although a number of researchers had investigated the sexual behavior of male and female by way of interviews and animal behavior studies—Kinsey, Ward Pomeroy, Krafft-Ebing—none could accurately describe the physiology of the human sexual response. The female response, which is less visible, was shrouded in mystery and misconception.

Freud, for example, had believed that in normal females orgasm was always produced by vaginal stimulation. He believed the clitoris to be the erotic center of activity only during the early stage of sexual development. A mature woman should have a vaginal orgasm, thought Freud. Clitoral orgasms were a sign of immaturity or pathology. To this day, many so-called marriage counselors try to solve marital problems by convincing the woman to adjust to the more mature vaginal eroticism. Maturity, they mistakenly assert, is synonymous with satisfying the male. If a wife is not orgasmic when the male is in the superior position, she must be immature. In fact, what such a woman may require is a position or foreplay which provides more clitoral stimulation.

The clitoris is not like a teddy bear—something which female children outgrow. It is the source of erotic pleasure for the female.

Dr. Helen Singer Kaplan, in a fine and comprehensive volume called *The New Sex Therapy*, points out that recent studies have provided compelling reasons to reevaluate this clitoral-vaginal orgasm concept. "The new evidence suggests that stimulation of the clitoris may always be crucial in producing female orgastic discharge during coitus, as well as during other forms of lovemaking. Masters and Johnson have aptly defined the function of the clitoris as the 'transmitter and conductor' of erotic sensation."

Dr. Kaplan also notes that the clitoris plays no role in the execution of the orgasm. The actual contractions are those of the circumvaginal muscles. So that it is now believed that "all female orgasms are physiologically identical. They are triggered by stimulation of the clitoris and expressed by vaginal contractions."[6]

All this may sound like so much medical mumbo jumbo. In fact, Masters and Johnson admit to having purposely made their first volume as complicated and difficult for the lay person as possible, in order to lend respectability to an area of research that most of the medical profession considered laughable or unethical. But one cannot underestimate the importance of the research into human sexual response and the truly revolutionary nature of these recent findings.

Some of our beliefs about sexual response have been as uninformed as medical practices of bloodletting and theories that "humors" controlled the body. If the female response could be evoked by the same means which triggered the male response—the so-called missionary position for intercourse—then the theory of female adjustment made sense. But now it turns out that Freud was a few inches off. The much-romanticized simultaneous orgasm might happen coincidentally, but could be impossible, and even undesirable for many couples, including those women who require several orgasms for satisfaction, those who do not receive enough stimulation with the male in the superior position, and many, many others.

It is important to understand how ignorant we and the medical profession have been about human sexuality. Only then can we realize why so many of us suffer from sexual dysfunction (estimates run to half the population) and why so many doctors and marriage counselors have, in the past, failed to provide information and encouragement for couples to achieve satisfaction.

When Masters proposed it in 1953, research on human sexual response was considered professional suicide. As late as 1961, even after the publication of the pioneer research by Masters and Johnson, not one medical school in the country was teaching future doctors about human sexuality.

Now most medical schools offer courses on this once taboo topic, and some teaching hospitals, such as Loyola University's Foster McGaw Hospital in Chicago, offer training programs which include courses and supervised experience in a sexual dysfunction clinic.

In spite of these recent efforts one can calculate that a large number of physicians and therapists, and the majority of clergymen, have a limited knowledge or a mistaken concept of the human sexual response.

Many volumes and paperbacks are now available to explain the research findings of Masters and Johnson. But during recent interviews they provided one of the clearest and most concise summaries of the views which have brought sex into the twentieth century.

MASTERS AND JOHNSON

Sex—what is it? Sex is a natural function which begins at birth (possibly *in utera*) and continues, even during sleep, into old age. According to Masters, who delivered hundreds of male and female babies before he gave up his $100,000 practice as an obstetrician-gynecologist, all baby girls lubricate (the female counterpart of erection) within six hours of birth. All male babies have an erection within that same period of time—many, according to Masters, show they are functioning sexually before the cord is cut.

What distinguishes sex from other natural functions—such as respiration and circulation—is its unique vulnerability to social and psychological pressure. A man in his fifties does not become alarmed if he can't run as far or as fast as his teen-age son. He doesn't believe he is suddenly losing his ability to walk, run, and breathe. But when he doesn't achieve an erection as quickly as he once did, he begins to doubt his masculine prowess—the beginning for many of an inadequacy syndrome. As Masters puts it, "When fear starts, a man is fifty percent on his way to impotence."

The double standard. None of us in our culture has had the privilege of living with sex as a natural function, according to Masters and Johnson. Either we have been influenced by the notion of sex as something a man did to a woman, or we regard sex as something a man does *for* a woman—a kind of gift. In both these versions, the responsibility for sex has been the male's. If the female's requirements were to be met, she had to give subtle, even subliminal signals, or have an unusually perceptive mate. While he was responsible for his sexuality and hers, she was responsible for making him feel good enough, potent enough, to give her "the gift." No wonder nearly 50 percent of this society was declared sexually dysfunctional!

Male sexuality versus female sexuality. While the old division of sexual responsibility seems arbitrary now, and even ridiculous, there is a difference between male sexuality and female sexuality. Masters and Johnson, Mary Jane Sherfey, and Helen Singer Kaplan make clear that there is no comparison between male and female. The female has an infinitely greater capacity for sexual excitement than the male. From a physiological point of view, the female is naturally multiorgasmic. The male is not multiejaculatory. "The greatest mistake we can make in our culture," says Masters, "is to put equal marks on the wall." And Johnson adds that oppression by the female who now demands top-notch "performance" is as bad as the old oppression by the male who claimed to be doing something *to* or *for* the passive female. "At any age, sex must be lived. It cannot be performed."

This statement brings us to the second part of the Masters and Johnson contribution, which is the development of a form of therapy for treating sexual dysfunction.

One of the lovely things about William and Virginia is their humor. Virginia's sense of humor is conveyed by a gentle, knowing comment which pokes fun but also offers sympathy and support. William Masters' jokes come as a relief from a rather severe mien. One can believe he has the knowledge to help people, but one is unsure about his ability to get down to the level of us common folk—unsure until he tells one of his delightful anecdotes, such as the one about the engineer who tried to learn sex from a book. The sex manual instructed the husband to find the wife's clitoris and "stay with it." The engineer followed instructions until the moment before orgasm when the clitoris retreats. Then he would turn on all the lights and shout, "I've lost it!" After the punch line the blue eyes of Dr. Masters twinkle, the nearly bald head with just a rim of white is stroked, and you believe that he is the sort of man who might be able to care about your problem.

Dr. Masters says he's never written a how-to book because he doesn't believe sex can be taught.[7] Most of these manuals, he says with disdain, are written by *men.* Realizing that men can't fully appreciate the nature of female sexuality, one of the tenets of the Masters and Johnson approach to therapy is the use of male and female co-therapists. The team approach works particularly well when the personalities of the pair are complementary. Virginia Johnson notes that "We're not attitudinally geared to hear what we're told." Our bias of maleness and femaleness is too great. A man-woman team—even with a homosexual couple—produces comfort which allows people to change.

It is also comforting to know that Virginia is a mother, that she has no degree from graduate school, having dropped out of Washington University's doctoral program, and that she apparently has no sexual hangups, being fortunate to have grown up where "no one ever told me it was bad."

Not that Virginia Johnson would discuss her own childhood, her divorces, or her personal life if you were to come to the Reproductive Biology Research Foundation in St. Louis for help with a sexual problem. You would wait with your partner in a pleasant outer office filled with framed cartoons from *Playboy, Esquire,* the *New Yorker,* and other magazines. In spite of your anxiety you would have to chuckle at the sketch of the sailor waiting outside the Masters and Johnson offices with a mermaid in tow. Masters and Johnson have collected all these cartoons on one wall to show that they can laugh at themselves and be playful with a subject which does, after all, have a humorous side. You might be able to tour the foundation where research goes on concerning hormones with costly computers and highly paid scientists—rather than paid volunteers—being observed for sexual response. Masters and Johnson would greet you in white coats, which is *de rigueur* in St. Louis. They would be cordial. But they would not attempt to become your social acquaintances.

Masters and Johnson do not believe in forming friendships with the couples who come to them for therapy. In fact, they discourage any type of involvement, friendship, or even social interchange. The focus is on the emotional interaction between the partners, not across the desk. There is no "coaching," no observation of sexual progress, no demonstration of technique, no surrogate used. If the individual seeking help is not married, he or she must bring their partner. Four years ago, after a blackmail attempt and a lawsuit for alienation of affection settled out of court, Masters and Johnson discontinued the program of supplying a partner for the single dysfunctional person during therapy.

Virginia Johnson told us, "We feel a person who offers their services as a surrogate [a substitute sexual partner] is exploiting, because a health care professional can't sustain that kind of support." And Dr. Masters adds, when asked for his views on extramarital sex, that he has never recommended it. Even though the requirement for monogamy in our society is honored in its exception, Masters and Johnson see their role as therapists in helping partners find what they want *within* the partnership.

Many couples who come to their clinic have had extramarital affairs, especially in cases of unconsummated marriages. (One out of eight of the marriages they see at the clinic is unconsummated; in the most extreme case this condition lasted for twenty-three years.) But they ask the couple to declare a state of neutrality for two weeks. They then proceed to teach something about communication and reveal or mirror back to the couple things about their ability, or inability, to communicate. As Dr. Masters points out, they don't treat the dysfunction. "There isn't one thing you can do to help the impotent man achieve an erection. Since sex is a natural function, there is no way you can teach it. You can remove the roadblocks. Time is on your side. Nature is on your side."

Even when time is a problem, sex therapy can work. The oldest couple treated by Masters and Johnson was a seventy-two-year-old man and an eighty-four-year-old woman. He was suffering from temporary impotence after a lifetime of satisfying sexual relations with his wife. She told Dr. Masters, "I know I don't have much time left, so I'd like to enjoy what little time I have." She did just that, since the therapy was successful.

Dr. Masters will be the first to tell you that there is no such thing as the M-J technique. "We preach no dogma. We treat each couple as a unique relationship, and we don't know what approach will be followed until we know what the particular problems are."

Most sex clinics do use an approach based on the program which Masters and Johnson set forth in their second volume, published in 1969, *Human Sexual Inadequacy*. Some of the basic elements are: male and female cotherapists who provide interpretation and explanation for the spouses and moral support; treatment of the couple and the relationship rather than treatment of so-called dysfunctioning individuals; an initial period of interview, analysis, and education during which the couple refrains from intercourse; followed by sensate focus exercises—massaging, stroking, caressing, except for the genitals; an emphasis throughout on pleasure rather than performance.

But be wary of sex clinics which advertise use of the "Masters and Johnson technique" or ones which incorporate the names of Masters and Johnson into their title—such as the "Willowbrook Masters and Johnson Sex Clinic." Someday we may see McDonald's-type franchises in the area of therapy—"David Reuben clinics," "Comfort Outpatient services"—but there is nothing of the kind now. Masters and Johnson have trained only eight therapy teams spending from four months to a year with each pair. (The names of these couples appear in the Appendix.) Many other therapists and nonprofessionals who have attended workshops in St. Louis for a week or two advertise themselves as being trained by Masters and Johnson. In one case we investigated, the training consisted of nothing more than one ten-day workshop. After the misrepresentation was exposed by us in a magazine, the clinic removed the "Masters and Johnson-trained" description from their literature and lowered their fee from $2,200 to $1,100. Others who call themselves Masters and Johnson disciples have merely read their books, *Human Sexual Response, Human Sexual Inadequacy,* and, most recently, *The Pleasure Bond.*[8]

Masters and Johnson have no exclusive hold on the treatment of sexual dysfunction. They are in a position similar to that of Freud when psychoanalysis was first used to treat mental illness. At one time the only analysts available were those who had been trained by Freud: among them Jung and Adler, Reich and Erikson. But soon there were a number of therapists all over the world, including those who had rejected many of Freud's teachings, and were adding their own interpretations and original ideas which greatly enrich our knowledge of psychology. Our knowledge of human sexuality is a new frontier on which Masters and Johnson are the first pioneers, but by no means the only ones.

Helen Singer Kaplan in New York, for example, has treated many couples without a co-therapist. Most sex therapists do not schedule intensive two-week sessions requiring a couple to leave their homes and stay in a nearby motel. The notion of concentrated therapy (averaging twelve consecutive days in St. Louis) is based on the idea that things can fall apart during therapy. "We have to be there on the morning after," says Dr. Masters. But he also admits that reversals can occur in the first six months after therapy. Unless a couple has the means to make long-distance phone calls and visits which necessitate expensive plane trips, they may be better off seeking help closer to home.

There is something to be said for getting away from the distractions and pressures of work, children, and in-laws. Using the radio analogy, Dr. Masters says, "Each sending set can be improved. The receiver set is inalterably prejudiced by life experience and by male/female bias. Added 'static' is produced by jobs and kids. That's why we socially isolate people during treatment, to eliminate, temporarily, the static."

But how many people can afford two weeks at a hotel, baby-sitting expenses, and two weeks away from their jobs? (Twenty percent of the Masters and Johnson clients are on some form of "scholarship" or reduced fee.) In fact, the total elimination of static is not necessary in treating sexual dysfunction. Many therapists encourage couples to have at least one night a week without the children. They insist that couples keep the TV set out of their bedrooms, reserving at least twenty-five minutes a night for quiet talk, with clothes off and defenses down. Mothers who must contend with continual demands throughout the day are required to set aside a quiet hour for themselves, each day, when they can be alone and do as they please. If one has had no relief from continual demands from children and husband, how can one have anything to give by the end of the day?

Another thrust of therapy which may actually work better when couples are not closeted in a hotel room or office is the process of individuation. All the couples we have interviewed who went through what they judged to be successful experiences in sex therapy attribute part of the success to the process of becoming separate persons, or "de-courting," as one therapist defines it. There is no uninvolved partner in a sexual relationship, but neither is one partner responsible for the other's sexuality. Says Dr. Masters, "No man can assume responsibility for his partner's sexual function, nor can a woman assume responsibility for her partner's function." There is no way she can ejaculate for you or he be orgasmic for her. "Our culture is finally accepting the concept that effective sex is something individuals do together."

This process of taking responsibility for one's sexuality and one's behavior is often the key to changing and improving a marriage. The two partners are more likely to emerge from sex therapy feeling this greater independence and self-esteem when the therapists deal with some of the psychological causes of the dysfunction. The causes are not necessarily tied to any deep psychological disturbance, but fears which block sexual communication are probably responsible for blocking other areas of life.

Sharon was lonely and alienated when she moved from a familiar town to a suburban bedroom community. Her normal self-reliance had no outlet so she took responsibility for her husband. Her husband's inability to give affection, his lack of maturity and his indecisiveness, were causes of an inadequate sexual relationship, but she took the responsibility. She became the patient, allowing him to avoid any change. Footbaths and body massages did not solve their sexual problem. Neither did therapeutic films. What made the change in their sexual behavior and their entire relationship possible was the revelation of the causes, the exposure of the process of sick dependency that had developed.

When therapy is conducted by individuals trained to recognize and understand the causes—the psychodynamics of human behavior—the treatment is likely to be more effective. As Dave Carlyle stated, "I received double help at the sex clinic, help with our sexual problem, but more important, help with becoming a responsible and loving person."

Most cases of sexual dysfunction are not caused by medical problems, but an estimated 10 percent do have some physiological basis. If one of the therapists has medical training, he or she can recognize any physiological causes or factors—such as the influence of drugs, prescription medicines, alcohol, hormonal imbalance, anatomical anomalies, and various illnesses—influencing sexual behavior. If there is an MD on the therapeutic team, medications such as antidepressants and tranquilizers, which may be part of the treatment, can be prescribed. Being an MD is not sufficient, since medical training has not included until recently training in sexual response and sexual inadequacy. But such training is another safeguard for you in a field which is riddled with frauds and exploiters. Virginia Johnson lacks a formal degree in psychology, but she had years of supervised clinical experience. And, of course, her partner is an MD. A couple or individual has every right to ask about the psychiatric training of prospective therapists.

Another way to avoid exploitation is to demand that the sex therapist be accountable to an established hospital, university, or social agency. Clinics which are affiliated in this way are more likely to offer a wide range of testing and other psychiatric services. An effective screening procedure may reveal that one of the partners or both needs separate counseling, that individual or group therapy would be more advisable than the concentrated program of sex therapy which works best when marital hostility can be set aside or neutralized.

CONTROVERSIAL PROCEDURES

But even if one insists on training, degrees, and accountability, unethical procedures can and do occur. Practices which can lead to exploitation should be avoided, or at least approached with great caution. Here are two such practices in use by a number of sex therapists, practices with potential for doing damage.

1. *Coaching, demonstrating, participation in/or observation by the therapists of sexual experiences between the couple.* Foot massages or footbaths and facial massages are commonly observed by reputable therapists as one of the first exercises in sensate focus bridging the gap between verbal and nonverbal sexual communication. But therapists need not demonstrate how to manipulate breasts or clitoris, how to use the squeeze technique on the penis to retard ejaculation, or how to have intercourse the "right" way. Masters and Johnson; the Payne Whitney Clinic, headed by Helen Singer Kaplan; the Forest Hospital Sexual Dysfunction Clinic in Des Plaines, Illinois; and most other reputable sex clinics throughout the nation rely on the couple's verbal reports or their written reports on their sexual experiences.

But our investigation confirms the practice of coaching and observation reported by Dr. Kaplan in *The New Sex Therapy:* "Some sex therapists actually observe couples in the process of caressing and stimulating each other. They then attempt to teach them more effective techniques by direct 'coaching' and even by personally demonstrating such techniques."[9]

We could see rather quickly how such practices could lead to exploitation, but we wondered how two responsible therapists such as William Hartman and Marilyn Fithian could advocate such a controversial practice.

William E. Hartman and Marilyn A. Fithian practice their innovative therapy at the Center for Marital & Sexual Studies in Long Beach, California, about one hour's maddening drive on the freeway from Los Angeles. There, on the fifth floor, Hartman, director of the center, a PhD with twenty years of counseling experience, and Fithian, associate director, licensed marriage counselor, may be in the process of observing how a man and woman touch each other. "We're there to direct," says Bill Hartman, a genial man with a roguish but always appropriate sense of humor. "Anybody can run their hands over a body. Basically, it's the difference between a massage parlor which massages you and getting a warm, intimate touch from somebody who is committed to you in a relationship."

As Hartman and Fithian observe a couple, they are "looking" for changes in breathing, changes in movement during the caressing, which provide nonverbal clues to what the person is feeling, what is exciting them. From these observations they encourage each partner to verbalize the sensations they are feeling. The caressing begins with the hands of the partner. "He can hold her in his arms," says Hartman, "but as soon as he starts his hands going, he doesn't know whether to titillate, to scratch, or what to do. We'll say to him, 'Now, John, we want it in slow motion,' and John starts to move. 'John, we want it in *super* slow motion.' Then is when the feelings start to flow, in the super slow motion. But the feeling is the thing. We're not running a massage parlor. We are talking about caress, and caress has to do with feelings, and you've to go slow, and you've got to touch in a way that will maximize warm, deep, positive feelings flowing.''

Hartman and Fithian will be looking for those same slow, warm movements as the couples caress each other's hands, feet, face, breasts, and genitalia. "It's important for us to watch a woman who can't touch her husband's genitalia to see what she does, not just hear how she grabbed him by the balls when she got him in the motel. If she can't touch him lovingly in our presence, why should we believe that all of a sudden she's going to be loving and tender in the motel? So we do that as part of the sexual caress here."

But no, Hartman and Fithian do *not* observe the couple in treatment having intercourse. In fact, if the couple is able to do a body caress satisfactorily, Hartman and Fithian will leave the room as the couple goes on to sexual caresses. Sometimes, Hartman says, "couples cop out." If they do cop out, then the therapists will come back in the room, observe, direct, and comment.

Marilyn Fithian says they tend to get "very complex, complicated kinds of problems" at the center, most of which are referred to them by psychiatrists or physicians. They have two types of programs—one is five days long for couples who have been married a relatively short time and where there is a basically good relationship. The cost for the program is $595 or $495 (the more expensive situation includes meals). A two-week program for people with more severe problems costs $2,500.

One rather "unique" (to quote Hartman and Fithian) aspect to their treatment is what they call a "sexological examination." As described in their book *Treatment of Sexual Dysfunction*,[10] the sexological examination, which Hartman conducts with a female co-therapist present, includes the following: "The breast is lightly touched and the nipple gently squeezed to determine physiological response, as well as eliciting any feeling of response in the vagina." Any response to this stimulation is noted and pointed out to the woman with appropriate comments. The clitoris is checked to see if it is freed of clitoral adhesions. Also, "What we attempt to do is get her to focus on the feelings in her vagina, with an examining finger in the vagina." This, the authors say, is a way to check if lubrication takes place, as well as vascocongestion, nipple response, and sex flush. Also other gynecological conditions are checked. Finally the husband is called into the room where the male and female therapists are conducting the examination. "We have him insert a lighted plastic speculum into his wife's vagina. This allows him to look into the vagina and see the vaginal walls and the cervix and its opening, and he is able to see the area that has been forbidden for so long in our culture.'' The male sexological examination is not as complex, but the penis is checked to see that the foreskin is loose and movable. The wife is later called in and with the aid of the female therapist she examines and is coached on how to hold the penis in the squeeze exercise. "We note whether she is able to touch her husband's penis and testicles. Some women have never touched the genitalia of their spouse and are quite uncomfortable about it and need to have help in learning how to do this.''

The reverse may also be true. Hartman cites the case of a man who was always grabbing at his wife's breasts. The wife had told the husband that she didn't like it, but he persisted. She reacted by keeping her husband away from her breasts, contributing to their dysfunction. Finally, in the second week of therapy, the wife grabbed the husband's penis with the same intensity as he had grabbed her breasts. "When his wife grabbed his penis, for the first time in his life he knew what his wife had been experiencing.''

Most of the people who come to the center are in desperate need of plain, old-fashioned sex education. Men fail to understand that there are other methods of arousing their wives other than through insertion of a penis. Women are told that there is nothing "deviant" about having intercourse when their husband's penis is only partially erect.

Although couples who come to the center watch films and videotapes of caressing and intercourse, the couples are never filmed or videotaped while they are having sexual relations. However, volunteer couples who are part of the center's ongoing research program do permit themselves to be filmed or videotaped during intercourse. Hartman said that one doctor and his wife spent a week at the center, researching as well as spending a couple of hours a day in consultation. One day they asked if they could videotape themselves having intercourse. They were shown how to operate the machinery, how to lock the door, and how to erase the tape when they were through. The next day the couple asked Hartman what he thought of their tape. "What tape?" Hartman asked. "Didn't you erase it?" "No," the doctor replied, "we'd like you to go over it with us. We'd like you to critique it and give us some feedback.''

Hartman realizes that there is no way he could do that with all their clients, but this couple, and perhaps others in the future, those with an adequate or even good sexual relationship who want an even better one, might benefit from this kind of assistance. "We should be ready, willing, and able to provide this kind of help," Hartman says, "but the motivation has to come from the couples. If the culture changes to the point where people won't see this as an invasion of privacy but an invitation for needed help, then, at that point, the therapist should be ready to move, always making sure it's not the therapist's needs that are carrying them in there but the client's needs for a clear, professional service that's being requested.''

2. *The use of surrogates or substitute sexual partners.* Another highly controversial practice which is handled responsibly by Hartma and Fithian, but irresponsibly by some so-called sex therapists, is the use of a substitute sexual partner. One wonders, what is the difference between a sexual surrogate and a prostitute? And how did the whole business gain any legitimacy in the first place?

The practice of using paid sexual surrogates grew out of the need to help people without mates who were suffering from sexual difficulty or dysfunction. At one time Masters and Johnson did accept male clients at their clinic and supply them with paid female surrogates, but they discontinued this practice in 1970, as we have noted.

But elsewhere the practice of using surrogates continues, predominantly in California. Approximately 200 women and perhaps twenty men work under the supervision of trained therapists. There are several hundred more who call themselves surrogates but are, in actuality, prostitutes, because they have no training and no supervision except that of the pimp or madam whose only interest is in the client's wallet, not his sexual response. We have also spoken to marriage counselors in New York and Michigan who use surrogates but refuse to admit to the practice for fear of legal or professional reprisals. In many states intercourse between surrogate and client is a violation of laws against prostitution and adultery. The therapist who has recommended the surrogate may be considered, under the law, a pimp or panderer.

Surrogates are supposedly trained in certain therapeutic techniques. At the Hartman and Fithian Center, surrogates are used only for single or divorced individuals—usually men—who come to the center with a sexual difficulty but without a partner. The surrogates are screened and trained by Hartman and Fithian, who view them as part of the helping profession.

"The most successful ones," says Hartman, "are mature and comfortable with their sexuality, with a life-style of pleasing primary relationships, so that this temporary thing is not likely to throw off what they've already got their roots well down into." He says the surrogate work is roughly analogous to that of a nurse in a hospital,

The Berkeley Sex Therapy Group, which claims in their brochure to have had "more experience with individual sex therapy than have other sex therapists," rejects the term "surrogate." They refer to a surrogate as a co-therapist, an equal member of the sex therapy team whose specialty is "direct body work," and who sees the patient in a "controlled sexual context" in daily sessions of two and one half hours. By "controlled sexual context," they mean that the person who specializes in the body work conducts one hour of therapy in a special room or apartment, "observing the patient's ways of responding." Therapist and client then go to a different office where they report the results to the other member of the team, the review therapist.

The cost for the two-week individual sex therapy program is $2,180. A married couples' program, also lasting two weeks but employing no surrogates, costs $1,440.

Martin Williams, PhD, a member of the Berkeley group, insists that anyone should have access to this form of therapy, even a married person. If the only way a person can manage sex therapy is without the spouse, then, according to Williams, therapy should not be denied. When we noted that Masters and Johnson no longer use surrogates, Williams commented, "Masters isn't a psychiatrist and Johnson isn't formally trained at all. The way they do sex therapy, especially the way they approach surrogate therapy, indicates a tremendous amount of naïveté about what therapy is and how to do therapy on people." While Williams believes that the dangers of exploitation with surrogate work are overrated, authorities such as Helen Singer Kaplan feel the effectiveness of such techniques has not been demonstrated and the ethics of such practices are highly questionable.[11]

We questioned the possibility of finding a surrogate who could be detached enough yet sympathetic enough to have intimate physical contact with numerous strangers and put the observance of the "body work" to good use. What follows is an interview with a woman who comes as close to fulfilling the objective surrogate-helper role as anyone we have interviewed or read about.

AN INTERVIEW WITH A SEX SURROGATE

Lana (not her real name) is a sexual surrogate who works with highly reputable therapists in Berkeley (not the Berkeley Sex Therapy Group). She charges $500 to $700 a case, which runs for ten to twelve sessions. Other surrogates often charge a great deal more. "I liked surrogate work because it was a fixed contract. You work with this person for two weeks. 'Hello, how do you do?' 'We do this together,' then, 'Good-bye.' At the end I would be free to go to Mazatlan if I wanted, or Spain or Portugal if I wanted, none of which has happened."

Lana's story is fascinating because of the intensity and depth of the insights she brings to her experience. She is a woman who has been able to penetrate the mysteries of man's sexuality, a woman who uses the techniques of pleasuring for her partner's as well as for her own satisfaction. At thirty-two, she is a sophisticated, sexually certain woman.

Yet there is a strange contradiction in her life. Her "primary relationship," as she calls it—the man she lives with—is a twenty-six-year-old student. He is a spoiled young man, given to tantrums and violent outbursts toward Lana. One moment he is screaming and the next, lighting up a pipe of hash, lying back and staring for hours at one of his many unsold sculptures which lie around their tiny house. His method for retaliating against Lana's "work" is to have affairs with many other women. She endures him, almost maternally, saying, "I'm in love with him."

Lana is naturally beautiful. She eschews all makeup save for some pale lipstick. Her eyebrows are full, her nose straight and narrow. Her long, straight, chestnut-colored hair is parted in the middle and hangs down until it touches the slopes of her breasts. She wears snugly fitted Levi's which mold her thighs and hips. Her voice is deep and full; not theatrical, but the tones rise and fall in harmony with the words she is using. Her gray eyes are always focused on your eyes.

Her background (with only a few of the highly specific facts changed so as to protect her identity) is basically upper middle class. She graduated from college with a degree in literature and philosophy. Her interest in writing led her to her first job as a writer for a small magazine, and then, for five years, as an editor for a weekly newspaper.

Here, in her own words, is the story of Lana, a sexual surrogate.

I'd lived in the same small town all my life. I had commuted to college. I had lived with my parents when I was going to school. I was married. I put my husband through medical school. We were living in the house that he grew up in as a kid, and I was very much rooted in one place. And I began to go through a period of "My God, am I this train that's headed straight for the void? I know exactly how it comes out and I'm only twenty-three!"

I pulled away from that and got involved in something that was pseudotherapy. It was moderately revolutionary, moderately therapeutic, and moderately visionary. There were encounter weekends inclined to confront people with the fact that we live in an oppressive society, confront them with the fact that there was a war in Vietnam and that we were not in control of our lives. It was a very visionary time of my life.

Part of what we confronted was sexuality—what are our sexual values and where do they come from? I went through a whole lot of physical changes about how I felt about my own body, lots of beating and screaming kinds of encounters. I became a kind of staff person for these weekend encounters.

The goal was not to make people into bisexual swingers so much as to make people into a community of change and alternatives. We were trying to gather people, and we were drawing primarily on a white, middle-class, youngish population who were mildly dissatisfied with their lives but not quite sure why and wanting to rev it up and create some motion.

I got involved in the women's movement and finally ended up leaving my husband, hitchhiking across the country with two other women, going through a period of my life where I blew out all the stops, became sexually very experimental. I would fuck just to fuck—threesomes and foursomes. I would fuck anything I could put my cunt around. It was liberating to me in a whole lot of ways. I have a sense of it being what probably would have happened to me if I'd moved away to college.

[After a few months of being on the road, Lana went to Arizona and worked at a drug crisis intervention center, acting as a kind of paraprofessional with several other volunteers and paid staff members. She then moved to Berkeley, living with a man for a time, not working at any steady job. She met a woman who knew a therapist, one who had been doing sexual therapy with surrogates, and suggested Lana interview for a job as a surrogate.]

During the interview with the therapists I told them, "I don't know if I can do this. I have no idea. I'm counting on you to interview me really hard. Don't go easy on me because I don't want to get in the middle of this situation and go 'Yikes! I can't handle this.' I don't want to misrepresent myself in any way. I don't know if I can do it. What is it?" Then we talked about what being a surrogate is.

I agreed to do it with the understanding and agreement that, more than in any other work, I was to tell the truth about my own experience. That seemed like an incredible win. At the very worst the truth would be, "This is really awful for me and I can't stand to do this anymore." Then there might be a variety of truths along the way.

Sexually, I didn't believe it would be like a whore because at the worst, a whore's job is to pretend that she's enjoying something she's not, to forget about her own feelings in deference to another's. I wasn't making that contract. I was making a contract to share with another person the truth of my body, to say what I liked and didn't like and to try and hear what they liked and didn't like and learn about that.

I think there are women in the Berkeley area who will call themselves surrogate partners who are probably just very kind, slow, patient prostitutes, and that's probably fine.

From my standpoint I would never work with somebody who has a mate or a wife. That's just where I am. I'm just not willing to be somebody that they go to and get cured and then go back and try to transfer to their partner. I'm in the business of making a contract with a person who has somehow gotten so confused about his own sexuality that he's unable to form a lasting relationship because that's always in the way. So at one level it's a contract to give a person an experience of himself that's sexually all right.

On another level what I'm doing is deconditioning his fear. In my backlog of experiences I had before I was a surrogate, I made love with a virgin. I made love with a man who'd never made love before and it was okay. We survived. We had fun. We got the giggles. We got it up; we got it down. I can do that and it's not scary to me. I know I can handle that situation. It's providing that kind of experience for a man who has had a lot of negative experiences. That's also part of the role of a surrogate.

The first person I acted as surrogate with suffered from premature ejaculation and secondary impotence, but primarily it was premature ejaculation. He was twenty-six or twenty-four, however old you are when your parents are putting you through school and it's taking a long time.

He was real, real uptight sexually and therefore not able to maintain a relationship with a woman. He was just super, super withdrawn from women, and he had tried all kinds of other therapies.

I walked in and met him. We went to dinner and sort of told each other our life stories. I told him a little bit about who I was and how I lived, that I lived with a man who was my, well, primary relationship. You see, it's very important to me to make clear that "I'm not here to fall in love with you or to marry you or to live with you. I'm here to practice bodies with you."

That's not a criticism or an antiromantic thing. It's building the fireplace so that when the fire comes it doesn't burn your house down. You see, in my own life I'm a very romantic person. My wish for each of those men that I've worked with is that they find a mate, that they can get comfortable enough with their own sexuality that they can do the real learning which occurs when you stay with a person over a long period of time. I have that bias because I have that in my own life and I value that highly.

This, in a sense, is what I tell them: "Be clear who I am to you. I'm here to show you as much as I can about who I am and how my body works and how a woman's body works and for you to learn how your body works. We will do what the therapists tell us. My contract is to meet with you for ten or twelve sessions, two- to three-hour pleasuring sessions in your own home. You don't come to my house. You don't call me. We don't have dates. We're doing this thing together, learning, doing practicing. Between each session we have, we come in to the two therapists and tell them as honestly, as completely as we can, what we thought and felt and what happened. And then those therapists put their attention on that and tell us what to do next, and then we go back and do it."

Well, we went to his house. We took off our clothes. We took a shower together and we touched each other's bodies in the shower. We took turns giving each other a back rub, a complete body rub. Breasts and genitals were excluded the first session. We gave feedback to each other, saying what gave us pleasure, what hurt. I remember it as awkward and pleasurable.

Then we came back to the therapists and reported. If everything had been awful and freaked out, the therapists would probably tell us to go back and do the same session all over again. The therapists don't let you take a step until you've already taken the step before.

The second session included show-and-tell, some genital pleasuring, but not focused on that. The third session was arousal—getting and losing an erection for him, and for me, just saying what I wanted during genital pleasuring. It included the squeeze technique, since he was a premature ejaculate—you know, stimulating him, then squeezing his penis to prevent him from coming too quickly.

When we had done enough sessions that he felt comfortable getting and losing erections and felt ejaculatory control comfortably outside the vagina, then I would insert his penis into my vagina. He would ask for a squeeze if he felt anxious. We worked on that until he had an orgasm.

After that I know he felt a lot better. I know he began to go out with other women and started forming relationships and stuff like that. But I don't do follow-ups. That's the therapist's job.

I worked with one person where he was having trouble, and the therapy dragged on for about three times as long as it normally would. Now I make a contract to work with someone for ten to twelve sessions and then stop because I need that. I need a time limit. I need closure.

I need to feel like I'm not making an agreement to stay with you until you feel completely like you could fuck any woman on any street corner in America.

When there's ambiguity, it begins to become like a regular human relationship, a regular marriage relationship in which you feel responsible and guilty and not free to say no. For a surrogate to be in that place is risky and dangerous, and that's what happened to me one time and it wasn't good.

I feel what I can offer as a surrogate is this: I will put my attention on you for these number of minutes. At the end of that, "Good-bye." It's not an unloving thing to do. I do the same thing with my mate sometimes—"Yeah, I'll rub your back for an hour and then I don't want to anymore." But I have to be really clear about what I'm willing to do.

To make a contract that "I will stick with you until you feel sexually well" puts me into a frame of "sick" and "well" which makes it my business to "cure" you. That's a frame where one or the both of us fails. It's not pass or fail. It's not win or lose. It's exchanging bodies and practicing some things that are really helpful when you get stuck.

Several cases I had like that are very clear-cut. They finally do it and they say, "Wow, I can do it!" It's something that never happened to him before and now it happens and so the man has information. "Oh, yeah. I can do that." The business of lasting longer, the premature ejaculation, is an iffier thing. Sure, he experiences that he can last longer, but it's not usually as miraculous a thing as somebody who finds he can come in a vagina.

When a man has his first orgasm inside my vagina, I don't turn around and say, "Don't fall in love with me." I just go, "Wow! Far out! Barry, I'm really pleased for you."

Different men, different ways. There was one man that I did just one session with. It was his first time and was an initiation rite for him. He took the decision upon himself. We came into the therapist's office afterward and the therapist said, "Well, you need more practice," and the client said, "No, I know I can do it now and I want to go out and do it with a woman I have picked out." He had it together.

There was another man I worked with for a long time. As soon as he had his first ejaculation inside my vagina, there was sadness. He said, "Okay, I want to stop now because I don't want you to become the source for that. I know now that I can no longer tell myself I'm incapable or incompetent or impotent or whatever. It's back on me. Thank you. You've helped me. Good-bye."

One man I worked with was, well, delusional. He had me as part of some fantasy world that he lived in. Throughout therapy he would continually slip out of the mode of what we were doing and say, "I want to take you home to meet my mother." Then I would have to re-form the contract with him. "I'm not that," I would tell him. "I'm not willing to be that. I see you, I care about you, but I'm not that to you."

I've talked to other surrogates who get all wound up in—"Oh, everything that I owe to him"—and then the man calls up in the middle of the night and they feel responsible and go over and care for him. I'm not coming from that place. Those kinds of feelings come from the fact that we have sex and love or sex and mateship so closely interwoven. In my own personal life I have love and sex just right there together. When my mate goes to be with another woman and I feel like it's love, I just eat it! It's really hard for me. I experience jealousy. There are some women that he occasionally makes love with where they're friendly with me and I know it's just real casual, and it's not threatening because they're not seeing stars in each other's eyes. It's still hard. But when he goes off with someone where there's any feeling that the romantic myth attaches, it's really hard. Obviously, I must be getting enough of what I want so that it's worth the loneliness. But in the end, alone is how I was born and alone is how I'll die.

Even if one were to find a surrogate such as Lana, even if a husband or wife suffering from a sexual problem would want to risk the considerable legal dangers of using a surrogate, is a surrogate likely to solve their sexual problems? Unlike the professional sex treatment involving the couple, surrogate work with an individual, even accompanied by psychotherapy immediately following each physical contact, does nothing for the relationship. The relationship involves the sexual functioning and the psychosexual behavior of *two* particular individuals. The married man who responds to a surrogate may not respond to his wife. The woman who has an orgasm with a male surrogate may still be unresponsive or downright hostile to her husband. The ability to sustain a loving relationship is different from the ability to respond to a trained stranger. It is that loving relationship—of which sex is one expression—that improves in the best sex therapy programs.

Some individuals may gain satisfaction from sexual experiences with a surrogate which they had not previously been able to achieve. But if your aim is the enjoyment of sex within marriage, or within a particular relationship, then it's you and your sexual partner who need to be in therapy, not you and a paid sexual surrogate.

GROUP SEX THERAPY

An entirely different approach to sexual problems which also excludes the partner is the new technique developed by Lonnie Garfield Barbach, PhD, in the human sexuality program of the University of California Medical Center in San Francisco. Barbach treats groups of six single and married women meeting together with two female co-therapists. The women in the group are "pre-orgasmic"—they have never experienced an orgasm, but as the term optimistically implies, there is no reason why an orgasm should not be open to them with the right education and practice. The treatment program developed by Barbach and explained in her book *For Yourself*[12] includes information about female anatomy and female sexuality, group discussion to ease embarrassments and feelings of isolation about the problem, homework exercises, and individualized instruction in masturbation. Orgasm through masturbation is the goal of the twice-a-week, five-week program. Many women lack a regular sexual partner, or are unable to bring their husbands, or fear the loss of control during orgasm, even with their mates. Barbach believed that the first priority was for such women to experience an orgasm; then they could go on to achieving orgasm with their mates if they wished to.

"Instead of looking at self-stimulation from an antiquated perspective, as a substitute for the 'real thing,' " says Barbach, "why not view it as one of many alternative forms of sexual expression provided by nature for a party of one?"[13] Barbach reports an incredibly high success rate, ranging from 91.6 to 100 percent. Up to 87 percent of the women "were capable of orgasm in partner-related activities within eight months posttreatment. In addition, the women showed increased enjoyment of coitus and sexual satisfaction and reported improvement in life in general sex, communication with their partners, and overall level of happiness and relaxation."[14]

Ideally we would like to see the Barbach approach used in conjunction with a couple therapy program so that the partner is not excluded and the relationship not totally neglected. Masturbation, which Barbach and other sex therapists regard as a learning tool, as an alternative form of sexual expression, has been hailed by some militant feminists as the best and only form of sexual expression.[15] Militant rhetoric which excludes the male or makes his satisfaction subordinate to the female's is not conducive to understanding and enjoying sexual responsiveness in a relationship. We would hate to see two thousand years of this new militant feminist double standard replace the old chauvinistic double standard. Sex between two unique, equally valued individuals seems to be the best promise of the new sexuality.

One of the most recent developments in sex therapy is the group treatment of dysfunction for men without partners, an approach influenced by the Barbach program. Bernie Zilbergeld, PhD, director of the Male Sexuality Program and a colleague of Barbach's at the University of California Medical Center in San Francisco, says, "As far as sexual matters go, men have it much worse than women right now." Zilbergeld's groups are composed of single men or men whose wives refuse to join them in treatment, men who are suffering from premature ejaculation and erectile problems. Most of the men Zilbergeld has treated feel incredible pressures to perform. "The man feels responsible for turning himself on, turning the woman on, taking care of her, and taking care of himself. Zilbergeld uses several different techniques in his group therapy approach. The therapist (or male/female co-therapists) encourage men in the group to discuss their fears and failures with the opposite sex. In this way, they feel less isolated and many are then able to discuss these problems when they do have a partner. Second, is a kind of assertiveness training where the men learn they have sexual prerogatives too, which include the right to say no to a sexual advance if they just aren't in the mood, and the right to tell their partner what pleases them and what doesn't. There are stop-and-start homework masturbation exercises to retard ejaculation or learn to lose and then regain an erection. Much of the group time is spent debunking male sexual mythology. All of the men Zilbergeld and others in the program have treated have unreal sexual expectations which they have picked up mostly from the so-called men's magazines. And the situation is becoming worse as certain of the women's magazines present pictures of superstud men who are supposed to be representative of "good" lovers. Zilbergeld reports a high degree of success with this treatment, success which persists and even increases after the twelve weekly sessions are completed. A similar program is just getting underway at the University of Colorado Medical Center, in Denver, under the direction of W. Charles Lobitz, PhD. (It was Lobitz who worked with Dr. Joseph LoPiccolo to develop what may have been the first group sex therapy program at the University of Oregon in 1971.) There are many ways to help men and women move towards a single standard of satisfying sexuality.

SETTING STANDARDS

At one time prostitutes were the only expert professionals when it came to understanding human sexual response. But, thanks to the pioneering work of Masters and Johnson and others, medical schools are establishing courses in human sexuality which stress the need of women and men to regard themselves as sexual beings as well as decent and honorable people. The women's movement and other cultural shifts have opened a new era. Men can exhibit affection, tenderness, and nurturing behavior previously consigned to women. Women can be open about their sexual preferences. A number of physicians, psychiatrists, psychologists, psychiatric nurses, and social workers are now capable of teaching people about human sexuality. Couples can now gain the permission and the understanding necessary to enjoy themselves in a setting of warmth and intimacy. They can choose among a number of sexual dysfunction programs, but they should have standards of integrity and experience in mind—standards which even today's medical schools may not guarantee.

Jessie Potter, who has been a sex educator for eighteen years, a sex therapist with Dr. Joseph Levin for three years, and who now gives courses in human sexuality at Northwestern University Medical School and the University of Illinois Medical School, believes that staid, ignorant physicians have done just as much harm as the "crazies." Even in the seventies, Jessie finds vast differences in the quality of sex education medical students receive. Jessie notes that some doctors are still being graduated from medical schools who are ignorant, moralistic, and uptight about sex. How could such doctors be comforting and understanding about their patients' sexual difficulties? asks Jessie.

The American Medical Association has talked about setting standards for sex therapists. The American Association of Sex Educators and Counselors have set up a program certification for sex therapists which includes education, experience, and the ability to pass written examinations. (See Appendix, Sex Therapists/Sex Clinics.) Our investigations suggest that licensing helps eliminate frauds but doesn't always guarantee therapeutic effectiveness. Jessie finds the area of sex education and therapy one that is particularly difficult to standardize and legislate. She recommends to her medical students two criteria for juding a sex therapist: (1) The therapist must be a person who has come to terms with his or her own sexuality, so that he is much more comfortable with sex than are the various clients. (2) He must have more information about sex than the patients.

As for innovative practices, Jessie is more open-minded than most well-established therapists. She believes a surrogate program might work for people who cannot overcome their sexual problem, initially, working with their mates. But since such a program is not socially acceptable, Jessie much prefers the Barbach approach, which works with people of the same sex who share a common sexual problem.

We always seem to be mythologizing sex, be it with the puritan myth that it was dirty or the current glorification myth which leads us to expect beautiful, sensational sexual experiences each and every time. We need people like Jessie Potter to give us a more realistic view of sex.

We have tried to present many alternative approaches to sex therapy, but our preference runs to programs which help couples improve their relationship. What Masters and Johnson call "the pleasure bond" cannot be forged in a weekend or even in ten or fifteen sessions. Such a bond of intimacy and enjoyment can be encouraged by trained therapists, but in the end it survives because the relationship has been sufficiently strengthened to endure on its own.

There are a number of practices which can be either ethical and helpful or unethical and damaging, depending on how they are executed. For example, a physical examination. We have seen how Hartman and Fithian use the "sexological exam." We shall also see how this technique can lead to exploitation or out-and-out rape.

But a "conjoint medical examination" is an entirely different and definitely valuable procedure. "Each spouse is given a complete physical and gynecologic and urologic examination, including the genitals and female pelvis, in the presence of the other spouse by a physician sex therapist."[16]

According to Dr. Helen Singer Kaplan, this exam gives the treating doctor basic information about the physical status of his/her patient and begins opening communications between the spouses and reveals special areas of sensitivity and inhibition. "It's also an opportunity for educating and correcting misinformation." Masters and Johnson estimate that one third of the sexual dysfunction in the country could be reversed by simple information.

Dr. Domeena Renshaw, director of the Loyola University Foster McGaw Hospital Sexual Dysfunction Clinic near Chicago, which offers one of the most reasonably priced programs of sex therapy in the country, claims that many couples who come to the clinic are ignorant about male and female anatomy. Many men, reports Dr. Renshaw, don't know where a woman's clitoris is, and some are even unfamiliar with their own genitals. One patient at the Loyola clinic didn't even know he was circumcised.[17]

Another legitimate way for therapists to gain information about the client's attitude toward his or her body is the "mirror technique," developed by Hartman and Fithian in California and now used by many sex therapists. In the Loyola program, during the third of seven intensive sessions (after giving their psychosexual history and seeing a number of slides and films), each individual is asked to give a feeling report on his or her own body in a mirrored room.

In the course of this anatomical journey, the individual is asked which part she/he likes most or likes least. During one of these sessions at Loyola, a totally anhedonic woman who was asked this question started to cry. She couldn't think of any part of her body she liked at all. Finally she said, "I think I like my hands because they work for other people."[18] During seventeen years of marriage she had never responded to her husband during intercourse. In the course of the seven-week program (which costs $350 for twenty-eight hours of therapy, four hours per session) this woman learned to let herself experience intimacy and joy in sex.

Another area of therapy which has been abused by certain therapists is assertiveness training, fair fighting, and other approaches to the healthy expression of anger. Here's an example from the Lefkowitz-Mindell Hearings into Abuses by Unregulated Therapists in the Mental Health Field which shows how the basically sound idea of helping people to express their emotions can be turned to sadistic purposes:

A twenty-nine-year-old woman testified that her "therapist" would engage in activities which he claimed would help her act out "the process of your anger. It was a painful kind of thing, bending people's arms, socking women in the breasts. When I saw him personally, he'd do things like that. He punched me in the breasts, banged my head on the floor, pulled out my pubic hairs. When I told him I didn't like it, he said I really had a problem with healthy play."

This particular therapist, practicing on the Upper West Side of Manhattan, was having sexual relations with a number of people who had come to him for help. He told one client if she ever told anyone what he had done he would say she was crazy and would have her put in a mental hospital. "He told me," said the client-victim, "if I told anyone, I would take the responsibility of putting the patients in a hospital because they would have a psychotic break."

The Mansonesque control that certain therapists can exert is absolutely frightening. But let's look at how legitimate therapists encourage couples with sexual problems to express anger and other emotions.

These are excerpts from the homework sheets of Tom and Sara, who came to the Forest Hospital Sexual Dysfunction Clinic in Des Plaines, Illinois. Tom had come from a home in which masturbation was strictly forbidden. At the age of thirty-four, after ten years of marriage, he had never been able to masturbate to orgasm. His wife, a "good" girl also from a rather strict home who had never engaged in any form of sexual activity, foreplay, or petting until she married Tom, had a great deal of difficulty expressing emotions, particularly feelings of a romantic or sexual nature. At the beginning of therapy, the female therapist offered Sara a nickel for every day she was able to keep from expressing anger, joy, or resentment. Five cents for each day of no emotion. Sara "earned" 35 cents that first week.

Being totally dependent upon Sara for his sexual satisfaction, Tom was hurt when he realized she was not interested in sex. Sara's lack of interest turned into real distaste, and during the past two years of their marriage she had become completely inorgastic. Thus the syndrome of hurt and rejection on Tom's part and guilt on Sara's part was set in motion.

The female therapist, Darlene Davis, was an unusually warm and outgoing person, an experienced registered nurse who had received one year of supervised training in sex therapy and taken special courses in transactional analysis and bioenergetics. Her husband and co-therapist, Jack Davis, is an obstetrician-gynecologist. They recognized three therapeutic goals for this relationship. (1) Both partners, but particularly Sara, must learn to express a range of emotions, including anger. (2) Tom must learn to pleasure himself in order to relieve the continual demands on his wife. (When faced with the common problem of disparate sexual appetites, sex therapists usually work with the individual who has the lesser appetite.) (3) Since both partners were trying to cope with rather severe parental prohibitions against sexual behavior, both would have to learn to become more childlike and spontaneous. They needed permission to be playful.

After the initial sessions—involving extensive psychological tests, private discussions between Tom and the female therapist, Sara and the male therapist, a conjoint medical examination, foot massages, the purchase of a queen-size bed to replace their twin bed arrangement—the couple was given an exercise to help them express anger.

Even at the height of their difficulty, this couple had never had an argument. They were always lady and gentleman to each other. In the privacy of their bedroom, sitting on a mattress holding a towel, each of them was instructed to take fifteen loud rapid breaths and, maintaining eye contact, to whack the towel down on the mattress, emitting a loud guttural noise. On the next turn, they were to take the fifteen breaths and hit twice, and finally they hit as many times as desired. This exercise was to be followed by cuddling in the nude.

In previous weeks Sara had been instructed to look at her genitals with a mirror. Now she was to continue visual and tactile explorations of her genitals with emphasis on locating sensitive areas that produced feelings of pleasure. "Thoroughly explore the clitoral shaft and hood, the major and minor labia, the vaginal opening and the whole perineum especially that area immediately adjacent to the clitoris and the clitoris itself. Concentrate on manual stimulation of these areas, using a variety of stroking and pressure and use lotion to enhance pleasure and prevent soreness. Pleasure yourself at least three times this next week for at least fifteen minutes when feeling sexually aroused. Fantasize."

While Sara was encouraged to explore her genitals and go with her pleasurable feelings, Tom was encouraged to pleasure himself to an orgasm. Far from being cold assignment sheets the therapists would add statements like, "Be gentle with yourself. You are a child of the universe and you deserve to enjoy life in all its fullness." After two weeks Tom was able to masturbate to climax. This was his homework, and thus he was able to permit himself this form of satisfaction. He could now be less demanding in his relationship to Sara.

On one assignment sheet the therapists told Tom, "It's apparent to us that Sara will be orgastic sooner in an atmosphere of *no* sexual demand from you—either overt or implied. Therefore in your days ahead together, linger in your body pleasuring, lick (flick) her eyelids, the inner aspect of her elbow, behind her knees; gently suck her fingertips; experiment playfully with no demand for response on Sara's part. (Sara will notice if you are watching her for response.) Lose yourself in the giving—close your eyes as you give and receive. Let Sara be the aggressor."

Meanwhile Sara was encouraged to increase the intensity and duration of her self-pleasuring, using "pornographic" reading material, erotic fantasies, placing herself in the fantasy and imagining various things happening to that woman. She was encouraged to purchase a vibrator and use it, along with the erotic fantasies. Tom would be allowed to pleasure her to an orgasm— only manually or with the vibrator, and only if she wished it.

During the course of the therapy, basic concepts of transactional analysis were explained, and they were encouraged to assign names to their three ego states—nurturing parent, punitive parent, and child. The therapists insisted that the punitive parent be left out of the bedroom. And on the assignment sheets one could see the notes to Sara: *You'll have to leave "Gertrude" at home for this one.* Or, to Tom: *"Bertram" will have to stay out of the bedroom.* Sara was encouraged to explore Tom's body with most of her senses—sight, taste, touch, smell, to experience being giver and receiver. Tom was to do the same, avoiding the genitals unless Sara requested pleasuring. Sara was to set aside some alone time during the day. She had three children, but did manage to find forty-five minutes to simply read and relax. They were to have one night out a week, without the children. "See an X-rated movie and go to an adult book store," said the therapists one week. "But leave Gertrude and Bertram at home!"

Though the footbath and the bioenergetic "anger" exercise was done with the therapists, none of the other assignments were observed by the therapists. Though Sara was encouraged to use the vibrator, she much preferred having Tom pleasure her. There was no forcing by the therapists to do anything distasteful, but intercourse was not allowed until the very conclusion of the program. Even though Tom and Sara had planned a spring vacation in the Caribbean, they were specifically instructed not to have intercourse. Here's their vacation assignment.

"Mutual pleasuring followed with quiet vagina. Experience the pleasure of being together in this way. Get with the new feelings. Slide your vagina slowly up and down the shaft of Tom's penis, delight yourself in this lovely new feeling. If the need for orgasm occurs, stop and withdraw. Pursue pleasuring elsewhere. Then resume penile-vaginal containment again, experiencing the unique sensations. Write a sexual fantasy that turns you on. Happy Vacation!'' Tom was encouraged to do the same, to enjoy the feelings of having his penis lovingly contained with only minimal movements. ''Be passive and let Sara be the aggressor in all your sexual sessions.'' He was also asked to encourage Sara. ''As Sara is giving herself more and more permission, it's important that you continue your loving support and building of her self-esteem with words of encouragement rather than criticism. She's relying on you now for these things and in doing them you won't lose her, you'll find her loving you more.''

Tom and Sara succeeded in resuscitating a lifeless marriage. The combination of specific exercises, including one to help Sara strengthen her vaginal (particularly the pubococcyges) muscles, and the therapists' use of many techniques to help the partners express a range of emotions—all contributed to saving this marriage. In fact, what happens during successful marital therapy is not a salvage operation, but the creation of a new relationship based on new self-esteem for each person and a greater sense of consideration for the partner.

Permission is a word we hear repeatedly from sex therapists and those who seek help. This is not surprising. We're a society of men and women who have grown up hearing don'ts: don't masturbate, don't touch yourself *there*, don't be a bad girl, don't let women run you, don't show your feelings, don't fail, don't make him feel bad, don't let her down, don't kiss it, don't hold it. No wonder we want permission.

One man recollects his first sexual experience as one in which he masturbated while wearing a leather jacket. As a married man, he had taken to secretly masturbating with his leather jacket on because he was ashamed to tell his wife that wearing this garment turned him on. During sex therapy the man admitted this hangup to the female therapist but begged her not to tell his wife. Two sessions later he told her himself. She said she didn't mind a bit if he wore the leather jacket while they made love. The more mutual pleasure the couple experienced, the less dependent he became on the leather jacket. By the end of the therapy, he had dispensed with this masculine symbol entirely. Dr. Helen Singer Kaplan reports a similar situation with a Superman fantasy. Again the man was ashamed to admit that thinking of himself as Superman rescuing a naked woman was a sexual turn on. Once he received permission to act out this fantasy with his wife, who said she didn't mind if he wore a Superman costume to bed, he found he was no longer dependent on this role for satisfaction. No, he didn't return to being mild-mannered Clark Kent. He learned to feel potent and powerful in his own identity.

Women often want permission to do and say things they have been taught are dirty or unfeminine. This can be anything from saying the word "fuck" to the act of fellatio. Women we've spoken to are particularly grateful when the sex therapist gives them permission to please themselves. Remember how surprised Sharon Carlyle was when the female therapist asked, "Don't you want anything for yourself?" She had been brought up to believe that she shouldn't want anything for herself, particularly in the area of sexual gratification. If a 1957 textbook in gynecological medicine states that a woman has no sexual feelings and another states that female sexual feelings are always subordinate to other needs, then how could we expect parents raising children in 1957, or 1947, or 1937 to encourage their little girls to feel good about fulfilling their sexual needs?

The whole concept of selfishness becomes a questionable one for women. If they can't openly ask for or even demand what they want, then how do they convey their sexual requirements? Often their very unselfishness becomes a distorted form of control.

Thus, when Kaplan gives sample instructions for a sensate focus exercise, she will stress that the woman be open and "selfish" about her demands: "I want you to focus your attention on the sensations you feel when he caresses you. Try not to let your mind wander. Don't think about anything else. Don't worry about whether he's getting tired or whether he is enjoying it—or anything. Be 'selfish' and just concentrate on your sensations; let yourself feel everything. Communicate with him. Don't talk too much or it will interfere with your responses—and his. But remember that he can't possibly know what you are feeling unless you tell him. Let him know where you want to be touched and how, and where his caresses feel especially good; and let him know if his touch is too light or too heavy, or if he is going too fast."[19]

Later Dr. Kaplan points out that "the passive-dependent, ultracompliant posture" assumed by one patient, the anxiety over any frustration of the husband's wishes, was actually a result of deep-seated hostility. A woman can be so ashamed of feeling anger that she bends over backward to hide the anger. This is one reason sex therapists will encourage patients, particularly women, to express anger, to be selfish. They are not encouraging women to disregard or hate their partners. They are simply trying to let them know that women, like men, are permitted to experience a wide range of human emotions.

SETTING GOALS

The goals of sex therapy should be set by the couple. While the goal is usually the successful treatment of a particular dysfunction, no couple should be forced or coerced into sexual behavior which is morally or physically repugnant to them. Sharon and a number of other women we interviewed were terrified of oral sex. They were afraid that the therapist would insist on oral sex and very relieved when they didn't have to perform fellatio. Other women and men want to be told that a particular expression is okay. Tom wanted permission to masturbate, permission which had been withheld from him by his parents. Therapists who encourage couples in a pattern of sexual "progress"—those who believe that a couple must move from monogamy to multiple sexual relations to group sex to bisexuality, for example—are not helping two individuals take responsibility for their sexuality. They are encouraging those individuals to submit to the control of an authority, an authority who may not be around to put the pieces back together when that sudden sexual progress leads to psychological pain. Withholding judgment, which is so crucial to sex therapy, also means allowing the couple to take the lead, not forcing them into some preconceived conservative or progressive notion of good sex.

We are so accustomed to performance and goals in all phases of our lives that many of us find it difficult to relax and enjoy sensual pleasures—even when we are instructed to do so by a professional counselor.

Sex therapy programs are more concentrated than other forms of marital therapy. Thirty hours of therapy—either concentrated into consecutive days as with the St. Louis program or spread over a period of weeks—is the average period most clinics allow for solving a sexual dysfunction. This deadline or pressure can be helpful in getting couples to commit themselves to working together on their problem. But some couples interpret their homework assignments as tasks which must be executed successfully. The performance of exercises which are supposed to deemphasize performance become goals which they feel they must achieve. Therapists should be sensitive to individuals, such as the wife who became so anxious about completing their "genital homework," she forgot to enjoy herself. The goal of sex therapy is not the successful execution of an assigned task. It is mutual pleasuring.

Virginia Johnson told us that, "We consider any failure our failure," but most couples who are unable to solve their difficulties with one therapist are convinced they have failed and are reluctant to try again. Because of the intensely personal nature of sex therapy and the special stigma our society has attached to problems in this area, a couple often has to summon up their courage in order to even enter the office of a sex therapist. No couple should feel they are doomed to live with a sexual problem. If they were unfortunate in their first attempt—because of an inadequate or exploitative therapist—they should not let feelings of fear and disappointment prevent them from gaining legitimate help elsewhere. The success rate at legitimate clinics we have visited is high—approximately 80 percent. But Masters and Johnson report that 85 percent of the patients they have seen in the past two years had experienced failure in previous therapy.

A rule of thumb for those interested: if at first you don't succeed with sex therapy, try—after carefully shopping and checking credentials—at least try, again.

DRAWBACKS AND LIMITATIONS OF THE NEW SEX THERAPY

The new sex therapy is not a panacea for marital problems. True, sexual dissatisfaction is among the ten most common complaints of the husband and wife who seek marital counseling.[20] Sexual problems are reported by as many as 75 percent of the couples who seek help with their marriage. Nevertheless, sex therapy is not always the appropriate treatment.

We have seen the dramatic change this relatively brief form of therapy can bring about. Tom and Sara, Sharon and Dave Carlyle, and many others we have interviewed after completion of a sound sex therapy program, note a marked "spillover effect." Not only are they able to enjoy newfound sexual pleasure, but they also find other forms of communication opening up. They feel a greater sense of independence and maturity. Tension is lowered. And they report that other relationships—with their children, their parents, and their friends—have become more open and honest. Sara, for example, who had had so much difficulty expressing emotion, feels that she now has a more positive attitude toward female sexuality, which she conveys to her two daughters, a feeling that the interest of young children in their own bodies should not be a source of shame. Thus she believes that the sex therapy has not only made her a better lover and companion for her husband, but also a better mother.

If so many couples suffer from sexual problems, why shouldn't sex therapy work for all ailing marriages? In his chapter on Sexual Dysfunctions and Marital Discord, Dr. Clifford Sager, clinical professor of psychiatry at the Mount Sinai School of Medicine, and psychiatric director of the Jewish Family Service in New York City, explains when sex therapy is inadvisable, and why it sometimes succeeds at the expense of the marriage.[21]

Sex therapy requires both partners to cooperate in maintaining "a sexually nondemanding ambience," says Dr. Sager, so that sex is not as easily used in the power struggle between the spouses. This means putting aside fights and hostility for a period of a few weeks, accepting each other as sexual partners, having a genuine desire to help each other, and possibly putting aside one's own gratification for several weeks so that husband and wife can realize their sexual potential.

If the spouses cannot accept each other as sexual partners, if they cannot declare neutrality, if they cannot give up other extramarital relationships or intramarital grudges, this form of therapy is not likely to work.

Here are some couples for whom sex therapy was inappropriate or inadequate.

A Midwestern couple had been married for eight years. Both were highly educated, sophisticated, and quite attractive. The husband was rather conceited about his good looks and erudition; the wife tended to feel insecure in spite of her many assets. The husband was given to infidelity and heavy bouts of drinking. During one such episode he had actually beaten his wife until she was forced to have the police come and intervene. Sexual satisfaction was at an all-time low and hostility had reached an unbearable height when they finally went to a marriage counselor. The husband continued an affair with a younger woman during the brief course of their marital therapy. The marriage counselor, a soft-spoken fellow with a PhD from one of the top universities in the country, told them at their first session to bathe each other's feet. With the husband sexually preoccupied, and the wife still smarting from her physical and psychic wounds, this exercise in sensate focus was hardly the treatment of choice. After three footbaths and a bit of role playing, the couple decided there was no chance of saving their marriage. They received a bill at the end of the month for $160. They had been charged for one extra session because they had not toweled off by the time their fifty minutes were up. When they sent a check for $120, the good doctor had his accountant mail them a note threatening to send a bill collector if payment in full was not received immediately.

This marriage would probably have ended in divorce no matter what form of therapy was used. But a therapist who recommends a footbath when alcoholism, infidelity, and brutality have to be dealt with is obviously not worth the parchment on which his PhD is written.

Sometimes sex therapy can proceed after certain roadblocks have been removed. Dr. Sager cites the case of a man suffering from impotence whose wife had recently begun to seek greater freedom in terms of a career and a wider range of outside contacts. The wife feared that if her husband became potent again she would be "locked into a relationship with a 'cocky' man who would not allow her to grow. She believed that to help her husband overcome his impotence was to participate in her own further exploitation." Dr. Sager was able to help this woman understand that her growth would be facilitated if her husband also felt adequate and in a position to grow further, that neither could develop for long at the expense of the other. This was the turning point of their treatment, treatment which resulted in greater potency for husband, wife, and marriage. Had the wife been unable to set aside her suspicions, or had she been sexually involved with another man, the treatment would not have been successful.

Sex therapy can be a test of commitment. In some marriages the partners will agree to sex therapy, but one will sabotage the treatment. Such was the case reported by Dr. Sager with one woman whose husband suffered from premature ejaculation. The wife encouraged her husband to enter her even though the therapist had asked them to avoid intercourse. The husband ejaculated and became depressed. In another session the wife insisted on performing fellatio instead of masturbating him. He was unable to control his ejaculatory response and again felt enraged. The marriage ended in divorce and the husband wound up coming back for help with another partner.

The man who continually says his inorgastic wife will "never come," the helping wife who gives her husband one extra stroke of the penis when he is trying to learn to control his ejaculation—these are individuals who cannot commit themselves to sex therapy. Either they have to be seen individually or the couple has to work on reducing hostility before attention can be focused on their sexual relations.

Masters and Johnson tell a story of one of their failures—a recently married man from a Middle Eastern country who had been accustomed to women in public places being veiled or very modestly dressed. When he came to America the sight of women in minidresses and braless silk blouses put him in a priapic state. He took to hitting his erect penis with his hand when he became overstimulated. When he arrived at the Masters and Johnson clinic, he had been suffering from impotence. When he was told that he could lose himself in his partner, that his wife should be with him throughout the therapy because there was no uninvolved partner, he ran from the room and never returned. He couldn't believe that his sexual response or lack of it had anything to do with anyone but himself.

Finally there are those rare marriages in which successful sex therapy highlights the emptiness of a relationship, the failure of other aspects of the match, and thus results in divorce. As Dr. Sager puts it, "Some couples, having overcome their sexual dysfunction, can no longer use this disability as a rationalization to avoid confrontation with other sources of discord between them. They either proceed to confront these problems more expeditiously or dissolve their marriage.[22] Translation: If I'm coming and he's coming and we still can't stand each other, it's time to split.

But Dr. Sager, and the majority of therapists and couples whom we've interviewed, find that effective sex therapy usually leads to a better, even brand-new marriage, with both partners feeling more hopeful and capable of handling other problems they may have to face.

Like all revolutions, the sexual revolution has resulted in certain excesses. Our new, more open attitude toward sexual behavior and sex dysfunctions has produced a number of highly effective sex therapists with high success rates. The new sex therapy has also spawned a number of practitioners who are unqualified, inept, or exploitive.

The American Association of Sex Educators and Counselors, the Eastern Association of Sex Therapists (EAST), and a professional conference recently convened by Masters and Johnson are among the groups currently striving to establish standards for sex clinics. But until strict licensing laws are passed and enforced, one must ask questions, check credentials, and refuse to submit to any instructions or activity which can be judged exploitative. In spite of some drawbacks, medical schools and teaching hospitals remain the best source for finding reputable sex therapists. We pointed to certain danger signs, certain questionable practices couples have encountered at so-called clinics.

We can't say exactly how much a sex therapist should charge. Clinics connected to large hospitals and universities may offer free therapy, or at least a sliding scale of fees determined by ability to pay. We have found $350 for twenty-eight hours of couple therapy with male and female therapists to be the most reasonable among the university affiliated clinics. The average fee for sessions at private hospitals and clinics with a male and female therapy team runs about $75 per session of one and one half to two hours, with a higher fee for initial testing and screening. Private clinics which offer concentrated programs of sex therapy with male and female therapy teams can run as high as $2,500. This is the cost of the twelve-to-fourteen-day program at the Human Reproductive Biology Foundation in St. Louis.

Any unqualified therapist or therapy team—no matter what their fee—is too expensive. The emotional cost of going to a clinic of questionable standards is too high for any couple to pay.

Remember, whether one is selecting a sex therapist or an interior decorator, *caveat emptor*—buyer beware—should be the motto.

5

Social Service Agencies

The social service agency is the most likely place for a couple to go for marriage counseling, particularly if their means are limited. In smaller cities and towns an agency may offer the only source for reliable counseling—an agency being any of the more than 350 Family Service Association agencies, counseling service affiliated with a church or charitable organization, or a national or federal organization.

What can a couple expect of an agency in terms of fees and services? Should a couple always avoid an agency if they can afford private help?

First we will show that agencies vary in size and responsiveness. Most agencies have a waiting list of two weeks to two months, though most will see a couple immediately if they feel their situation is desperate (for example, if alcoholism, suicide, or severe behavior problems are involved).

Because most agencies are overloaded—the demand for therapists exceeds the supply—couples will usually be assigned to the therapist who happens to be available, not necessarily to the one who is best suited to their problem. The other drawback to an agency is the possibility of getting an inexperienced therapist, someone who has just completed academic training.

Finally, a couple may feel intimidated because they are paying so little for their therapy. They may think they have no right to speak up if they have questions or complaints. But they should remember that the therapist at an agency is being paid a salary. The therapist has chosen to work for the agency rather than devote that time to private practice. All the client owes the therapist is a reasonable amount of cooperation and courtesy. Neither the couple nor the therapist will benefit if the two are badly mismatched.

If you choose to go to an agency, you can be confident that you will not encounter a fraud. Agencies have academic standards and periodical reviews of cases. You will be paying much less at an agency than you would for private counseling. The fees are usually based on a sliding scale, but we could be talking about the difference between $10 a week and $50 a session. An agency may offer a number of simultaneous treatment programs, so that a marital problem which is linked to or exacerbated by a related problem (hyperactivity in a child, alcoholism or psychosis in one of the mates) can be attacked on several fronts at once. Finally, an agency offers consumer accountability. Agencies are backed up, by a large association, by a hospital or charitable institution standing behind the therapist and ready (if not always eager) to hear any complaint you may have.

Since agencies are so numerous we can only offer here a sampling—from the oldest and the largest of them, and the newer, smaller, and more avant-garde ones—and a number of personal experiences couples have had at these different kinds of places. (Information about locating an agency in your area can be found in the Appendix.)

Because of the enormous case load of agencies, they also tell us something about the kinds of marital problems people have and the various crises that affect couples at different stages in their lives.

NORMAL CRISES

The Philadelphia Marriage Council has a case load of 1,200 people a year, making it one of the largest agencies of its kind in the country. Neville Vines, assistant director of counseling education and therapist at the Marriage Council, finds that adults have certain types of problems at certain stages in their lives, something known as "age-specific problems." Vines, along with a number of researchers around the country, believes adults do not remain static, but continue to grow. Psychiatrist Roger Gould at UCLA, one of the authorities on adult life-stages, summed up the static view of adulthood this way:

"Like a butterfly, an adult is supposed to emerge fully formed and on cue, after a succession of developmental stages in childhood. Equipped with all the accoutrements, such as wisdom and rationality, the adult supposedly remains quiescent for another half century or so. While children change, adults only age."[1] Taking his cue from Erik Erikson, who was the first to conceptualize adulthood in stages, Dr. Gould is gathering evidence to show that adult men and women grow and change, and thus have their developmental tasks at each life stage.

The developmental view of adulthood has profound implications for the way in which adults see themselves and the way therapists and marriage counselors evaluate adult problems.

For example, a twenty-nine-year-old woman is married, the mother of a twenty-four-month-old son whom we shall call Johnnie. When Johnnie says no to everything, his mother is not overly concerned. She knows that the two-year-old period can be a negative stage, a time when kids assert their independence. Yet she may regard her own emotional changes with alarm. Her yearnings to be recognized in the adult world, to be more than a wife and mother, and her fears at risking the secure arrangement she has—these stirrings worry her and may even make her feel abnormal, especially if her husband also views her dissatisfaction with alarm. A marriage counselor who holds the static view of adulthood might see her as abnormal or neurotic. But one who sees adults as developing, changing, going through different stages, could quickly recognize that Johnnie's mother is undergoing a normal transition.

Getting back to the research of Roger Gould, we find that the "terrible twenty-nines" are as common as the "terrible twos." In Gould's survey of 524 adults between the ages of sixteen and fifty, reported in *Psychology Today*,[2] the first high problem period for marriages seems to be in the late twenties. The adult at this stage feels, "I wish my mate would accept me for what I am as a person." At the same time, that adult begins to disagree with the statement, "For me, marriage has been a good thing." (Forty percent of those who come to the Philadelphia Marriage Council are between the ages of twenty and twenty-nine.)

The man on the brink of thirty needs his wife to be more of a companion to him and less of a substitute mother or child bride. The woman on the brink of thirty is likely to be torn between wanting to grow and become more a part of the adult world and wanting to hold onto the security of her domestic role as caretaker of her children and moral support for her husband. Gail Sheehy, in an article on adult life-stages, has identified this dilemma as "Catch-30."[3]

Gould found that "the thirties are a period of very active psychological change" characterized by concern about money as well as a tendency to blame parents for personality problems which have failed to vanish with age. According to Gould's respondents, the mid-thirties is the time when couples are least likely to feel that marriage has been a good thing. (This, too, seems to be reflected in the Marriage Council data which reveals over one third of their clientele, 35 percent, to be between the ages of thirty and forty.)

Between forty and forty-three Gould finds personal comfort decreasing and marital comfort remaining at a low level, with the added anxiety that comes of passing the halfway point and realizing for the first time that there is not plenty of time left to do the things one wants to do. Later in the forties comes a period of stability and acceptance, corroborated in the Marriage Council figures by a significant dropoff of forty-to-forty-nine-year-old adults coming in for help with their marriages.

We think there is sufficient data now, from Gould and others, including Bernice Neugarten at the University of Chicago, Daniel Levinson at Yale, and David Guttman at the University of Michigan, to confirm the view that adulthood is a process of development—not a fait accompli. It follows then that marital problems, far from being abnormal, may be signs that one or both partners needs to move on to the next stage of development. Agencies like the Philadelphia Marriage Council, which see adulthood as a process of change, will not mistake these growing pains for sickness. Instead of trying to keep the marriage static, they will try to help the partners grow together.

As marital problems—aired on TV, discussed in newspapers and magazines, seen in films—become part of normalcy, the old stigma attached to seeking help with emotional and marital woes is disappearing, particularly among middle-class couples. Many of the people who come to the Philadelphia Marriage Council, according to its director, Dr. Harold I. Lief, do not look upon themselves as patients. They are beginning to see the therapist as a source of information and education. Many come to the council's enrichment programs not because they are troubled, but because they know marital rough times are inevitable. This change in attitude is particularly striking, according to Dr. Lief, in the area of sexual problems.

Dr. Lief has also noticed a change in the kinds of people now being seen by his staff. "More people come in directly complaining of sexual dysfunction. Not because there is any more sexual dysfunction but because of the openness of society in regard to sexual mores, sexual behavior, plus the fact that people recognize that help is possible." That "help," according to Lief, is recognized as short-term rather than the therapy of psychoanalysis, which lasts several years.

Lief also feels that sociopolitical forces have triggered a change in the kinds of people and problems dealt with at the Marriage Council of Philadelphia—specifically the women's liberation/feminist movement. "There are more women desirous of personal fulfillment, and this produces both internal and interpersonal conflict," he says. "Many of these women are programmed in the old way, so they have the inner conflict that often produces a kind of bizarre behavior on their part since they are ambivalent about moving out of the house and into a job situation or going to school. If they themselves are not ambivalent, but are dedicated to this, it may create problems with the husband who has been raised stereotypically." Lief has also seen what he calls an "interesting variation" on this theme: the husband who pushes his wife into "liberation" because it grants him more autonomy and freedom while the wife rejects and resists the whole idea.

The Marriage Council actively promotes its programs for marriage counseling, divorce and separation therapy, and sexual dysfunction therapy to the general public. It reminds people that marital problems are not abnormal, that psychological growing pains at various life stages are bound to put stress on a marriage.

The growth and development of adults can be at least as negative as the terrible twos, as adventurous as the threes and fours and "curiouser" than the questioning fives. Agencies like the Philadelphia Marriage Council are helping men and women to deal with the normal crises that growing adults encounter.

Los Angeles does not burn as Nathanael West envisioned in *The Day of the Locust*. The heat generated these days emanates from carburetors and piston valves—of relationships shifting gears and consciousness being raised. The Angelean treats his soul almost as well as his car, caring for it, burnishing it, massaging it, having it encountered, eroticized, transacted, transcended, processed, and trained. In the midst of this spiritual traffic jam is an unlikely old Packard—the American Institute of Family Relations. It is the oldest and largest nonprofit marriage counseling institute in America.

Founded by divinity school graduate Dr. Paul Popenoe as a one-man, one-office marriage and family support agency, AIFR now has a staff of fifty licensed marriage counselors operating out of thirty-two rooms in Los Angeles, as well as four large branch offices located in South Bay, Orange County, Woodland Hills, and San Gabriel Valley.

As author of the monthly magazine column, "Can This Marriage Be Saved?" and disseminator of pamphlets including *Are Virgins out of Date?*, *Are You the Perfect Husband?* (rating scale included), and *Are You the Perfect Wife?* (rating scale included), Popenoe projected the image of the marriage counselor as the rescuer of shipwrecked souls. During his twenty-year reign as marriage counselor for *Ladies' Home Journal* readers, Dr. Popenoe has made "adjustment" (with the wife adjusting a bit more than her spouse) and the salvation of the marriage the keystones of counseling. The "savior" image still plagues sophisticated counselors and therapists. Some feel it necessary to point out on the first visit that the needs of the individual husband and wife will not be sacrificed on the marriage altar.

Dr. Popenoe has been "promoted" to the emeritus position of AIFR founder and chairman of the board. The new executive director of the institute is Jerold R. Kuhn, PhD, a psychologist concerned about keeping the bigness of AIFR from becoming dehumanizing.

Although he carries a heavy administrative load, Kuhn still sees patients, charging them the usual AIFR rate of from $11 to $30 a session, based on their ability to pay. He is very concerned with "reductionistic" therapies. He has seen the Masters and Johnson approach and the transactional analysis techniques of Claude Steiner used by other therapists with little regard for the total person. "We're not sending therapists to school anymore to be human beings," he says. "We're sending them there to be researchers in human sexuality or sexual therapists or transactional analysis therapists. We're missing the whole point. Therapy is merely a one-to-one equation, and that's where health occurs as far as I'm concerned. That's where treatment begins and ends—not all the techniques you can toss." Thus the therapists of AIFR, while they may intellectually subscribe to the basic theoretical boundaries of one kind of therapy, make use of all kinds of other techniques to resolve the problems people come to them with. Adapt the therapy to the person rather than changing the person to fit the therapy—that's the AIFR philosophy.

Kuhn told of a case involving a woman who had so far failed to achieve orgasm with her husband. Barbara was married to Rick. Both were college educated, in their late twenties, and they had a two-year-old adopted daughter. She sought help because she felt she was letting her husband down by not having orgasms. After the first session with Barbara, Kuhn said he wanted to talk to Rick alone. Rick came in and, according to Kuhn, said, "I don't really see what the problem is. All I care about is that she has a climax and enjoys sex four times a week. That's all I need since she's a wonderful mother and cook and all that."

"I could immediately see in Rick a lack of responsibility," commented Kuhn, "a lack of any kind of insight to any degree of depth on his part, as well as a misunderstanding of his role and his wife's role and the possible tie-up between his virility or lack of same and his need for frequent relations with his wife."

Kuhn saw Barbara for five more sessions without her husband, taking a more historical approach to developing the case. He took what sex therapists call a "psychosexual history," examining relationships to the parents, early sexual experiences, early sexual fantasies, first sexual experiences recalled, first sexual experience with Rick. Then Barbara suggested that she might like to have her husband attend the sessions because, as Kuhn put it, "One of her problems when she initially came in was, 'It will never be solved. I don't even want to face Rick with it because he'll just get excited and then I'll let him down again.'"

Kuhn saw the relationship this way: "Her emphasis in her sexual relationship is on performance, and she rates herself. She's so uptight before she starts that of course she's going to fail. So I get Rick in and we have maybe six or seven sessions together. One obvious goal with him is an understanding of the dynamics of the relationship—the sexual side of their relationship, what kind of expectations he puts on her, his need to be virile, his not being able to get her pregnant, as well as her inability to communicate her problems to him in the first place, her inhibitions and fears."

After twelve sessions with them together, Kuhn helped Barbara and Rick achieve breakthroughs on several levels. "One, she initiates a sexual relationship a couple of times a week. Two, she is able to talk to her husband about it and about her performance after the relationship. Three, his response begins to shift slightly, at least surface change to the extent that he appears to her to be more accepting and generous in his praise even though she hasn't climaxed. He is saying, 'Hey, look. I understand this now, and I don't need it as much.' I say to them at the end of the twelfth session, 'Look, I could probably see you forever. I'd like you to go try certain things,' and I give them a couple of books to read, a couple of exercises to try, different forms of pleasuring techniques, and tell them to go home for a month and try it out.''

Kuhn is strongly opposed to therapy that fosters dependency and reporting to the therapist, which is why he told Barbara and Rick during that time not to call for a month. The relationship collapsed. "So we got them in again and worked on other things, sex included, but the major item was communication—expressing feelings at the time they're feeling them rather than building them up and letting them out on each other when they make love or on the weekend when they're home." He moved them away from their emphasis on performance and into pleasuring and sexual activity for two sessions until they both felt they could make it on their own. "That's where they are now. The last I heard, things were going fine. He has cut down on his workload and shows her more attention outside the bedroom. A typical kind of case.''

Most of the therapists at AIFR resist sex-role stereotyping in counseling, and they argue about the contention that a woman seeking help can be best served by another woman rather than by a male therapist. "Can I counsel a paraplegic if I'm not paralyzed?" Kuhn asks somewhat rhetorically. "I think those kinds of analogies are really ridiculous.''

AIFR also helps people who live at a considerable distance from a therapist by offering what they call intensive therapy. Norma Walters and David Pounds, two therapists at AIFR, saw one couple for six hours in a single day. Tom and Bernice were both in their fifties, college educated, and they were having financial difficulties, in-law conflicts, sexual problems, and their children were into drugs. "I guess they covered every area as far as problem situations were concerned." Tom and Bernice took the bus to Los Angeles, and at nine in the morning sat down with Norma and David. Since the therapists had decided much of the couple's problems centered around an inability to communicate, and that both desperately needed to "ventilate," the first several hours were spent just letting the two talk about their relationship.

"We allowed them to ventilate where they were," Pounds said. "We interpreted as we went along. We expressed and gave empathy. Then in the afternoon we taught some communications techniques—making 'I' statements rather than 'you' statements. Each was seen separately, and then they were given some rather interesting assignments.''

Norma Walters told Bernice to write down seventeen areas in which she really felt loved and cared for. The idea is that love is a nebulous word, and love is really action. "For me," explained Walters, "love is when my husband stops and buys me a crumb doughnut with glaze. It's being able to sleep late. It's his answering the telephone when maybe it's a call for me.

That's how I feel loved. In my own marriage my husband and I did this. I had been loving him for years in the way *I* wanted to be loved, and it really didn't mean much to *him*. *He* was loving me in the way that *he* wanted to be loved, and it wasn't meaningful to me. So the idea is to get in touch with what are the ways that *I* feel loved and cared for—and vice versa. We found out, and now I can give him the ways that he feels loved and cared for, and I know how he likes to be loved.''

David Pounds carries the "love list" idea a bit further. He has the couple write out a list of the ways each spouse wants to be loved. Then each chooses one thing from the other's list that they're willing to do the next week. Pounds also uses a "caring day list" which he says he "stole" from Richard Stewart, a Canadian therapist. "The list is made of little things that can be done—greeting at the door, bringing a card or a rose, fixing a special meal, rubbing her back—that kind of thing. I have each of the people make a list as long as they possibly can in one session. Then I say, 'Okay, tomorrow one of you will choose as many things from your spouse's list as possible and do those things for that person. Then, the next day, the other. You'll alternate.' Then this kind of thing goes on, and usually within a week they forget whose day it is, and they're both doing as many things off the list as possible. This really makes people begin to focus on the positive aspects of the relationship rather than the negative because it seems difficult to reduce the negative kinds of things but much easier to increase the positive."

Norma Walters told of one case she was rather proud of. Sylvia had just given birth to a girl. She came in complaining that she was feeling like a "typical housewife." She was feeling frustrated taking care of the newborn infant and, on top of it, was receiving pressure from her mother to divorce her husband. The mother had an intense dislike for her son-in-law, partly because he was Spanish and partly because her daughter was pregnant at the time of their marriage. One of the first questions Norma asked Sylvia was, "Do you really want this marriage?" and Sylvia's reply was, "Yes, I do." Norma began working from that premise. The next step was helping Sylvia stand up to her mother. After that Norma helped Sylvia realize that her attitude of "If-only-he-would-be-this-way, if-only-he-did-that, if-only-this-would-happen" was a kind of passive-aggressive behavior pattern that did neither of them any good. So Norma worked with her on developing open communications with her husband, giving "I" messages, sharing her thoughts with him, letting him know when she was angry. Not once did Norma see the husband. Twelve visits later Sylvia came in and said, "I really don't feel like I have anything to talk about. When do you think I'll be finished?" Norma replied that she was ready when she thought she was ready, and Sylvia replied, "Now."

Norma smiled remembering the incident. "I said, 'Great. I trust your judgment.' She was accepting her role as a mother. I'd given her some articles on housekeeping, so she wasn't just overwhelmed with that. We'd worked with communications, having fun, making time for friends and, most of all, making time for her husband. I never did see the husband, and yet their marriage had improved so much, she was feeling very positive. And the relationship with her mother improved as well.''

Walters, Pounds, and others at AIFR have strong disagreements with those therapists and counselors who believe it is very difficult, if not impossible, to truly change a marital relationship if *both* partners do not receive therapy. The therapists at AIFR, like those of many clinics around the country, have to deal with the realities which face them—which means at certain times either the husband or the wife will refuse to come in for help. What are clinicians to do—refuse to see one party to the marriage who asks for help unless he or she can cajole the other spouse into coming in also? ''I don't believe that one person can change without changing the basis of the relationship,'' says Pounds. That may create a threat in the relationship, but it can also bring about some positive changes in both husband and wife because they learn to respond differently.''

There is another party to marital disputes, particularly in sprawling urban and suburban Los Angeles—the automobile. Charles Ryder, a hip young AIFR therapist, and Allen J. Brown, director of the department of counseling at AIFR, both point to the car as a precipitator of problems for married couples.

Brown believes that there is an ''absolute saturation of opportunity'' available in Southern California. The husband has his job; the wife has her part-time work. He has his basketball and she has her tennis. It takes him an hour to drive to work and she spends two hours taking the children to drum lessons, dancing lessons, and baseball practice. They can drive to the ocean for swimming and fishing or the mountains for hiking or skiing. Thanks to a totally inadequate public transportation system, middle-class families are forced to bear the financial burden of buying and maintaining two cars, which means more gasoline, more time spent in the car going to and fro. And, of course, because Los Angeles is so spread out, it takes even more time to go to the dentist, the doctor, to visit Aunt Millie . . . whatever. Ryder sees the tone of Southern California as ''Rush, rush, rush, run away from your problems—just keep going and get caught up in all of it. Pretty soon your problems won't hurt as much.''

Brown gave an example of a couple in their late thirties who had been married for twelve years. The husband, Byron, was an attorney who drove through miles of traffic each day to and from court, to law school three times a week where he taught, and to conferences all around the country. His wife, Emily, had a college degree but chose to stay home with her two young sons. After coming home from a hard day's work, Byron retired to a workshop because he basically was a shy, introverted kind of guy. Emily, at the end of her day, had had it with the children and wanted some attention for herself. But all Byron wanted was a little peace and quiet. So Emily ate . . . and ate . . . and ate, eventually tipping the scales at 250 pounds even though she had been a slim young woman while she was in college. Emily went to a psychiatrist and gained enough insight to realize that she was competing with her sons for attention from her husband. She wasn't totally uncomfortable with her weight situation, so she broke off from her psychiatrist. Then Byron came down with hepatitis, and she not only had to care for her children but for her husband as well. That was when she started to go through a two-pound box of chocolates in ten minutes.

They came to AIFR and sought counseling. Brown worked to have them each explore how the other felt, and after several sessions Byron and Emily sensed a certain degree of success. The two were spending at least five minutes together in the morning before he left for work, but those five minutes were "quality time," without coffee and newspaper. They stopped therapy. Three months later they came back for a "checkup" because they had begun to slip back into their old patterns. He had begun to spend more time in the workshop or mowing the lawn when it didn't need it, and she had begun her compulsive overeating.

Finally Brown said to her, "Look, Emily. I really think what's going on with you is that you've never had a mother to pattern after. You don't really know how to hack it with a couple of kids. You're constantly vying with them for attention from Byron, and he doesn't have that much good stuff left to give. You've got him wrung dry all the time. He can give it to the kids, but when it comes to a big girl like you, he just can't put out any more." Brown suggested that she get some individual counseling in a women's group at AIFR where she could do some patterning and modeling. "In a sense the case is a success," says Brown. "In another sense it's a continuing education of growing, of conditioning that she never had as a kid."

That old notion that adjustment is more the responsibility of the wife than the husband was not retired with Dr. Popenoe, but it has been modified. Such modified progress is both the safety valve and the drawback of large social service agencies. They choose to refine the tried and proven counseling techniques rather than taking chances with radical innovations. Conservative pressures from the bureaucracy within, and time pressures from the waiting list without, put creativity in a bind. As more and more couples refuse to settle for an unhappy relationship or an unfulfilled sex life, the demand upon agencies such as AIFR increases. Will they be able to keep mediocrity at bay? Couples who choose the safety and economy of the large agency will want to ask that question as they go to their intake interview.

Even large bureaucratic agencies can and do respond to the creative efforts of determined individuals. Psychologist Sheldon Star of the VA hospital in Palo Alto is such an individual.

The Veterans Administration Hospital on the outskirts of Palo Alto, California, is architecturally like most sprawling governmental institutions: oppressive and dehumanizing. In 1968 it functioned like the rest of the VA hospitals around the country: veterans presented themselves for hospitalization and hospitalized they were. But Sheldon Star, PhD psychologist, who trained with Virginia Satir and Don Jackson, decided to start a family therapy and conjoint marital therapy unit, with the help of only one trainee. In 1976 the Palo Alto facility remains the only VA hospital that has a systematically organized unit to deal with family and marriage problems.

The section or clinic is not designed to replace the psychiatric unit at the hospital but rather to complement it. When there is a psychiatric problem, the patient—usually the man—will be admitted. But more and more doctors—from psychiatry as well as from medicine, surgery, neurology, and internal medicine—are realizing that many of the people who present themselves for admission for medical problems are really in the middle of a severe family crisis.

Star describes a typical case as a man and woman who are in their forties. The man may have sought admission sometime before, possibly for depression, but now, when he presents himself at the hospital, the diagnosis suggests a marriage problem. "The most typical problem is the feeling of a kind of deadness," he says. "It's what everybody goes through, that feeling of 'Okay, so we've been married for twenty years, and we find a kind of emptiness between us.'" Sometimes there are problems with children, sometimes not, but these men have reached a point in their marriage where both they and the marriage have fizzled out. They had believed, as Star put it, in a "Doris-Day-this-is-what-marriage-should-be-like," and it never panned out that way. "They are in a midlife crisis."

Star describes the general technique he and his twenty full- and part-time colleagues and trainees use with the couple. First find out what is "missing" between the two. "Then you need to know, was it ever there, and if it was, when did it erode away? Because if it was never there, you've really got problems. If it was never there, how the hell do you get something that never existed? That is pretty tough. In other words what can we do for these two individuals that would be beneficial for them in the way they define it? Sometimes they can't define it, and that's our job, to help them define the problem."

After there is some kind of definition of the problem, therapy will begin. "We use any modality we think will work," Star says, which includes the use of videotape. But then there is the kind of hard questioning which forces some kind of resolution to the problem: "What do you want?" is what Star calls a "tough question for everyone, especially when you're between forty and fifty, you're married to the same person, your kids are almost independent." Then there are questions like, "How would you like things to be?

How was it at one time?" Star finds out about the wishes and hopes they once had. Have they been frustrated? How did they lose what they once had? He might ask, "Do you want it to be that way again? You once described yourselves as being very close. What was that like? Do you want it to be that way again? What do you tell yourself about why that got lost?"

The cost to the patient is exactly nothing—a factor which Star feels is an impetus to the therapist to work hard and swiftly since there is no economic incentive for keeping the patient in therapy.

Star's example should encourage other VA hospitals around the nation to begin setting up family support units similar to the one in Palo Alto.

THE AVANT-GARDE AGENCY

Ten years ago, after working with the government sponsored "helping system" at the San Francisco Health Department, Dr. Joel Fort became convinced that the conventional therapeutic model used to aid psychologically disturbed people was actually hurting them rather than helping them. "All the problems we were dealing with were being poorly dealt with by society," he says. "The problems were either being ignored or handled in a punitive manner, and I thought there needed to be a new approach which included a social perspective." So five years later, after much work and planning, Fort Help came into existence—complete with some very radical innovations.

The first thing one notices when they walk in the reconverted warehouse that is Fort Help is the informality. Off to one side, an elderly woman is bending the ear of an attentive, bearded young man while they both sit on a brightly colored, comfortable couch. On the other side of the room there are more brightly colored chairs and couches where mostly young people freely "crash," rest, or read.

In the office young men and women, all of whom are wearing blue jeans, bustle to and fro, answering the phone with "Fort Help, may I help you?" and jotting down messages. Half the people working as "consultants" or "helpers" are volunteers and are not paid; the other half of the staff members do draw salaries, but not what one would call comfortable these days. There are no secretaries or clerks because the model from which Fort Help works is based upon participatory democracy rather than the typical hierarchical medical model. Secretaries and clerks are viewed as sexist jobs, and besides, when people have to do their own paperwork, they write fewer memos.

Although Fort seems to display a lack of modesty in calling his organization the "National Center for Solving Social and Health Problems," it would be a mistake to dismiss Fort Help as just a monument to one man's ego. Fort has been, and probably will continue to be, if not in the center of some controversy, at least on the outskirts. From his long-standing interest in crime and violence as a social problem he has testified as an expert witness at the trials of several mass murderers—most recently the Charles Manson case in Los Angeles. He has written extensively about the problem of drugs and, much to the dismay of many, has labeled alcohol the most abused drug. He has acted as a consultant to established agencies, including the U.S. Justice Department, the U.S. Senate, and the World Health Organization.''

The informality, the openness, which permeate Fort Help are built into the agency for a specific reason; it's not just a spontaneous manifestation of San Francisco-style behavior. "The humanization of the helping process we have achieved here," Fort explains, "is fifty percent of helping somebody. Sometimes people with difficulties lack self-esteem; they feel insecure and dependent. By responding to them as persons, as individuals, or as guests— and by getting rid of titles and false professionalism, the white coats, the stethoscopes, couches, or sitting behind desks, all of which we've dispensed with here—that is half the battle of helping someone. They feel good about you and the program they're coming to, and where they're not further beaten down with the kind of negativism or stigmatization of diagnosis and treating people as *patients*—that's when you wind up helping people.''

"Guests" come to Fort Help with a whole panoply of "social problems": marital and family difficulties from heterosexual, homosexual, and even a few transsexual marriages. (Fort eschews the term "gay" because it implies that heterosexual is "sad.") People come to Fort Help feeling suicidal, lonely, and alienated. Then there are the drug abusers (and here Fort classifies the use of alcohol and tobacco as "drugs"), those who are obese, and those who must face the problem of death and dying.

Just as there are a wide range of problems, so too are there many kinds of therapies practiced at Fort Help. Fort calls it a "smorgasbord" approach, valid, he believes, because of the varieties of problems coming through the door. But there's another reason behind the eclectic approach to therapy at Fort Help. Diversity, Joel Fort believes, equals freedom of choice, something which is not available to the typical mental health clinic, the kind of place with a this-is-what-we-have, take-it-or-leave-it attitude toward the client. At Fort Help if a "guest" wants a "helper" who is male or female, heterosexual or homosexual, married or divorced, if they want co-therapy, family therapy, or couples group therapy, Joel Fort feels that is the guest's prerogative and the center's responsibility to meet.

So, naturally, the kinds of therapists at Fort Help run the psychological spectrum. But because they are a diverse bunch, it would be a mistake to believe that anyone who wanted to be a "therapist" could just volunteer his or her services and start practicing. Before a person is allowed to "help," the potential helper is subject to a peer review during which he is closely screened. Degrees or the lack of them are seldom given great consideration.

What is given great weight is the potential helper's attitude: does it fit well in the freedom-of-choice, participatory-democracy plan of the clinic?

"It is my personal view," says Fort, "that ideally a person who counsels others should have shown in his or her own life an ability to carry out a sustained relationship with another human being. And it is my experience that the majority of people doing marriage counseling and therapy have been unsuccessful themselves in marriage." Those who are admitted as helpers to Fort Help are continually subject to supervision inside the clinic by their peers, and they are also advised to seek further supervision from other therapists outside the Fort Help community. The emphasis on informality, both in terms of therapy and the relationship between helper and guest, extends to the point at which it is not unusual for a counseling session to end and then for the helper and guest to have a social drink together. But there are two very firm rules which are strictly enforced: no sexual involvement with someone who is being helped, and no "poisoning" of someone by blowing cigarette smoke in his face while he is in the center.

Joel Fort has definite "political" reasons for structuring Fort Help along democratic, nontraditional lines. Fort believes that the traditional governmental mental health approach to therapy has combined with a conservative, psychiatric model into which all who seek help are forced. And although this medical model has fallen into disrepute, says Fort, it is nevertheless maintained to protect those "in power," namely those who run the mental health establishment.

Fort believes the traditional psychoanalytic techniques (patient on the couch, lying down, and thus vulnerable while the therapist sits on a chair, out of sight, silent and powerful) are just one typical example of how those in power use "magic" to enhance their stature. "Those kinds of rules," says Fort, "are designed to keep us ignorant of the best-kept secret in America, which is that those who rule us are incompetent. Mayors, governors, and Presidents use the same system to separate themselves from everybody so people won't realize how terrible they really are."

Fort is not alone in these beliefs. Thomas Szasz, professor of psychiatry at New York State University at Syracuse, believes the psychiatric community for all too long has had the power to stigmatize whole groups of people just by their—the psychiatrists'—definition of what is sane or insane. Szasz does not believe in the term "mental illness" because the definition of what is "well" as opposed to "sick" is made by psychiatrists who respond to the prevailing values of society. In 1928 a middle-class housewife who wanted to pursue a career in law or medicine rather than stay home with her husband and children might have been considered "sick." Today she would be called liberated. The therapist can never be totally freed from the values imposed by society and his own personality. But the therapist can overcome some of these limitations by treating the patient as a unique individual to whom he must accord dignity and decision-making powers.

Ralph Robinson is one such helper who classifies his approach to psychotherapy as a "casserole" of various styles, techniques, ideas, and philosophies, fitting neatly into Fort's smorgasbord concept.

The thirty-eight-year-old PhD came to Fort Help because he liked the lack of hierarchy. "I believe too much of psychotherapy is a rip-off, and this is my community contribution." Robinson is paid $250 a month for devoting half his working time to Fort Help. And although he has a positive feeling about the democratic procedures at Fort Help, he nevertheless understands that it has its drawbacks, including a certain degree of inefficiency as well as some inexperienced helpers. There are some people at Fort Help, Robinson says, whom "I would *not* give a client to."

A typical case of a couple who came to Fort Help was Frank, twenty-eight years old, a contractor, and his wife Cindy, a housewife, twenty-six. They had been married five years and came to Fort Help because they believed they had a sexual dysfunction. The problem was that they were having sexual relations very infrequently and were arguing a great deal. When they argued, Cindy would usually win because she was more articulate, louder, and more sophisticated. Frank would even the score by refusing to have sex with her. Cindy would try to get one up by initiating sex when Frank was engrossed in watching a football game on television. He would refuse her. Then, later that night, after she had cooked dinner and put their five-year-old child to bed, Frank would initiate sex, and Cindy would refuse, saying she was "too tired."

Robinson had the couple write out their complaints about each other, and not so surprisingly, they both wanted to have more sex and more sexual foreplay. During the first session Robinson told the couple that he expected them to show significant improvement after the first five sessions and that if there were no improvements he would either send them to another therapist or try another technique. He quickly followed this statement by saying that in almost all cases the couples he sees do have significant change within a relatively short time. In this manner, Robinson explained, a couple begins to change because their therapist expects it.

Robinson immediately established his "power" position with Frank and Cindy by ordering them to stop blaming each other by using "you" statements and instead start using "I" statements. To reinforce his dominance over the couple as well as to alleviate a great deal of anxiety, Robinson insisted Frank and Cindy have no sexual intercourse. He gave them "assignments" including lots of touching, stroking, one partner guiding the hand of the other partner in the most pleasurable manner—but no intercourse. "Of course, that's usually a turn-on as soon as you forbid it." He smiled. "Usually a couple will come in the next session rather sheepishly, giggling, and say they had fantastic sex the night before, which of course is a positive reinforcement.''

Then Robinson told them they were never to have sex unless both partners really wanted it. He did this not only because Cindy was on a kind of round-robin guilt trip (feeling guilty about not having sex, then having sex out of a sense of duty rather than pleasure and desire, which in turn triggered guilt, which caused her not to want to have sex) but because it gave Cindy and Frank the knowledge that when they did have sexual intercourse, both genuinely wanted to have it. The so-called sexual dysfunction vanished after three sessions.

Robinson then brought in a co-therapist and began to work on the couple's communications problems. The female co-therapist and Robinson "modeled" an argument, and Frank and Cindy saw that a couple could fight and yet have a great deal of respect for each other. After seven sessions Frank and Cindy left. Eight months later they returned, not because of any sexual dysfunction but because each wanted to learn a bit more about communications. They had three more sessions, left, and reported later they were doing just fine.

Couples also come to Fort Help seeking "permission" to divorce. Ralph Robinson will give them permission as well as his best talents in helping them deal with that traumatic experience. John was an engineer in his early forties; Patricia had just finished her bachelor's work in sociology. They had been married nineteen years and most of that had been hell. Robinson saw them for three sessions, working mainly on their lack of communications. They returned for the fourth session saying they both now wanted a divorce. Robinson then turned his attention to helping both deal with that problem. He told Patricia not to bottle up her feelings of depression and sadness but rather "to go with it," to put on the melancholy music and understand that her tears were a natural release. Although John wasn't very much into his feelings, Robinson nevertheless counseled him so that as the divorce proceeded, John and Patricia began to communicate with each other and, because their expectations for each other no longer mattered, actually became pals. Patricia went into a women's rap group; John went into "est," an acronym for Erhard Seminars Training, which one trainee describes as a distillation of Gestalt, Zen, scientology, the Bible, and Dale Carnegie. Robinson was satisfied that each had gone as far as they wanted, that both were much, much happier than before.

"Although I draw heavily from Gestalt theory," says Robinson, "I am an extremely eclectic practitioner." His approach embraces the family therapy concepts of Satir, Jackson, Haley, and Ackerman, as well as using an array of tools and techniques drawing from Gestalt fantasies, dreamwork, and dialogues; communications systems, behavior modification, and transactional analysis.

But Robinson also believes the clients have a responsibility for the success or failure of the therapy. "I think it's important to let clients understand their share of the responsibility for therapy, that I haven't got a magic wand, and they are ultimately responsible for change. I let them know that they will only change as much as they want to, which imposes a paradox on them— that if they don't change, it means they weren't motivated to change. Whenever I suggest something for a client to do, I let my client know where I'm coming from and explain the process to them. I don't want to covertly manipulate them."

Fort Help, with the vision of Joel Fort and the work of people like Ralph Robinson, represents a forward step toward accountability of therapists and marriage counselors to their clients. Those at Fort Help are not without their flaws (nor are those at any other mental health institution). But Fort Help offers something which one does not see at many other places: the freedom of choice by the client.

THE RIGHTS OF THE COUNSELED

Pamela Barnham, born and raised in England, described herself as the kind of woman who always had a list of demands when she visited a doctor. But when her marriage was falling apart and she called the Family Counseling Service of Evanston, she made no demands. She put up with an inexperienced, insensitive therapist for nearly one year until the man was fired— through no complaint of hers. She never expressed her dissatisfaction to him or anyone else. He had made her feel ashamed of having failed.

The Family Counseling Service of Evanston and Skokie, Illinois, is one of the most reliable suburban agencies in the country. Each of the fourteen social workers has a masters degree. The agency promotes husband and wife involvement in choosing a therapeutic program and generally strives for appropriate matches of therapists and couples.

But no agency can have a foolproof matching system. Some agencies are so overloaded they simply assign the case to any therapist who is available. The client must be the one to pass judgment on the therapist. The couple must decide if they feel respect and trust for the person assigned. Even if a couple is paying very little for marriage counseling, they are wasting their time and money and the agency's time and money if the therapeutic match is a bad one. Pamela's description of her therapist should encourage consumers of agency services to stand up for their rights.

I went into the agency cold and wound up with a young man, a psychologist with an MS whose experience had been in some sort of state mental hospital. I later learned that he had been fired.

I went first by myself. Finally I persuaded my husband to go. He had a separate session. I guess the man went into my husband's childhood or his hangups. My husband said, "The guy is crazy. The guy is mad. If you want to go and waste your money, fine; you go. But I'm not going." It scared him so that he never went back.

As far as putting the marriage back together, I think that could have been done because we both wanted it. The very fact that my husband would go at all, I think, showed it could have been done. The thing he did that I really can't forgive the marriage counselor for was to frighten my husband so much that he wouldn't even consider going back.

The therapist spent an hour once a week trying to make me angry so that I would react. Unfortunately, in my husband's and in my own case, we both went to English public schools. Now, nothing in this world will make us angry if we don't wish to be angry. We're trained so that we simply will not show emotion. So he was wasting his time. Finally I asked him, "Why are you doing this?" And he didn't say anything. I said, "But you know, really, all I can say is you're making it so bad we can't communicate at all. I mean, half the time we sat in silence. And I thought, "My God! I'm paying this guy all this money, and we sit in silence."

Actually he was not a marriage counselor. I think he was trying to do something that he was not qualified to do, but I was too stupid to see it. I don't think he was concerned about the marriage at all. I think he was practicing what he had learned. He was very young.

That's one of the mistakes that social agencies make. They get these young kids there who have a degree in sociology, and they think they know everything. I know they have to learn on people, but sometimes when things are really rough, you feel like saying, "Don't learn on me!"

I think in fairness he should have said to me at the outset, "This is what I can do, and this is what I cannot do, and this is what we will try and do," or, "This is what we'll work on," and see if it was agreeable. I should have trusted my instincts which I usually do and said, "This is not right for me," and looked for somebody else.

He wanted to talk to my children. He thought it would be good to study the whole unit. I didn't mind suffering with him, but to touch my children was quite another thing.

I thought to myself, "If I think he's so bad for my children, what am I thinking of in going to see him myself?" But this was sort of unconscious. In other words, if he's that bad that I'm afraid to have him deal with any of my children, what must he be doing to me?

I suppose if one learns anything, it's trust your instincts. I was so ignorant in that area. I never thought about damaging my psyche because it never occurred to me that I had a psyche.

Many therapists are coming around to the point of view that the "failure" of the patient to respond, to feel better about himself or herself, may in fact be the fault of the therapist and not the patient. Patients, increasingly aware of their rights, are beginning to question therapists about their backgrounds, their life-styles, their value systems.

A husband and wife came to see Denver psychiatrist Dr. Michael Solomon. At the first session Dr. Solomon asked the couple how they felt about being there. The wife answered, "I'm here with my husband and you—two men and one woman—and I'm not sure just how sensitive you are to my needs. I don't know if you're married, if you have children, whether your marriage is any good. I don't know if you just happened into this because there wasn't anything else to do, whether you actually know what you're doing. Do you find my concerns unwarranted?"

Dr. Solomon replied that he did not find her concerns unwarranted and added, "We have to find out how you are going to come to a decision." The wife answered, "I just want you to know it's going to take time. I'm not coming in here and spill out my guts until I come to some conclusion about you as a person. If I have a good feeling, I'll tell you things. If I don't have a good feeling, I'm not coming back." Many therapists, locked into the traditional modes of therapy, would have bristled at the very idea that a "patient" would dare to make such demands. But Dr. Solomon replied to her, "That's a good place for us to be. I'm not going to sell myself to you. But I'm going to do my thing and you will decide."

Patients do have a right to decide. World-renowned family therapist Virginia Satir urges people to leave therapy if they feel they are being humiliated or denigrated. But Satir is very clear and very precise in having people differentiate between humiliation and denigration and the normal kinds of anguish and distress which come from self-revelation. "Don't confuse the presence of anxiety or pain with humiliation, because most of the time in therapy, when you make new overtures, you will feel some pain."

An outstanding Chicago psychiatrist, Dr. F. Theodore Reid, leading a group therapy session in which a recently divorced Jewish man had finally expressed his interest in starting a new life, looked at the gloom on the man's face and the sadness of the group and said, "Look at us. We're all sitting *shivah* [mourning] at a birth."

THE PAIN THAT PRECEDES CHANGE

Elsa Leichter, a petite, soft-spoken product of Wittgenstein's Vienna, has practiced family and multifamily therapy with one of the most overburdened agencies in the nation—the Jewish Family Service Agency in New York City. She and the JFSA are committed to family therapy because it is the most "economical" brand of therapy the agency can use and because it "works."

Ms. Leichter has found that families often have an unspoken agreement, a "pact" whereby the family acts as "a fortress against outsiders." One aspect to the resistance to therapy is that they believe—correctly—that there will be much unpleasantness. There are couples who fear being open, who fear to say things their spouses do not want to hear, for the very simple reason that they cannot tolerate any anxiety in their mates.

"To tolerate anxiety, pain, in others, is something that has to be learned," says Ms. Leichter. "Even the most banal communication between spouses, if it is open and honest, sometimes has to be learned. The ability to come home from a rough day's work and say to your partner, 'I had a rough day,' and not have to have your spouse *do* anything, but just to hear it, with perhaps only a gentle touch. Nothing has to be said or examined or analyzed but just to have a person be there.

"When you work with families or couples, there's the child's expectation that the other has to be a mind reader. We have to work a lot on that. A person has to be able to ask for what they want so that the other can understand and then give more easily. A couple or a family can be a team, yes, and get jobs done without all the to-do about it. But space must be given to each person; individuality must be allowed. And that is a hard thing to learn."

It is a hard, difficult thing to learn, which is why there is pain and resentment in the therapeutic process. ("If I understand process—out of bitter learning, sweat and blood, and from having experienced the same reactions—then I can say with great conviction that I understand what's going on. I don't get thrown. On the contrary.") Ms. Leichter constructs this imaginary but very realistic portrait of the pain a couple may feel while in therapy:

WIFE: You're not helping me. Things are getting worse instead of better. What the hell is going on? You egged me on to communicate, to really express what I'm feeling, and when I do express what I'm feeling, what do I get back? Shit!

LEICHTER: All right, you started to communicate. So you threw in your dime and you didn't get chocolate yet. You got just the opposite of chocolate. So your husband's not there yet. [To the husband] You have always complained that she didn't express herself. Now that she does, you don't like it.

WIFE: I knew it wouldn't pay. I'm getting just what I got as a child. When I opened my mouth, I got a slap.

LEICHTER: Yes, you took a risk, but your husband isn't quite there yet. It is true you took a risk, and it didn't pay off, and you think I stink because I led you down the path. But I would like you not to give up.

Ms. Leichter explains the pain this way. "Often things have to get worse before they get better. For things to get worse should *not* be a signal to the couple to run. Therapy is not pleasant. If things get worse, it hurts and it's hard to understand. For instance, a couple may have held a lot in—she's a *nudger* and he's a withdrawer—and suddenly they have fights with each other, they grapple with each other. And when they start to do that, it doesn't occur in, well, harmony. One of the pair may first have the courage to do it and then gets the wrong answers back—just what he or she was afraid would happen—retaliation. And you may get a setback rather than some progress."

But if the therapist can understand the pain, in a sense identify with it, a couple may begin to successfully deal with the problems that have caused their relationship to deteriorate.

To go through all this for marriage—is it worth it? Elsa Leichter wants to know the same thing. "Why people are expected to know how to be married, I don't know. It's not necessarily a totally natural thing. My feeling is that in our time, in our society, and in the changing world in which we live— women's lib and all that—marriage and the family is an almost impossible institution."

The impossible institution of marriage persists even as divorce rates soar. Marriage is the life-style that most unmarried people and the majority of the previously divorced still choose.

Yet, even with effective and sensitive people like Elsa Leichter who devote a lifetime of work to improving the quality of human relationships and married life, the almost impossible institution of marriage is becoming more impossible as Americans become more mobile.

THE AGENCY AS AN EXTENDED FAMILY

From a country of close-knit communities where families and individuals shared common experiences we have become, in Vance Packard's words, "a nation of strangers." Once upon a time a family moving to a new community had a good chance of remaining together. The move created a sense of solidarity for the entire family, a sense of shared adventure, shared excitement. Now, as families move from Iowa to California or from New York to Florida, the journey is made in relative isolation. The impersonal moving van has replaced the covered wagon just as the little house on the prairie has been bulldozed to make way for the condo near the shopping center.

What gives the seventies-style frontier such a temporary rootless quality is the sure knowledge that another move is just around the corner. The average American moves once every five years—more often than any other national group except for refugees of war-torn countries.

Sinking roots is one of the most important tasks for adults as they move into their thirties and forties. But with forty million Americans changing their home address each year, the once easily accomplished goal of settling down now requires an extraordinary effort. Marriage and the family often buckle under the strain of these traumatic moves from friends and familiar places. The community social service agency is frequently the only buttress available for the shaky family structure.

To find out what kind of support an agency can offer the mobile American, we selected the Henderson Clinic of Hollywood, Florida—a community filled with transplants, a community whose sudden influx of people has transformed it almost overnight from a small resort town into a new American city.

The white stucco one-story building is at least forty years old—one of the oldest in the town of Hollywood, Florida. Underneath the lighted plastic bell button is the name "Royal Palms Hotel." The sleazy "Hot-L Baltimore" establishment with small rooms, frayed carpets, and dank smell of disinfectant was converted in 1953 into the Henderson Clinic family mental health service. In the years since the Royal Palms became the Henderson Clinic, the population of Hollywood, Florida, has tripled. The Hollywood branch of Henderson treats 1,500 patients with a staff of fifteen psychiatrists, psychologists, and social workers. In 1974 a 90-10 matching grant from the federal government which would have established a new enlarged mental health complex for the entire Broward County area was lost because the county couldn't come up with 10 percent of the funding. There are very few traditions in this south Florida region; taxation to support community services is not one of them.

At the desk of the Henderson Clinic a clean-cut-looking man in a cheap, short-sleeved sport shirt is paying his bill for two visits. He hands the receptionist ten dollars. He receives one dollar in change. A shy, frightened-looking young girl whispers to the receptionist that she has just been released from the hospital and has an appointment. The receptionist gives her a three-page form to fill out. Even though the reception room is full, she takes the time to tell the girl with great kindness that she can help her fill out the form or explain any questions that are unclear. On this 98-degree day the women are in halters and shorts, the men in khakis. One hears a Bronx accent here, a Brooklyn intonation there—as one Hollywood cabdriver put it, northern and middle Florida is the South; south Florida is New York City.

In the crowded waiting room the patients sit passively, watching *Secret Storm.*

In spite of their enormous case load, Henderson people, from the receptionist to director Hugh Nestor, all manage to treat their patients with consideration and dignity. Most of the staff members follow an eclectic approach—Freud as the classical base, a little behavior modification here, a dash of Masters and Johnson there, Gestalt, TA, Szasz, and Thoreau to taste.

The overriding philosophy is first, help as quickly as possible. (Patients who feel desperate for help are seen immediately.) Second, encourage patients to help themselves. Most city agencies around the country don't encourage long periods of dependency. But many of them do make the patient go through a number of intake interviews and hours of red tape before help is given. Others are staffed by intimidating caseworkers, each jealously guarding a tiny fiefdom, each more concerned with propitiating their department straw boss than appealing to the patient's dignity. At Henderson, staff members are willing to work together at weekly "boiler room" sessions so that new cases can be assigned to the best-qualified and most interested staff member. The staff seem to share a basic belief in the germ of sanity that exists in all people—even those who have just been released with the warning label, psychotic.

Henderson Clinic in Hollywood, Florida, shows what can be done in a community that has an escalating need and a small pocketbook. It shows how some agencies remain in touch with the needs of the community and how a limited staff maximizes its efficiency without becoming rigid.

Margaret Kennedy, an attractive woman in her forties who had been married for nineteen years, heard about Henderson Clinic in her work as a medical technician. On her first visit she came with her husband, who had behaved childishly and often irrationally throughout their marriage. The social worker saw Mr. Kennedy, gave him certain medication, and later described his behavior as psychotic. Mr. Kennedy refused to return to the clinic for treatment and usually refused to take his medication, the result being behavior which was so immature and obstreperous that it embarrassed the four Kennedy children, particularly the oldest daughter who had just turned seventeen.

Margaret Kennedy continued to see the social worker periodically for help with her husband, but an episode occurred which convinced her to bring the whole family into therapy with Henderson psychologist Dan Jackson. The two Kennedy boys, nine and eleven, stole baseball hats from one of the department stores. She made the boys return the merchandise, but the episode made her realize that the problems at home—the marital problems and the father's irrational behavior—were beginning to take their toll on the kids.

Margaret is finding Dan Jackson's multiple-family sessions effective. His blend of unlikely ingredients—including Ralph Waldo Emerson, Albert Ellis, Thomas Szasz, Carl Rogers, and Socrates—strikes her as eminently understandable and practical.

Shortly after Margaret and her four children began attending the family sessions, her nine-year-old boy, with a history of petty thievery including money from his mother's purse, stole a book from the clinic. Margaret brought this to Dr. Jackson's attention. So at the next session Dr. Jackson said, "Has anyone here stolen anything?" Although Mrs. Kennedy indicated by whispering and pointing that her son was the culprit, the boy did not admit the theft. Dr. Jackson waited, and after a moment of silence simply said, "Well, we don't have to worry about it because the people here who haven't stolen anything have no problem. And the person who has stolen something has to live with a thief."

The boy didn't say anything. But Mrs. Kennedy reports that this was her son's last theft. Dr. Jackson's remark, which made the boy responsible for what he did, signaled the end of his stealing behavior. The boy secretly replaced the book he had walked off with from the clinic, and he hasn't stolen a penny's worth since that family session.

Mrs. Kennedy felt Jackson offered her children and herself another way of being and a greater degree of autonomy. She claimed she's able to think in terms of greater independence, in terms of being good to herself and not always feeling responsible for every action, every fight, every misbehavior on the part of her children.

Her husband came to a few family sessions with the social worker, but his behavior on those occasions was disruptive. Margaret is beginning to believe that getting a divorce is the only acceptable alternative to endless suffering. She will continue to attend the family sessions because she finds herself feeling stronger each week, and she believes her oldest daughter needs help in dealing with her hostile feelings toward her father. Before one family session the social worker, whom Margaret continues to see, asked the daughter how she felt about her father. She answered, "I hate my father." Margaret felt that her daughter would definitely have run away from home if they had not gone into family therapy at Henderson Clinic.

The Kennedy marriage was not saved, but the Kennedy family was given "other ways of being"—alternatives to stealing, running away, unending hostility. Margaret found that she was no longer trapped in a desperate situation. She has alternatives and a degree of freedom to choose. When the statistics are tallied, the Kennedy marriage may be considered a failure. But in terms of individual self-esteem the therapy has been triumphant.

Psychologist Dan Jackson is particularly astute at pinpointing problems of rootlessness and new beginnings—problems which may be more pronounced for Floridians but are common throughout our mobile population. "Out here in the center of Florida," he says, "you don't see any big oaks." The lack of familiar roots, traditions, and value systems often aggravates dormant marital and family problems. Dan Jackson sees many couples and families going through such crises. He doesn't act as though the people who come to him at Henderson Clinic were patients. He behaves as if they were all quite capable of making decisions.

Dan is an unusually independent and adult person whose confident manner is even more impressive because of his own physical handicap—a withered arm and a decided limp. Dan treats people with a psychological problem or handicap as if they could behave with as much assurance and good sense as he. As Dan puts it, "I don't need my clients sick; I need them well." Maybe that's why so many people are able to leave Dan's office feeling healthier and more autonomous than when they came in.

JACKSON: I don't try to solve people's problems for the simple reason that if I solve their problems, the next time they get a problem, they'll just come back and I'll have to solve another problem. What I actually do is try to show them systems for setting priorities and solving problems and resolving interpersonal conflict to their mutual advantage.

There are a lot of games that married couples play. For example, they play twenty questions. "Where were you last night?" That's twenty questions. Twenty questions is a game, hide-and-seek, peekaboo, cops and robbers, keep-away. Keep-away is a wonderful game that they play with sex. They treat sex as if it's something they can draw interest on if they put it in the bank. They don't treat it as a universally available free agent that everybody has and that is in tremendous supply. So they play keep-away and twenty questions and hide-and-seek, peekaboo—and children can join in this too—and they can play confusion. Whenever they want to get me confused, I go ahead and say, "Look. You all go ahead and confuse each other or yourselves. I'm not going to get confused just because you are. I won't be drawn into your confusion." I have a choice of whether to do that. Along with this, I'll go ahead and say, "There are some grown-up games which grown-ups can play better than kids. They are more fun than kids' games." Grown-up games are where everybody wins and nobody loses. If you and I are playing an honest game, then we'll both win. If it's a dishonest game, then somebody will get exploited. But a game where everybody wins and nobody loses is quite easy to play.

Many families come to the group because their children have behavioral problems. But I find very often when children have problems, parents get into a triangle, one parent siding with the child and the other feeling locked out. It's two against one. In a bigger family it might be two against two. So we talk about who chooses sides. I'll say, "All right, now. You all get into a big fight about this. Now, who wins?" And that's a dirty question because if you and I were to get into an argument right now, who would win? Nobody, because I would end up mad at you and you'd end up mad at me. I would be trying to put you down; you'd be trying to put me down. See, my assumption is that you need me smart and I need you smart. If it's a husband or a wife, you don't need the other one stupid. You need him smart.

If I call my wife a bitch, I'm calling me a name because I was stupid enough to marry her if that's what she is. Or if she calls me an SOB, it's not saying anything real great about her because she was dumb enough to marry one, if that's what I am. I distinguish between being something and acting like something some of the time. I can act like an SOB periodically as one of my many roles, but it's not a permanent characteristic.

We act like SOB's because it has worked. In other words, when we've had temper tantrums before and acted like a spoiled brat, somebody gave us what we wanted. Somebody thought it was easier to go ahead and give the little brat his toy than it was to say, "Look. If you act like that, you don't get your toy."

In my system I show that grown-ups have a lot more fun than kids do. I can do things that my kids, with all of their energy and imagination, can't do, and not only that, I can afford it. And I've been around the track enough to know how to do them more expertly. So I'm pretty well convinced that grown-ups have more fun than kids. This is one of the foundations of my belief.

Secondly, I will very quickly get families or marital groups to figure out who is controlling whom. If a wife can get the husband angry, then for the moment she is controlling his behavior. It's all right if he wants to let her control him by getting him to regress in his emotional level. But he doesn't have to do it. If you want to let me get you angry, that's all right. But you don't have to do everything I want. If somebody wants to defeat me, I usually allow them to do it because there's nothing more boring than having defeated a person without a fight. I don't fight fights that aren't worth fighting. I say, "Yeah, you're right. Here, take the nickel and go." I won't fight over a nickel because I like my tranquillity.

People come because of marital problems, because of their children too. They're facing power struggles. They're basically trying to live full, rich lives even with kids in there. It's really rather hard when you've got three or four or five kids in the family and the adults act like children too.

One of the young daughters in the multiple-family group complained about her parents having the final word. "Well, it isn't fair," she said. "It isn't just." And I said, "That's right. But nobody promised you fairness. Nobody promised you justice. Your parents got here first, whether you like it or not. And they can do a lot of things just because they got here first. They never promised you it would be fair."

Parents stop oppressing their children not out of fairness but out of self-interest. I tell them I side with my wife in my own family, not because she's always right but because I need to side with my wife. I need her and I don't need my children. The first thing I ask these families is: "Do you need your children?" And if they say yes, I say, "Oh! No wonder you've got problems." Because if I need my children, what am I going to do? Quite logically, what's the extension of that? I'd live vicariously through them, plus I would try to keep them children. And if I keep them children, what am I going to have? I'll have children. Now, if I don't need my children, then I'll let them grow up. Again, if I love my wife, whom am I being good to? Me. It's fun to love her. It's not much fun to hurt her. It's not much fun for her to hurt me. And if a woman emasculates her husband, what has she got? A steer. Whom is she being mean to? Herself. Benign behavior comes about not because somebody's so wonderful but because you don't need that other person diminished. You need that other person maximized. For your own self-fulfillment you need the other person in good shape.

Jackson seems more like a teacher than a therapist, teaching people to transplant what solid roots they have, aiding them in developing new traditions, new value systems, which maximizes their freedom to be whole, happy people.

WOMEN'S PROBLEMS

One advantage of a social service agency or clinic is its diversity of personnel and therapies. Confronted with a husband who acted like a child and a child who was stealing, Margaret Kennedy was able to find individual counseling and multifamily therapy at the same place and at a price she and her truck driver husband could afford. Another mode of therapy offered at the Henderson Clinic is the women's group run by psychologist Faye Mitchell.

Faye is a fine example of the feminist therapist—a new breed of therapists who are particularly sensitive to the effects of role stereotypes which often result in problems for men and women. The feminist therapist realizes that no man could possibly conform to the machismo American male image, nor could any woman be the passive, emotional, altruistic little lady that tiptoes through the American consciousness. Faye doesn't call herself a feminist. She believes therapy is "asexual." And Faye is certainly not guilty of any man-hating or destructively militant behavior. But she does see the difficulties when the "John Wayne" husband won't do the dishes and the wife has a job, kids, and house to maintain. She understands that, in many ways, the man is as much a victim of the culture as the woman. "Culture," says Faye, "has kind of boxed the man in, and in order for him to get out of that box he's got to understand that it's possible to have a good self-concept, to feel male enough without the old wrappings."

She cites a case of a couple married twenty-five years who came in for a sexual dysfunction, supposedly *his* dysfunction. He was a quick ejaculator.

But the minute the man approached his wife, she made sure that he would have a quick ejaculation. As Faye describes this complicity, it was the wife's way of emasculating him, encouraging him to ejaculate too soon so he would never be able to satisfy her. Faye even told her once, "A stud couldn't get it up with you." But the woman had changed radically since their therapy—suddenly blossoming out from a withdrawn person into an extrovert who wanted an exciting, overt type of guy. Her husband *had* become more flexible, but basically he was the efficient, steady, conservative person, protective of his wife—the man she had needed when she was nineteen. The couple is now in the process of divorce.

But Faye doesn't believe that the changes in our culture have to bring destruction of the family or the species. She has studied too many cultures to believe that "Mother Nature" had one set plan for men and women. "How about societies like the Siberian society in which the woman takes a child and brings up the child and then marries the child when it's an adult? And the mother becomes the wife. Then there's a society where they practice lesbianism, and the male is used only to get children, but he's not acknowledged. That African tribe has survived."

Though Faye Mitchell appreciates the relativity of role values, she agrees with Hugh Nestor, director of Henderson, that once a model of male and female has become entrenched in a society, changes in these roles come about slowly and with great pain. Says Nestor, "It is hell to violate the rules of your culture and unsettle things that are as accepted as day and night. When a woman starts acting differently, when she suddenly says, 'Get your own beer'—there's trouble in that marriage. Yet as long as he said, 'Get me a goddamn beer now!' and she got the beer, that marriage seemed stable." Now people want more than stability, that kind of stability; they also want friendship. People who come to crisis points in their lives, such as the departure of their children from the home, suddenly realize that they are two strangers coming face to face for the first time. If this radical change is accompanied by a total change in environment, such as a move to Florida, the seeds of potential marital trouble are sown.

Another therapist at Henderson, Tony Fallon, a former Catholic priest who went into social work and is now earning his doctorate in public administration, sees many retired couples. "Most of the problems I see among the older people," says Fallon, "is that for a good number of years the type of jobs and the type of lives they led somewhere else provided just enough insulation between the two of them. But when they get into retirement situations, they have to face each other for the first time in a long time. They now have seven days a week together, when before they may have had only the weekends, if that. They now have no distraction of children, just each other. They become conscious of themselves and conscious of that other person, their spouse. And they look to the other person for help, for fulfillment, for everything. And sometimes there seems to be nothing there; just an empty void.''

Whether the couple is facing a retirement crisis, a problem of infidelity, disruptive behavior by children, or sexual dysfunction, it's usually only one of the partners that approaches the clinic. Says Fallon, ''You don't get couples coming in saying, 'We need help.' It's usually the wife, saying that her husband 'just refuses to come in. What should I do?' ''

At Henderson, though they would prefer to see the husband and wife together, they will not insist on it. They will try to establish some type of contact with the person who calls ''so they don't feel like they're completely alone.''

Faye Mitchell finds it quite a feat to get a husband to come in and admit that someone else is going to tell him what to do. Of course, Faye has no intention of giving husbands or wives any orders. In fact, *if* the husband would show up, she would tell the couple on the first interview: ''You're going to do the work. I can't fix things up. I'm not God. I'm not a witch doctor; I'm not a power. I can clarify the dynamics going on. I can clarify and interpret and show you what you're doing. [She has done this from time to time by taping a number of sessions so they can hear what's going on.] But if you want to make changes, you will be the ones to decide which changes you'll make, if any. Either you can work hard and try to arrive at a new compromise, or remain as you are, or you can decide that you don't want to get together—that you'd prefer a divorce.''

Last year Faye formed a women's group which meets once a week. Four of these women, Maria, Sheila, Helen, and Lilli, agreed to discuss the nature of their marital problems, why they came to the group, and how the therapy is helping them cope.

TWO TALES OF INFIDELITY

Maria has large, dark brown eyes and dark hair pulled back into a ponytail. She looks younger than her thirty-four years. She came to Florida from New Jersey, but she is originally from Italy.

''We had been married sixteen years,'' began Maria. ''We have four children. And I never suspected my husband. I thought he was the kind of man that had never done anything wrong and never would. It was a shock when he left me. All of a sudden I find out that he had another woman and a child. Two months from the day I found out, I decided to come here for help. My girlfriend had been coming here for almost two years because she almost had a nervous breakdown, and she told me wonderful thing they do for her. Because I was very shaken. I figured I have four children—four boys—and I need to be strong. If I started like crying or doing something bad, who was going to take care of my four children? I don't have nobody down here, not in this country. I'm from Italy, and everybody's there. I only have my mother-in-law, who lives in New Jersey. Here everybody was understandable. They understand me. Because I have to be the strong one.

"When I came here, they gave me an appointment right away with a doctor. I went to the doctor and he said I didn't need any pills or anything. He said I was a strong woman. All I needed was somebody to talk to. But my husband is back. He's back, but we don't know how it will work. We're trying."

Maria has been coming to the group for seven months and feels it has helped her. "It's somebody to talk to, to advise you what to do. Now and then you hear other stories, and you compare your story with the others, and you feel a little better. It makes you able to go on for another week, or two more weeks."

With four children ranging in age from two to fourteen years, Maria feels she can't go to work. She has never known another man. Marrying at eighteen in Italy and having had no teen-age life, she cannot entertain the idea of going out with another man. Yet she does not believe the woman must be subservient. "The woman," says Maria, "has to be independent, because I am, really. In my marriage I've been like a man and woman. See, the bad part with me is that I only know my husband; I do not know another man. That's bad for me. That's why my thinking is always old-fashioned. In Italy the life-style is different."

In spite of her belief in independence, Maria sees the women's movement as very cold. "I don't think they have feeling. They think of themselves, themselves, and not enough about others." So Maria, for the time being, is staying with her husband and taking care of her four sons. "Now," she says, getting ready to return to her children, "it's really up to me. I have to be now the understanding wife, cute little wife, keep my mouth shut. I don't know. Maybe it's good if I become like those other women; it's up to me with the marriage. Last year at this time, November fourth, that's when I had the shock."

While each individual's story of marital strife has its own unique characteristics, the problems tend to repeat themselves—the jilted wife and the unfaithful husband being two of the characters making repeated appearances. The stories are kept from banal melodrama only by the palpable pain on the faces of the narrators.

So when forty-four-year-old Sheila, petite, small-boned, and pretty in a fragile way, begins her account of her husband's philandering, one might flash back to a recent study conducted by the Family Service Association of America. One might picture their graph indicating one out of four couples complaining of infidelity, three out of nine fighting over money problems. Sheila is already on the charts. But her resentment, which emerges slowly and politely, never quite surfacing into full-fledged anger, is real and potentially malignant. No matter what course she chooses—divorce or a compromise continuation of the marriage—she needs help and permission to expose the anger, to assert in the face of sometimes humiliating circumstances, that she is a person rather than a puppy dog.

The so-called feminist therapist, then, is not involved in a man-hating campaign, but rather brings to therapy an understanding of sex role stereotypes, of what women's place has been and how that's affected women. As another feminist therapist put it, "A good therapist doesn't lay her values on someone coming to her for help. But a woman cannot be a product of this culture without having a one-down feeling. She is lucky if the marital relationship doesn't heavily cement that feeling."

So here is Sheila's script. A timid girl leads a very protected childhood in a small Midwestern town, does very little dating and in her teen-age years takes care of a domineering invalid father. She marries at eighteen, and even though her husband turns out to be weak and indecisive, she remains with him for fourteen years, finally leaving him with the approval of her teen-age daughter—"It's the only thing you could do, Mom." She then meets an attractive man who seems to know exactly what he wants. As Sheila puts it:

"I thought I would be glad to have someone tell me what to do for a change. He was entirely different from my first husband. That's what attracted me to him in the first place. He's such a domineering person. Before, I was the dominant one and I carried the load of everything. And the responsibility just got to be too much for me all the time. The way my husband now treats me—never letting me have enough money even though he makes twenty thousand a year, discouraging me from working, going to school, even selling Tupperware—well, he has always treated me this way. But before, I hadn't seen it. I just ran along like a little puppy dog and did what I was told."

Sheila describes a series of affairs her husband conducted while on his many business trips—one with a young woman who lived close by and was practically a member of the family. Sheila walked out on her husband when that one came to light, taking their two sons with her. But she returned when the boys begged her to go back, and her husband, playing on her guilt feelings, said, "You see what you're doing to the children?" She returned, and another affair, this time with an airline stewardess, was soon in progress.

"One time," reports Sheila, "I did try to catch them together, but a mutual friend told him I was on the way. I locked him out of the house down here then. I locked all the doors before I left. He had no key. But he broke into the house and he was in the house when I got back. I filed for divorce then. That was two years ago. He had said then it was finished. However, it never did finish."

Here again, Sheila's situation of total dependency upon her husband made action impossible. She became ill at this point and had to have an operation—nothing life-threatening, but still the hospital bills added up to over $3,000. At the helm once more, her husband told her that he knew she didn't want a divorce, that the whole idea was "silly." As soon as Sheila went into the hospital, he went back to his twenty-five-year-old stewardess. Two months later, when Sheila learned of this episode, she was driven to seek help at Henderson for what she saw as a "no exit" situation. "I didn't know what I wanted to do. I didn't know whether to go ahead and divorce him. I had no skills, really. I have never worked other than in a big store or something. I can't make a living, not in this day and time. And I'm from Kansas; I have no family at all here. So what do you do?

"It seemed to me there was no way out, because if I divorced my husband, I felt that I could not keep our home together, and my boys idolize their father, absolutely. I had to decide what I was going to do and I couldn't do it myself.

"When I first came to the group I felt that nothing could be worse than the situation I was in. But when I listen to the other women, their problems are so much worse than mine, that mine looks better. It's easier to face. It makes you feel that, well, you aren't so badly off after all."

Lately, home and security are not receiving the top priority they held for so long in the woman's scale of values. Some people even admire the woman who can chuck it all and take off for the big apple and her second chance. But this is not the right decision for all women. And a good therapist, even if she is a feminist at heart, is on the scene to facilitate awareness, not to dictate decisions. As Faye Mitchell puts it, "I deal not with some objective reality, but with each individual's perception of reality." At this point Sheila perceives that security and home mean more to her than most other things: "I've decided to strive towards keeping the family together. And my husband, of course, has told me many times he won't leave me. Faye says, 'Why should he leave? He has it made.'" And Sheila, who has tried dating other men and found the thought of sleeping with another man repugnant, states with rue that has not yet turned to gall: "He has his cake and is eating it, too. He has a home life, a pleasant home life, and he has his play."

WHAT DIFFERENCE DOES MARRIAGE COUNSELING MAKE?

The kind of "adjustment" that Sheila is making was once the only advice offered by marriage counselors and is still the most common path recommended by priests, ministers, and rabbis. But this picture is changing. Marriage and family counselors are beginning to appreciate the needs of each member of the family to satisfy his or her best interests. Separation and divorce are no longer viewed as an indication that the couple or the counselor has failed.

In one of the few extensive studies of marital counseling, Dorothy Fahs Beck and Mary Ann Jones surveyed 3,956 cases from 266 family service agencies in the United States plus a Canadian sample of 150 cases from seven Canadian agencies. The Beck-Jones study, conducted in 1970 and published as *Progress on Family Problems* in 1973, clearly reveals this new attitude toward divorce as an alternative and the wife's interests as worthy of equal consideration with those of children and husband.[4]

With admirable lack of pretension, Beck and Jones first point out that marriage counseling in the majority of cases does not dramatically alter the direction of a marriage. More than half the couples surveyed were planning to remain married when they came for counseling and planned no change in this respect when they terminated. How many of these might have moved toward separation without professional help with their marriage is not known. Another one in four was separated at intake and planned to remain so at termination.

Marriage counseling did alter the course of one out of four couples, and in these cases where a change was made, the change tended to be in the direction of staying together rather than separating.[5]

But now Jones and Beck ask a daring question: "In whose best interest were these changes?" and come up with an equally daring, but soundly documented answer:

"When the interests of different family members were separately assessed, counselors reported remaining together or reuniting as most often in the interests of the husband, next most often in the interests of the children, and least often in the interests of the wife." This does not mean a divorce is always better for the wife. It means that in that small percentage of cases where the interests of the family members are in conflict, divorce or separation is in the interest of the wife, remaining together better serves the interest of the husband.

Fortunately, most decisions—divorce or reuniting—are in the best interest of all family members. Reuniting was more often in the interest of husband, wife, and children. But "even moving toward separation was seen as in the best interests of all family members for 65 percent of those who chose this way out."

Divorce, then, has become a legitimate option which can sometimes serve the best interests of all family members. When marriage counseling does alter the movement of a particular family, the change is usually toward reunion. There is no evidence that marriage counseling results in divorce. But there is evidence that marriage counselors are encouraging the wife to think of her best interests instead of always adjusting or subordinating her needs. There is evidence that in a small but significant minority, divorce may be the most favorable outcome for all the family members.

"From these findings," conclude Beck and Jones, "it is obvious that the success of marital counseling cannot be judged by whether a marriage is 'saved.' '' This standard, which once was the sole criterion for successful marriage counseling, is gradually changing. Their study demonstrates that the breakup of a marriage may be unavoidable or may actually be in the best interests of all concerned.

In an increasing number of agencies the marriage counselor is no longer seen as the rescuer of lost souls from the damnation of divorce. And marital therapy is no longer the therapy of adjustment. For marital therapy, or any other form of therapy, the two cardinal professional principles should be those set down by Beck and Jones—"the client's right to autonomy and the counselor's obligation to work solely in the best interests of his client."[6]

According to the Beck-Jones study it is more difficult to achieve improvement with marital problems when the marriage is of long standing. But even when the marriage has lasted more than twelve years, over a third of those who considered their main problem a marital one reported improvement after counseling.

Helen had been married twenty-one years before she finally came to Henderson Clinic for help. "I wanted to come for marriage counseling years ago," says Helen, "but my husband wouldn't hear of it." She waited, and things got worse. Five children are now in the complicated picture. Children definitely do not alleviate marital troubles; they exacerbate them.

Helen's marriage started out with a problem of poor communication between husband and wife, sharp differences in ambitions—he being content to remain a virtually illiterate blue-collar worker while she entertained ambitions of economic and social upward mobility. Helen stubbornly refused her husband's generous offers of cooperation in raising the children. Her children's problems included bed-wetting, stealing, and some potentially dangerous and destructive behavior such as lighting matches. Helen put up with all of this, continuing to spurn her husband's offers of assistance, until her sixteen-year-old daughter became pregnant. "I had a terrible time facing that," admits Helen, who finally came to Henderson one year ago and now is a regular member of Faye Mitchell's group sessions.

"We didn't have that much money," says Helen, who seems animated compared to the others in the group. "Henderson fits our pocketbook. To me it's been a lifesaver."

Faye Mitchell was able to see Helen on two occasions with her husband. This experience, plus the group interactions, have made Helen, who admits to being inflexible, realize that their marital problems are not all her husband's fault. "I felt that my husband was all in the wrong, and he's not. He's a good man. He's not an educated man. New ideas come very hard to him. But it was really a shock to me when I realized that I was provoking him and causing a lot of the problems that we're having. [Joan of Arc?—no. Personal heroism?—yes!] I have such a one-track mind that I have had a hard time of trying to change my way of doing things. But coming here has been a big help, for the whole family, really."

Helen is trying now not to sabotage her husband's efforts at cooperation, trying to accept his offers for help with the children and the housework. And as she works on her marital problems, her children are also getting help at the clinic on the psychological and medical levels.

For example, her twelve-year-old son was still wetting his bed when she came to Henderson. Helen admitted that all her children wet their beds, the two girls stopping only when they were in their teens. The doctor at the clinic put the boy on medication which included an antidepressant. "I didn't realize that he was depressed," Helen said. (This was the same boy who constantly lit matches and "thought nothing" of taking a ten-dollar bill from Helen's wallet.) Helen claimed that her son became an altogether different boy after the medication and separate therapeutic sessions at the clinic.

The medical and psychological help Helen is receiving for herself and her children could have cost her over $100 a week were she to see private practitioners. At Henderson she pays approximately $12 a week.

Helen is genuinely trying to be more flexible in order to solve her marital problems, but change would have come much more easily if she had sought help earlier in her marriage.

In terms of family functioning, things usually don't become more harmonious as children grow up; they become more complicated, with marital and parenting problems peaking during the adolescent years. According to the Beck-Jones study, 90 percent of agency families have marital and children's problems when the children reach the teen-age years. This is why marriage and family counselors recommend early treatment of marital problems. "For maximum effectiveness and for the sake of the children," their study notes, "young couples must be reached early in their marital careers or even in the courtship stage."

The study also notes that family service agencies are beginning to offer early prevention through marriage enrichment programs. But couples who have been married for many years should not feel it is too late for them. Men and women in their forties or fifties may have twenty more years of married life together. Why should they resign themselves to a life of hostile words, disenchantment, and resignation? Those years when the children are launched on their own lives need not be empty. It could be that the stranger who stares across the void when the kids are gone is a person you should get to know, a person you might be able to love and cherish again—with a little bit of help.

Sickness and health, normal and abnormal, crazy and sane, are words which are often misused to the disadvantage of patients. We have seen many cases of "sick" behavior which could be understood and altered by understanding the family relationships and the family history. Despite the relativity of such terms, there are certain standards of social and moral behavior which are universally accepted.

The husband or wife who recognizes what seems to be "crazy" behavior in a mate can try to seek help as a couple. But if the spouse who is psychotic, alcoholic, drug addicted, or sociopathic will not admit to needing treatment, the chances for a satisfying marital relationship are virtually nil.

The therapist can, as Dan Jackson noted, continue to look for the vestiges of sanity and tranquillity in such a person. But the mate who is united to a destructive personality cannot always maintain autonomy. Sometimes it's a case of abandon ship or go under. This was the situation with Lilli and Craig.

Lilli, the fourth member of Faye Mitchell's group, is a strikingly attractive woman who admits to being fifty-three though she looks years younger. She has had a spotty career as a nightclub singer. One can easily imagine her, glamorous yet vulnerable, singing Helen Morgan torch songs.

Lilli had been widowed for five years when she met Craig. In him she thought she had found the perfect lover. As she described it, "Sex with him was beautiful. We were like two kids, kissing each other good-bye in the morning, making love almost every night."

Craig had been married twice before. He was delinquent in his child support payments. He manipulated people at work and exhibited flashes of hatred toward those who crossed him. He had once gone to a nearby pond and killed the ducks there with a bow and arrow, taking pleasure in watching them die slowly. But Lilli failed to see these flaws until she was finally made painfully aware of the fact that Mr. Right was deeply troubled.

THE ULTIMATE TABOO

I had been married twenty-one years when my first husband died. The kids were grown and, let me tell you, it just got lonelier. I had three or four relationships with other men—which were bummers—but when I met Craig, he was very understanding. First of all, I must tell you he's a very, highly intelligent man. He's a professional man, an insurance actuary, and he's got a mind. He's got a high IQ. He's a manipulator, and he manipulates minds, too. He's very good at that.

When he met me I was afraid of men because of the three others who hadn't worked out. And he, being a manipulator and knowing the mind, just knew how to handle me. He knew just how to build up the faith and trust in him.

He had been married twice before. I didn't pay too much attention to that. He had four children in Colorado and four in Pennsylvania, but I didn't pay too much attention to that either because I looked at him as the individual I knew. He told me the other wives were both mentally unstable women, psychotics. So I said to him, "What makes you think I'm going to be any different?" He said, "I took a long, hard look at you. You're all together." So I never paid any attention to the wives. I never asked questions about his past.

I must tell you that for three years this man treated me beautiful. He was the typical gentleman, and he has finesse with women. And we were compatible to the nth degree. He said I was the best sex partner he ever had. So this has nothing to do with sex.

We were like honeymooners. I would kiss him good-bye in the morning—go outside and kiss—and the neighbors would say, "My, what a beautiful thing to see." We would throw kisses, you know. I would treat him beautiful and he'd treat me beautiful.

Last year in August one of his daughters—twenty-one, from his first marriage—started to call up. She was on drugs and she tracked him down. I don't know how. I was going to be this good, good wife that he said his previous wives weren't. So when his daughter, Kathleen, started calling up, I would talk to her and I'd try to get her head together. I accepted her over the phone.

After a while I said to him, "Why don't we help this girl of yours. Why don't we send for her?" He said, "Gee, I'm glad you said that." He didn't push her; I did. So we planned; we sent her money. She was in the hospital drying out. We wanted to get her as soon as she got out of the hospital so she wouldn't go back to the dope, because she had been mainlining. She has a five-year-old son and she's twenty-one.

Anyway, Kathleen finally got here at the end of August. We went to meet her at the Greyhound terminal and she had this sleepy little child. I hugged her and I kissed her and I accepted her immediately. I was really happy to see her because I loved my husband and I thought, "I'm doing something great for him." So I gave her a room and she was very happy.

He told me he was going to get her head straight, try to get her off the drugs. He was into the head scene, and he had read about Sigmund Freud.

At the beginning it was father, mother, daughter, grandson. We would walk to the mall together. I would be holding his hand, and she would be walking with the child. Before you knew it, he was walking with her and I'd be in back with the boy. And I noticed at the dinner table all the conversation was geared to her and I was the left-out, and every night after dinner they would sit in the corner like two kids. He was getting into her head. He's getting into her head so he can help her, right?

Then started a business about him buying half a gallon of wine every night, and between her and him, he would feed her the wine. He told me he had to give her a substitute for what she was withdrawing from. I bought it, you know. A good father is going to help his daughter. He also smoked pot with her, which I didn't like, but I felt maybe he had to get to her level. I'd try to understand everything.

Then he started sleeping in the Florida room. He didn't sleep with me anymore. After one night I said, "Craig, why are you sleeping in the Florida room?" He said, "Oh, I don't want to disturb you. I have to get up too early in the morning." I even bought that, the dumb nut that I am. I bought that. I could never visualize what was happening.

Every morning he'd be sitting on her bed feeding her coffee, but still I didn't see it. But I did start feeling very rejected.

One night I felt so rejected I took my blanket and my pillow—he was sleeping on the sofa bed in the Florida room—and I laid my pillow next to him. (I'm going to cry, remembering . . .) Came four o'clock in the morning, four thirty, she gets up. And I had a teapot in the same room. She gets up—I guess it was her job at that point to make the coffee. She just walks around me and sits with her father and gives him the coffee. That used to be *my* little nicety to him, *my* little luxury, to bring him coffee in bed every morning and wake him up. Well, after that, I picked my blanket up—neither one of them saw me—and I went into my room. That's the day I went to the marriage counselor.

I found a marriage counselor in the phone book. I explained the whole thing to him. He said, "You've been displaced," but he didn't say any more than that—displaced, whatever that meant. I didn't know. I still didn't see it for what it was, and this counselor—he told me he was a psychotherapist—he just told me to keep my cool. I kept trying to keep my cool. I kept my cool; I really did.

Kathy began coming home with a stomachache. One time I said, "Come on, Kathy, what's the matter?" She said, "Oh, it's so hard; it's so hard." I said, "Kathy, come on." So she said, "Let's go for a walk." We went for a walk, and she said, "My daddy is freaking me out." I said, "What's the matter?" I used to notice if she had dates, Craig would be very jealous and angry, and he'd wait up for her. In fact, he waited up one night until three in the morning, and he told me he put her over his knee and spanked her, and she was shocked. Anyway, she said, "My daddy is freaking me out." I said, "Why, Kathy?" But at this point she didn't say it all.

I know now. All the pieces fit together now.

Finally she told me. She called me into her bedroom and said, "Lilli, I wasn't going to tell you this, but I have to tell you. You're a lovely person and I love you very much." So she told me that Craig loved her as a woman and he wanted to live with her in an apartment. He didn't love her as a daughter, but as a woman. She said he would give her soul kisses when I wasn't around and "hold his body close to mine." He would say, "Okay, hold your daddy. You've got to hold it this way." And then he would push his body up against hers, and he would hug her and give her soul kisses, and she'd try to turn away. And he'd say, "Look, that was taboo years ago, but today it's acceptable." She said every time I was around, he would kiss her. And when I wasn't around, he would get on a sex kick. In the morning he would wake her up by unbuttoning her pj's, and she'd try to push him away. And he'd say, "You're my little girl. Your daddy has a right to look at you. You have a beautiful body."

I had asked Kathleen, as a favor, would she come to my counselor and repeat to my counselor what she had told me about Craig? Since he had told me his two ex-wives were crazy, he would try to say the same thing about me.

At that point I wanted him back. I wanted to understand the situation. I wanted him as a person. I loved him, and maybe I still do. So I took Kathy with me to the counselor. Kathy told the counselor she wanted to bring out the whole thing in a rap session with the three of us—me, her, and Craig. The counselor—I feel he was very wrong—said, "Look. Your father is a very sick man. He sounds like a borderline psychotic. Don't hurt him any more. Just write him a thank-you letter. Leave town. Go to Colorado. And then never see him again." She was glad to get this advice. But I think that counselor was wrong. To let this man to get away with what he's been getting away with. This wasn't the first time, it turned out.

When Kathy was walking out, her bags packed and everything, he said, "Aren't you even going to hold your daddy and kiss him good-bye?" Kathy tried, but she couldn't.

So I took her to the station, and I cried all the way, and she said she felt very bad for me. I stayed with her until the train left.

I walked the streets that night. I didn't know what to do. I figured, "I can't take it." The next night he didn't want any small talk. I made his dinner as usual, went to bed; he faced his way. That night I was desperate. I said, "Honey, do you love me?" He turned around. I said, "Do you love me?" I wanted to know because I needed an answer at that point. He said, "Possibly." I said, "Do you love me?" He was like a madman. I also saw a bad face, a drawn face, a face that I'd never seen before.

When I said, "Do you love me?" for the third time, he got up in bed and sat up. He said, "You lay on that pillow, and lay there for five minutes, and maybe I'll tell you." I reacted like a puppy; I lay down there. I still didn't understand what was happening. So I got up and said, "Honey, do you love me?" He said, "It's only three minutes. Get back there." When he did that, I changed my clothes and I walked the streets again.

That night I decided to go to a motel. I wasn't going to go back home. I called him up and he must have been sleeping. I said, "Craig," real quiet. I said, "Craig, do you believe that a man should have incest with his daughter?" He didn't answer me. He said, "Why do you want to know that?'' I said, ''Just please answer me that.'' I've forgotten the exact answer he gave me. It was some kind of an answer by which he evaded it. So I hung up and went to a motel. I couldn't sleep. It was seven in the morning, and I was pacing the room like a crazy lady. So then I thought, ''Let me go back home.'' I went back home and I lay on the couch where he used to sleep. He was in bed, sleeping away like nothing had happened. He was sleeping. Here I'm the one that's going through all the hell, and he's sleeping. He woke up and he went to work without a word to me.

That night he came home and started quizzing me. He says, ''You mean to tell me incest is abnormal?'' He was starting to talk to me. I said, ''It sure is.'' He said, ''Well, you don't condemn lesbianism?'' I said, ''I don't condemn that, no—because it has nothing to do with me.'' I don't condemn a lesbian. If that's her bag, fine. He said, ''And you don't condemn gay fellows, homosexuals?'' I said, ''No. To each his own, if that's their bag.'' He was using his logic again, trying to manipulate me.

In the meantime the phone rings. It was Kathleen's mother who answered. When I said, ''Hello?'' she said, ''Lilli? You don't know me, but I'm Kathleen's mother.'' Craig's standing right near me. He doesn't know what's happening. She said, ''I'm Kathleen's mother, and I was very surprised to see Kathy back here. I thought she was going to stay up there. And when I asked Kathy why she was home, she said, 'Because I don't believe in incest.' '' She said, '' 'Lilli, is that true?' '' When I told her it was, she said, ''Thank you. This happened when the girls were fifteen and sixteen, but I didn't believe them. I didn't want to make a scene, and I didn't believe them. I thought they were on pot.'' She said, ''Thank you,'' and hung up.

When I heard that—man, I couldn't stay with Craig anymore! It triggered to me all that impact of what I went through. So I picked up and I went to my girlfriend's for about a week and a half. All this time I'm going to a private marriage counselor. The marriage counselor is telling me to go home.

I had sessions with the marriage counselor for about two months. Some sessions he charged double for because it was twenty dollars for thirty minutes and that was it, cut and dried. Once that time was up, I couldn't even ask him another question unless I paid for two sessions. Otherwise, it was ''Make another appointment.'' He wanted me to keep everything inside, never confront Craig. But later, when I went to Henderson, Faye Mitchell told me Craig was destroying me. But this counselor in Miami said, ''Look. Go back home. It takes awhile for a man to come out of this. He will. Go home and pretend nothing happened.''

So I went home singing. I went home pretending. I made his favorite dishes. I tried to make conversation. But inside of me I was living a hell.

So I prayed; I prayed. I'm not a holy person, but I prayed for guidance.

I read books. I got pamphlets upon pamphlets—*How to Deal with Your Problems, It Can Work.* I got a million things that I kept reading. While he was sleeping I would keep reading and reading. I couldn't sleep. I kept reading all these things in the hope of finding a solution.

Well, it finally dawned on me one night, after getting all this rejection, that he didn't love me. One night I was reading and it suddenly came to me that, "Hey, if this man does not love you, you can't force someone to love you. If he loves his daughter and I try to hold him back, I'm going to lose a marriage anyway." I just suddenly, after praying and trying to read, came up with this. "Well, if I hold him back from his daughter, he's going to hate me and he's going to leave anyway." Either way, he was going to leave.

So the next morning, when he woke up, I made his coffee as usual. I said, "Craig, would you be willing to talk to me today? I really want to talk to you." he said, "Okay." So he sat in one chair and I sat in another. I said, "Craig, I've come to the conclusion—this is my opinion and my opinion only," and I made sure that I stated that this was my opinion. I said, "I feel if you love your daughter that much and I hold you back, I'm going to lose you. And if you love her, I'm going to lose you. Whichever decision either one of us make, I'm losing you. I'm letting you go out of love."

He thanked me and he said, "Well, I feel better. I think I could have sex with you now. I couldn't have sex with you before." He said, "I think I could be aroused now." Well, he and I had such a beautiful rapport. We had no hangups at all. I don't think I'll ever find another sex partner like him, and I don't think he'll ever find one like me. He said, "You were the best sex partner I ever had in my life." And he's been around. He said, "You were the best woman I ever had. I had four of the most beautiful years of my life. You're a good person." And I'm thinking, "What the hell does it get you?"

Later, I called Craig's second wife again. She told me everything. It was because of Kathleen the second marriage was split. Kathleen came up to their house. She was fifteen. Craig had told me his second wife didn't want him to help Kathy. She was pregnant at fifteen. Craig told me his second wife kicked Kathy out because she was hanging around with some boys after school. But that wasn't so. He had this situation going on with Kathy with the second wife, when Kathy was fifteen. He wanted the second wife to move to Colorado so he could be near his children, but she wouldn't go. So he went down there for three months, and he lived with the two girls—not the boy—the two girls, right? And they were fifteen and sixteen at the time.

I called him the next day. I said, "Craig, I heard that you did something like this when they were fifteen and sixteen, when Kathleen was fifteen."

He said, "No, they walked in on me. I was feeling Kathleen's tummy. I wanted to feel the baby kick." Later Kathleen said to me, "Bullshit! He was manipulating my breast and telling me I had to get used to this if I was going to nurse my baby." That's when they were caught. He was manipulating her breasts.

I also talked to Kathy's mother, Craig's first wife. She said it happened. She said she didn't believe the girls when they came back from Colorado. I talked to Kathleen's sister, who's a lesbian. "He's a crazy man," she said. "I never wanted to tell what he did to me. But now that it's out, he used to come in my room and give me soul kisses. He used to manipulate my body in the dark all the time."

It was a pattern. It all fit in. When I was moving, I found a pair of Kathleen's panties. When he has sex with someone, he keeps their panties. Because when I met him and I first went to his apartment, he had these black panties—see, it all fits in now—he had these panties Scotch taped on his wall. I said, "What's that?" He said, "Oh, those are my old girlfriend's panties. She wanted me to keep them."

His second wife told me one more thing. She told me it was on record in the courts, and he had no permission to see his children. It had to do with a one-month old baby. I asked Craig about it. He told me that he got caught cleaning the child's labia with a Q-tip. He said, "You know how clean I am." He said, "At least I saved the Q-tip." I don't know what that meant. I became frightened, talking to her, afraid that Craig would do something. He used to say, "I never get mad, but I get even." He got fired two years ago, and this man's name was Hansen. And he said, "It might take me ten years, but I'll get even with Hansen." And one day he came home and he said, "Well, I started my thing on Hansen. I heard he had a little bit of an accident." For all I know it's just talk, but it frightened me. So I stopped talking to her. I wanted to run away because it was so sick, all of it. I thought, "What the hell are you fighting here?"

I went to my doctor. I was very nervous. The doctor said, "You'd better get on tranquilizers." My stomach was so bad I couldn't even drink water. He told me to see a psychiatrist. I said I couldn't afford it. He said, "Well, go to Henderson Clinic." I explained the situation to Faye Mitchell, and she told me to come to this group session, and I've been coming.

I told Craig he had to seek help. "Admit what's happening, Craig. Seek help and I will stick by you." I told him he'd have to come with me to Henderson Clinic. So he came, just once. He said he'd do anything to get me back. Faye acted as if she didn't know too much. She asked Craig why he was there. He said, "I want to see if we can get back together," but he didn't say anything else. So I started telling the story about Kathleen. But Craig said, "That's only hearsay. That's only hearsay from Kathy." He told Faye he was only trying to help his daughters . . . with their heads.

She asked him if he was qualified to give this help. He said, "I want to know your qualifications." It became a heated thing. Faye asked, since it was hearsay, if he would be willing to have Kathy come in so the three of us could discuss this. Well, he changed immediately. Faye saw it and I saw it. He said, "I haven't got time to come here and waste my time. I haven't got time. I'll lose my job." Craig is an executive. He has his own hours. But he kept saying, "I haven't got time," like he was in a panic that he was going to be exposed.

He's living with a twenty-year-old chick now. I don't know if it's revenge. Faye told me, "Lilli, this man is destroying you. Get away." I haven't communicated with him. When the divorce came through, I went way downhill. Even now I'm still emotionally attached. I'm still questioning what I did. That last little thing is not cut yet. Only when I find someone else, I think. If I find a replacement, I won't dwell on him. I dwell on him continually. And I know if I had someone that I cared for or someone that's halfway intelligent, which I can't find, I don't think all that time would be spent thinking and wondering and being jealous.

I love people. And sing with a band once a week. If you would see me dressed up, you wouldn't know it's the same person. They pick me out for thirty, thirty-two. I'll tell you what I wouldn't tell anybody else. I'm fifty-three, but when I'm dressed, they say I'm a knockout.

I don't need very much. I need an emotional relationship more than anything. I'm a giver and I want to give and I want to feel. I think love could cure everything. They have told me at the Henderson Clinic that Craig's incapable of really loving. They called him something, a sociopath, incapable of really loving.

I recognize it. But when you're alone and you're lonesome, and then when you meet all kinds of creeps, that's the hardest part. It's not that Craig was a handsome man. But he knew how to get to me. And, like I said, he's got that charm that it takes, you see, because he wasn't good looking. I guess he really worked on his other points, and he knows. That man opened the car door for me, and he still lights women's cigarettes— all these little niceties. He used to send me a rose every week, one rose. I dug that. I'm a romanticist. We ate by candlelight. . . .

6

Alternatives to a Dull
Marriage

The main reason people will continue to seek out the services of marriage counselors is this: most Americans prefer marriage to any other life-style. The high divorce rate does not indicate that people no longer wish to marry; rather, it shows that an increasing number of Americans are unwilling to settle for less than a vital and complete marital relationship.

A 1974 Virginia Slims-Roper Poll of 3,000 women and 1,000 men shows 96 percent of the respondents still believing in marriage as the cornerstone of life. In spite of the enormous publicity given to living together without marriage, living alone, living in a commune—only 4 percent of those questioned in the Slims-Roper poll would prefer those alternative life-styles. In another poll conducted by the Chicago *Tribune,* 7,000 Midwestern women returned questionnaires: seventy percent of those responding chose marriage as the ideal life-style. Both the *Tribune* and Roper polls do suggest a changing view of marriage, one which we would call a "family-lib" or partnership-style marriage.

"There is a strong pull among women toward bonafide partnerships in marriage. Nearly half the women surveyed prefer marriages in which both husband and wife work and share the responsibilities of household and bringing up children. Over half of those polled are in favor of combining marriage, children, and career. Since three of five women under 30 feel this way, it is very likely to become a strong trend in the future," notes the Slims-Roper poll report. And the *Tribune* poll confirms the trend by indicating a 52 percent majority in favor of the equalized type of marriage. Despite the liberalization of divorce actions and the prevalence of no-fault, the *Tribune* poll notes that the majority of their respondents are not in favor of a quickie divorce.[1]

There are some excellent practical reasons for avoiding divorce. The breakup of a family usually results in a lower income for the new, single-parent head who, in the overwhelming majority of cases, is the mother. In 1973, for example, the median income for all families headed by a male with wife present and at least one child under six was $12,000. The corresponding figure for a single-parent female-headed family was $3,600. These nation-wide statistics collected by Professor Urie Bronfenbrenner of Cornell University[2] are only part of the grim financial picture for the majority of divorced women. Alimony is awarded in only 2 percent of today's divorces. Child-support payments are considered generous if they cover even half of what the mother will need to clothe, feed, medicate, and educate her growing children. Even with the 1975 child-support legislation in effect (Public Law 93647), we cannot expect all the court-ordered support payments to be honored. When the new support law was passed, 42 percent of parents so ordered were defaulting by the first year and 87 percent were no longer paying support after ten years, just when many of the children would be incurring more clothing and educational expenses. Four out of five people who divorce eventually remarry. But according to Paul C. Glick, senior demographer in the Census Bureau's Population Division, the remarriage rate among divorced men is five out of six, while the remarriage rate among divorced women is three out of four. Even if we allow for a certain number of women who do not wish to remarry, this clearly leaves thousands who would like to remarry but can't find another spouse.

While women suffer more obvious adverse consequences when divorce occurs, men without mates appear to be in relatively poor psychological shape. Their incomes go down; their mortality rate goes up to three and a half times as high as divorced women. Divorced men are more likely to commit suicide than married men, and they are more likely to have mental disorders. In fact, mental illness is higher among both men and women who are divorced.

So we have a situation in which marriage is preferred by the vast majority and apparently more conducive to their psychological and financial satisfaction. We have a rising divorce rate—and virtually no incentives to prepare young people for marriage or to keep the marriage vital once it has been joined. The practical reasons for remaining married will probably have no more effect on the divorce rate than the venereal disease statistics are having on premarital and extramarital sex. With society offering few supports for marriage, and the media providing many inducements to at least experiment with other, supposedly more fulfilling life-styles, we can hardly expect marriage counseling—even at its best—to fill the breach. As it is utilized in this country, marriage counseling often comes too late with too little. Marital therapy tends to occur one short step before a divorce action—a step taken only as a last-ditch effort to save a relationship that has been deteriorating for years. Yet, even under these unfavorable circumstances, we have come across many success stories. Couples who have been able to establish better emotional and sexual relations behave as if they were given a new lease on life. Couples who underwent therapy with a reputable marriage counselor are less ecstatic, but they generally claim that the therapy helped them to cope with the divorce and its aftermath, to resolve long-standing personal problems, to make a better mate choice the next time. The investment, which averages $350 to $500, was regarded by most couples—still together or subsequently separated—as money well spent. But among the divorced couples and with many of those who have salvaged and improved their marriage, we noted a wistful "what if we had gone earlier?" attitude.

After spending the last decade in a defensive posture, retreating into the fortress of the nuclear family, resisting the siren call of women's liberation on the one hand and sexual experimentation on the other, married couples have finally begun to emerge with new strengths of their own. They are taking stock of the dangers and joining forces with other vulnerable couples to invigorate their relationships and equip themselves for the inevitable conflicts. With a spirit closer to Peace Corps than Pentagon, hundreds of thousands of married couples are seeking enrichment, preventative counseling, joint awareness, and consciousness-raising designed to keep their marriages from crumbling after the first crisis. They are trying to avoid the continual fighting of the "conflict-habituated" marriage, the boredom of the "devitalized" marriage, the insipid pleasantness of the "passive-congenial" relationship.[3] More than ever, men and women are looking to make their marriages open and total.

THE MARRIAGE ENCOUNTER

Amy and Ted, married for ten years, have three children, and live in a modest bungalow, the mantel of which was covered with Ted's tennis trophies. There was nothing seriously wrong. But much of the zest had gone out of their marriage. Many of their friends were beginning to have marital problems; some had already divorced. One day a call came from close friends raving about something called Marriage Encounter. It was a weekend retreat which was inexpensive and apparently rejuvenating to relationships such as theirs. Ted and Amy were soon amongst the estimated 500,000 adults who had been "encountered."

They had no critical marital problems, but they were beginning to exhibit what the Marriage Encounter literature calls "symptoms of spiritual divorce." On a checklist of these symptoms given out during the weekend,

Amy checked the following: "Feelings of disillusionment, boredom, emptiness, loneliness in our relationship; indifference to each other's problems,
interests; occasions of coolness toward one another; feelings of insecurity,
jealousy; not enough personal conversation—most communication mechanical, routine, and on the surface; feeling used, feeling in a rut." If there
is a marriage that never suffers from such symptoms of malaise, we haven't
heard of it. The Marriage Encounter movement has recognized the normal
crises and dissatisfactions of marriage and provided a setting for couples to
work those issues out in advance of serious problems or separation. The religious aspects of the movement are not important theologically. There is no
attempt to convert the large proportion of non-Catholic couples who come
to the weekend conducted in the Catholic expression. But the spiritual aspects, the sacramental attitude toward marriage, invests the simple proceed-
ings with a profound meaning for most couples who attend. A higher purpose in life that appeared to be impossible of attainment in the post-Viet-
nam, post-Watergate era suddenly seems within reach.

"There's no way to describe how it feels to discover yourself, who you
are, to discover your spouse, what she is"—this from a short, retiring, gentle young man, a mechanical engineer who admits to having been a "workaholic" during most of the twelve years of his marriage. Burt was beginning
to weary of his 100 hour-a-week work schedule. Then a new boss came in
and Burt was passed over for a promotion. At home things weren't much
better. He got along well enough with his wife, Laurie, a buxom girl who
looks physically the more dominant of the pair. In the course of one year,
Laurie's grandmother died, their son was hit by a car, a new baby arrived,
and their dog passed away. In the midst of this maelstrom of misfortune
Burt's old college friend called from Dallas. "Burt, I want you and Laurie to
make plans right this moment to go on a Marriage Encounter weekend. You
must do it. It has absolutely changed my life. You know how I used to travel
all over the South, making big commissions, never seeing my wife or kids?
Well, I'm through with that. I've gotten a transfer to the Dallas office. My
wife and I are devoting all our spare time to Marriage Encounter. Burt, I'm a
new man."

Burt and Laurie went to a weekend conducted by Jewish Marriage Encounter. "I discovered what I was doing was not worth very much. Who I
was, who my children were, these things were much more important. I now
work less than half the hours I used to put in. I consider my relationship with
my wife and family more important than going in on Saturday morning and
every weekday night. I simply decided that a cash register was not a worthwhile monument to my life."

For Eileen and Marty Millman (their real names), the reasons for trying
Marriage Encounter were somewhat different. Marty had been working and
going to night school during the seven years of their marriage. Eileen Millman still retains a slight Brooklyn accent and the no-nonsense air of a city

kid who has decided exactly what she wants out of life. She had been teaching school and bringing up two daughters when she met Steve and Nicole VanderVoort, Chicago Marriage Encounter leaders. Eileen was impressed with Nicole and Steve. They seemed full of empathy for many other people, very much at ease with each other, and anxious to share their good feelings. Eileen looked on the encounter weekend as an insurance policy. "Since Marty graduated from night school, we were getting the first chance during the years of our marriage to actually examine ourselves and our relationship. Marty and I had had very little conflict in our marriage. But it was scary to perceive what was happening to other couples. We wanted to guarantee that we weren't going to wind up at sixty like some other couples. We were looking to grow." And grow they did. After attending the weekend conducted in the Catholic expression by the Chicago branch of National Marriage Encounter, Eileen and Marty decided they wanted to become actively involved. They served on the board, helped to start a Chicago chapter of Jewish Marriage Encounter and now are trained as "presenting couples" —those who attend the weekend and lead off portions of the weekend by sharing with the group a personal experience which altered and cemented their marriage.

"Our life-style of a few years ago centered on our family," said Eileen. "Now we find a great deal of satisfaction in making the weekend available to other people. We find couples have a need to experience deep feelings and share them with other people. People in America don't have the sense of belonging to a larger group that, say, the Japanese may gain from their loyalty to their place of work. The Marriage Encounter weekend is one of the few places that provides sustained feelings of community. It's no panacea. But I've never known the weekend to do any harm. There may be some couples who can evolve the same open communication on their own, but very few."

Maureen was an aficionado of pop psychology. She had been through individual therapy, attended a few encounter group weekends, and was serving as an instructor for Parent Effectiveness Training when she and her husband, Vic, visited Vic's family in Boston. Maureen noticed a change in her sister-in-law. She seemed happier, much more enthusiastic about her husband and their married life. A Marriage Encounter weekend was the reason. But Maureen was concerned about the Catholic aspects of the weekend. Would they have to sleep on cement floors? Would there be somber monks shuffling about in sandals and swinging crucifixes? At the very best Maureen suspected the weekend would be too regimented and dogmatic for her taste. She wondered if there was any point in looking into their relationship since they had recently done a considerable amount of soul searching. "Maureen had suffered a sudden cardiac arrest a few months before," said Vic, who is blond and stands at least a foot taller than his frail, kinetic mate. "We had already reorganized our priorities."

During the weekend Maureen thought the priest was a hippie who had somehow managed to come without his wife. She described the presenting couples as "modeling happiness. There's a glow about them. Other couples want to get into it. They want a piece of that good feeling." The only religious difference she noted between Catholic and Jewish couples was a subtle difference in attitude. As Maureen put it, "Catholics are brought up in an atmosphere of 'I will.' Jewish couples ask, 'Why should I?' " By the time the weekend was over, Maureen felt she knew what it was like to be a religious person. "It was unlike any other psychological experience. You come off the weekend feeling loved. Your self-image is better. You say to yourself, If my husband can care that much about me, I must be okay. I couldn't stop talking about it. You feel like an evangelist. You want everybody to go. Vic and I have already sent twenty-five friends and our parents on Marriage Encounter weekends."

One look at the literature passed out during the Marriage Encounter weekend—the simple guidelines for couple dialogue, the symptoms of spiritual divorce, the subjects for understanding which include money, sex relations, children, relatives, death, the marriage evaluation sheets and the plan-of-life form—and one wonders, What is there about the weekend that turns skeptics into true believers, that transforms workaholics into family men and changes ho-hum marriages into love stories?

Since most of the weekend is spent in private husband/wife dialogue and much of the experience depends upon spontaneity and the pleasant surprises planned by each organizing team of couples, it would be more of a service to describe what the weekend isn't.

(1) Marriage Encounter is not an encounter group. A group of couples retreat to a place free of work/children/TV/time/in-law/ peer distractions. Within the simple structure of introspection and sharing on basic issues, the husband and wife spend their time delving into their own thoughts about themselves and their relationship. The sharing is mainly on the part of the team couples and the religious leader, who lead off each session by imparting some relevant personal experience. Meals and a few other moments designed to heighten warmth and sentiment are shared by the group of twenty or so couples. But the primary focus is on the husband and wife, with no invasion of their intimacy.

(2) Marriage Encounter is not marriage counseling. On each encounter weekend, usually held at a retreat house or motel, the priest, minister, or rabbinic couple is available at all times for those who wish to consult or confide in them. But couples who have serious marital problems and individuals in need of psychiatric help are urged not to come on the weekend. Some degree of dissatisfaction, boredom, communication breakdown and/or desire to grow may prompt couples to choose the weekend. But those who are on the brink of divorce would do better to seek help from a reputable marriage or family counselor.

(3) Marriage Encounter is not designed for religious conversion. Marriage

Encounter took off in this country in 1967 when Father Calvo, who had developed the movement in Spain, addressed a gathering of the Christian Family Movement at the University of Notre Dame. The World Wide Marriage Encounter developed from that meeting with a bit more dogmatism than the National Marriage Encounter. But whatever the expression of the weekend, religious aspects are not oppressive. Jewish, Protestant, and agnostic couples who have attended Catholic encounter weekends report that they could easily translate the few Catholic references and ceremonies into their own terms. Two years ago a Jewish Marriage Encounter movement formed in New York. Since then 10,000 couples have attended Jewish encounter weekends. Several Protestant denominations, including Episcopalians and Methodists, have begun to organize weekends. And no doubt the renewal of marriages will have a rejuvenating effect on churches and synagogues. But for the present, the movement is low on theology and high on evangelism.

The word spreads like wildfire. Each couple coming from a weekend urges its friends and families to sign up—with no thought to the generation gap. The couples we interviewed had insisted that their parents, brothers, sisters, and friends of all ages attend. The confidential, voluntary contribution of "as much as you can afford" to cover the expenses of approximately $70 or $80 per couple allows any husband and wife to attend the weekend and keeps commercialism from polluting the newly encountered group.

What is emerging from Marriage Encounter with 500,000 "encountered" Americans and thousands more each weekend is a new sense of community, a ready-made extended family. In fact, "Family Encounter" weekends are the newest outgrowth of this burgeoning movement. The weekend experience creates a bond and the bond is reinforced by "rookie" renewals three weeks after the weekend, monthly dialogue sessions, and "anniversary" weekends.

Some couples now regard the Marriage Encounter movement as a calling and have devoted their lives to it. Others, like Eileen and Marty Millman, have reordered their priorities, making relationships number one in importance. Success, in terms of material possessions and social status, is subordinated to the mutual emotional needs of husband and wife. The prime time of the day is not devoted to lunch with the boss, mixing with the right people, or even doing for the kids. The best twenty minutes of the day are devoted to the relationship—ten minutes for writing love letters which husband and wife exchange and discuss in ten minutes of considerate discussion called "dialoguing."

IMPROVING MARITAL COMMUNICATIONS

The marriage enrichment movement—of which the Marriage Encounter is the fastest growing but by no means the only force—is part of what Sherod Miller calls "the new spirit in the land." A student of family therapist Virginia Satir and noted University of Minnesota family sociologist Reuben Hill, Sherod Miller has developed a package of coping tools for couples which is part of a nationwide program called Minnesota Couples Communication Program.

MCCP—developed and directed by Miller with colleagues Elam Nunnally and Daniel Wackman—offers weekend-long workshops to train instructors, usually men and women with masters degrees or family counseling experience, to run the program of four three-hour sessions. The basic source book used is *Alive and Aware: Improving Communication in Relationships.*[4] But much of the value in this program comes from the interaction of the five to seven couples all taking their relationships seriously. The male/female leaders keep the interaction focused on improving communication skills so that the lessons in speaking openly and directly will have a transfer effect on marriages long after the four sessions have been completed. The format has more stress on cognitive tools than heightened emotional atmosphere, partly because of Sherod's personal experience with encounter groups.

"Encounter and sensitivity training was a new and exciting idea but we didn't know much about the casualties. Usually, you went to an encounter weekend alone. The wife took care of the kids. You expressed feelings; you touched people and felt them; you felt good. You went home with the key to the universe. It didn't work at the front door. It didn't work at the office. It created distance in my marital relationship because the experience couldn't be translated. The only place you could get this emotional high was at the encounter group, so we created sensitivity bums." As for couples' encounter groups (not Marriage Encounter weekends) Sherod notes that there was usually very little structure and so there was no assurance that a couple would go away with useful skills that they could transfer to their home situation. Too often encounter groups would encourage individuals and couples to be obnoxiously aggressive in their feelings and judgments. In an effort to get people to "let it all hang out,"encounter groups often encouraged a total disregard for the next person.

At the opening session of one MCCP group meeting, leader Ann Weir realized she had just such a pair of encounter fugitives on her hands. They had been to many sensitivity groups, which, ironically, rendered them insensitive. They went around the room passing judgment on the other couples. "We picture you two breaking up. You're just like my mother, a ball buster. You're a milquetoast like Dad." Rather than dismissing them from the group, Ann Weir put a "limit" on them. She simply asked them to hold off their comments. By the last session of group meetings, this same couple had finally gained some real sensitivity. "We had thought we were open. We were actually speaking for everyone else, putting labels on people, not being open about ourselves at all. How come you didn't throw us out?"

This is the type of couple Sherod Miller or Ann Weir might have seen for marriage counseling, or even divorce counseling, if they had not attended the communications program. "I used to do marriage counseling," says thirty-four-year-old Sherod. With his blond hair and blue jeans, this maverick therapist/theoretician who has to be pressed to reveal the title he holds of assistant professor of medicine at the University of Minnesota Medical School doesn't look old enough to use the phrase "used to."

"I would see a couple for a few months. They would begin feeling better about their lives. Within a year they'd come back." Sherod began to wonder if most of his energy should be devoted to "saving" the sickest relationships when there were so many well marriages which could be kept well by preventative education. "Like the Bible story of the hundred sheep, one gets out of the fold and the shepherd goes to save that one. But what about the ninety-nine still in the fold?" Sherod began to think in terms of the well individuals who stood such a good chance if they could be taught to deal effectively with problems that came along.

Fortunately, he was at the best place in the country for such thinking. The University of Minnesota's Family Study Center, under the direction of Reuben Hill, had developed the most comprehensive program of family research, marriage-counselor training, and family-life education in the country.

It was at the Family Study Center that Gerhard Neubeck had instituted his course in human sexuality, the first of its kind, in 1967, sensational enough to cause a full-picture spread in the then-popular *Look* magazine. Innumerable research, community service, and training projects had gotten under way at the center—most of them with the thrust of understanding and helping the well family.[5]

During this pioneering era, with Reuben Hill as his mentor and Elam Nunnally and Daniel Wackman as co-workers, Sherod developed the couples communication program as a project to prepare engaged couples for marriage. The Minneapolis Family and Children Services and five other agencies, also trying to move from a strict problem orientation to a well-family supportive approach, participated in the project. The research results on MCCP indicated that the program had improved communications among participating engaged couples. They were speaking more directly than they had been before the program, and they had a more accurate understanding of what their partner was expressing.[6] Sherod and his colleagues began organizing workshops to train leaders and thus make the program more widely available. Unlike the Parent Effectiveness Training Program and the Total Woman Courses, which operate on a semifranchise basis with each group returning a portion of money to the central organization, MCCP charges only for its materials. The average $70-per-couple fee goes to the two instructors. As with the Marriage Encounter weekend, MCCP is not designed for the disintegrating marriage, but as a means of improving communications and thus enriching marriages. As a tool for upgrading couples who are reasonably stable, this program is, as Reuben Hill puts it, "a major contribution."

THE CENTER FOR FAMILY LEARNING

Another significant advance in the area of preventative marital and family care is taking place in the upwardly mobile suburb of New Rochelle, New York. There, on the grounds of an old estate, is the Center for Family Learning, a unique place where families who want to improve relations, who want to reduce the normal conflicts and tensions which accompany all marriages, can go to learn "techniques" for coping with their problems.

Mrs. Papp, director of a community project with the Center for Family Learning and a therapist with the Ackerman Family Institute in New York City, had long believed in "well-family" clinics, the idea being that just as we go for checkups to the doctor or the dentist, without waiting for a heart attack or for our teeth to rot, so too should married couples and families begin to go to a kind of family-life-counselor who would be able to spot the first signs of "distress" and give aid—in a preventative manner. Yet while society allows men and women, even encourages them to spend several years studying in order to pursue a career, the same society provides little or no education in preparation for marriage and family life. Thus, most couples and families wait for a psychological "heart attack" or for the relationship to "rot" before seeking help. And often one member of the family is singled out as the scapegoat, the person responsible for the problems in the marriage or the family. Yet, as we have seen, men and women go through certain "stages," encountering "typical" kinds of problems, predictable life crises.

"I feel there are thousands and thousands of families who need this kind of help and not profound psychiatric help, not something very costly or very long-term. They simply need to talk to somebody about some of these stages that they are going through," says Mrs. Papp.

Believing in preventative mental health, Peggy Papp applied for and received a grant from HEW that made the center possible.

Like the professional she is, Peggy Papp doesn't believe in sitting back and waiting passively for "well families" to come to the door. Instead, she goes into the community, actively seeking out families, much as Canadian social workers set up booths at wedding fairs, competing for the attentions of engaged couples with merchants who display sterling silver, fine china, and wedding linens. They have thus managed to interest nearly 20 percent of Canada's engaged couples in premarital counseling.

In presentations before PTA's, churches, and temples in the New Rochelle area, Mrs. Papp dramatically brings home the idea that all of us, in this complicated and frustrating society, can use a little help.

Through her technique of "sculpting" Mrs. Papp presents a little playlet about family life. She will ask for volunteers from the audience to pose as father, mother, daughter, and son. The four are to pose this situation: Father comes home from work irritated and wants to withdraw; Mother has been waiting for Father all day and wants to tell him about the children. This first act is entitled Who Has the Problem?

As Father sits down in the chair and reads his paper, Mother grabs Father. The more Father withdraws, the more Mother pulls and grabs him. Each falls to the floor, Father pulling away, Mother pulling Father to her.

Then Son comes in and turns on the TV. Mother, frustrated by Father, takes her anger out on the son twice—once for her and once for Father. The younger daughter comes in and the son pulls her hair.

At this point, Mrs. Papp turns to the audience and asks, "Who has the problem?" And of course the answer is everyone in this family. The problem is not *within* the people in the family but *between* them. Mrs. Papp then introduces the second act, entitled The Harder They Try, the Worse Things Get.

Mrs. Papp tells the four people on stage to "try more of the same thing, more, more, more!" So Father withdraws more, Mother grabs more, Father pulls away, Mother yanks back, Father withdraws, Mother screams at her son, and the son pulls the daughter's hair, and Father yells at Mother about what a lousy parent she is.

Act three is entitled Treating the Symptom. With this action going on, all the members of the family have to develop symptoms. Father develops migraine headaches; he goes to a doctor. Mother develops acute anxieties, calls her girlfriends on the phone and complains about the insensitivity of men. The son fails in his school courses even though he has an IQ of 140; he goes to the school psychologist. The daughter becomes hyperactive and she goes to a physician who prescribes pills.

The fourth and final act is called All Come Back. Mrs. Papp asks Father to do something which makes him more comfortable. So Father confronts Mother with the reality of the situation. In order to answer Father, Mother has to stop pulling on him and cease yelling at the kids. Of course, once Mother has stopped yelling at her son, the son stops pulling on the daughter's hair and the children's hassling abates.

Mrs. Papp then tells Mother and Father to "negotiate" different positions in their "drama." So Father reaches out and takes Mother's hands. Mother, in order to take Father's hands, lets go of the children entirely. Thus, for the first time in the life drama, there are Mother and Father, united as they should be, and their two children next to them.

Although the "drama" does not take long to present, it has a mesmerizing effect on audiences, who identify with the characters immediately. After witnessing the presentation, many families make appointments at the Center for Family Learning.

There, once a week, fifteen families meet with the staff. Through conferences, through videotape or lectures, families will discuss general problem areas such as discipline or one-parent family difficulties. Then the families split up into groups of three families with one "facilitator" and discuss the specific subject in greater depth. The approach is more educative than thera- peutic. Thus, the stigma of therapy, which still lingers in many quarters, is avoided.

Mrs. Papp believes that just as it is the community's responsibility to pro- vide psychiatric care for families, the community also has an obligation to provide well-family clinics so those not desperately in need, but still hurting, can receive attention.

ACME

There are numerous other enrichment programs of varying quality prolif- erating under the umbrella of ACME (Association for Couple and Marital Enrichment), founded by David Mace and his wife, Vera. A marriage coun- selor for thirty years, David Mace sees these enrichment groups as strength- ening marriages before "the seeds of pathology" take root. Another way to look at enrichment programs is to see them as opportunity for two people to grow at a similar pace, sharing a number of experiences designed to rein- force their marriage.

Our old ideas about successful marriages had little to do with personal or mutual growth. Longevity and fulfillment of traditional roles (good pro- vider/good housekeeper/good mother) were the criteria, as David Olson points out in his article, "Marriage of the Future": "Many couples today are becoming increasingly frustrated because they have rejected the more tradi- tional definition of a successful marriage and yet are having difficulty achiev- ing the mutually actualizing relationship."[7]

OPEN MARRIAGE REVISITED

What we have seen in hundreds of interviews with couples and marriage counselors is the phenomenon of uneven growth which destroys the mar- riage. It used to be the man leaving the more limited wife behind. Now it is frequently the wife, with a new awareness of her own possibilities, leaving the husband behind. Enrichment programs give the couple a chance to grow together, to develop their capacities for communicating feelings and ex- periencing intimacy, together, and yet to do this in a way which does not strangle either partner. If we read the opinion polls and marriage statistics correctly, it seems clear that most of the couples in America want to develop together rather than separately. The difference between the togetherness of the fifties, which Betty Friedan exposed in *The Feminine Mystique,* and the togetherness emerging in the seventies is that one suffocated the wife, the other lets her breathe and grow at least as much as the husband. One wants to find a label for this new style of marriage. George and Nena O'Neill certainly hit a responsive chord with the title *Open Marriage*. The book became the first volume on family life to make the best-seller list in twenty-five years. "Open marriage is *not* sexually open marriage," the O'Neills told us, "but rather a model for growth-producing, man-woman relationships." They feel their efforts have been misinterpreted by the media, by some therapists, and by many couples. Thus the term "open marriage" has come to mean a marriage in which other sexual relationships are sanctioned.

We saw how such "openness" rendered Ben Parks temporarily impotent . . . and spoiled any chance for sexual and emotional satisfaction in his marriage. The therapist who recommended this "solution," a man we have referred to as Eli, admitted to us that his open marriage requires constant attention. Eli and his mate must spend hours of discussion, much of it tape-recorded and played back, to resolve the problems that come of openly dating and having sexual relations with other men and women.

George and Nena O'Neill told couples what they should do, but they did not tell them how to do it. As Sherod Miller notes, "It takes a lot of energy to make a relationship between two people a source of learning and mutual renewal. When other relationships are brought in there is a geometric expansion. For every person added to the marriage network, there needs to be more time spent. If husband takes a lover and wife takes a lover, there are six relationships. If one of those relationships breaks down—if the husband can't tolerate the wife's lover or vice versa—the whole setup becomes unstable and untenable." If husbands and wives didn't have to work, didn't have to raise children, cope with aging and sickness among their own parents and relatives, perhaps sexually open marriage would work. At this writing, there is little evidence that the sexually open marriage is anything more than a transitional stage between the intimacy of one pair and another. The O'Neill book may have given permission, though inadvertently, to couples who wanted to try other partners or those who had been having clandestine affairs and wanted the relief of admitting to them.

Sexually open marriage can be a useful way to maintain distance in a relationship. As one husband told us, when he admitted a longstanding extramarital liaison to his wife, "I felt like she was my sister." The wife has since had a series of her own affairs which the husband knows about and encourages. Thus the pair can continue, more like siblings than spouses, avoiding the pain of divorce, co-parenting their two children, and carrying on their sexual activity with others. An additional sexual relationship can also be used, as marriage counselor Ann Weir told us, to make or break the marriage. The threat of another relationship will either liven up or kill most marriages, with killing being the more likely outcome.

While sex within marriage and multiple sexual relations openly engaged in by married couples have received little in the way of extensive scientific attention, extramarital sex has been the subject of a number of recent investigations. Thirty years ago Kinsey found half the men and 26 percent of the women had had an affair by the age of forty.

EMS: EXTRAMARITAL SEX

Today women apparently have sexual relations outside their marriages at an earlier age than women did in Kinsey's time. One study of 2,372 married women conducted by Robert R. Bell and Dorothy Ann Peltz shows that 26 percent of today's married women are adulterous before the age of thirty-five. The other study, of 1,500 married men and women conducted in 1972 by the Playboy Foundation, shows that while in Kinsey's day only 8 percent of married women under twenty-five had extramarital experiences, today 24 percent have.[8] A recent study by Robert Whitehurst (1969) makes it seem that men are having fewer affairs than in Kinsey's day.[9] Of the 112 upper-middle-class business and professional men studied, 67 percent had no extramarital sex, 9 percent had some EMS but no serious sexual involvement, 16 percent had short-term affairs, and 3 percent had lengthy affairs. The men participating in the greatest amount of extramarital sex tended to be alienated personalities—socially isolated with feelings of powerlessness. Johnson's 1969 study of 100 middle-class couples revealed that 28 percent of the marriages were involved in at least one affair. Husbands who indicated a low level of sexual satisfaction were more likely to become involved in affairs. Among husbands and wives, "perceived opportunity" led to EMS in 40 percent of the cases.[10]

What is one to make of all these studies and statistics? (1) Women and men are beginning to participate in extramarital sex in equal proportions. (2) The majority of couples do not have extramarital affairs. (3) Affairs are often an indication of sexual dissatisfaction or social alienation, and they usually occur when there is something called "perceived opportunity." Does a person perceive an opportunity if he or she is deriving strong sexual and psychological benefits from the marital relationship? This question has not yet been answered. Certainly the greater openness about sex and the prevalence of women in the labor market and out of the home will create more opportunity for interaction on every level. Whether men and women take advantage of this opportunity to a greater extent is not certain as yet. But we can make one generalization about "the affair": affairs create distance in marriages and they often lead to divorce. To put it another way: marriage equals love plus limits. Those limits used to be imposed on husband and wife by religious belief and tradition. Now the strictures are loosening; the limits tend to be self-imposed.

When asked what an affair means today, Connecticut marriage counselor Fred Humphrey hesitates at first. "I don't know anymore what an affair is. Ten years ago I thought I did." Humphrey, who worked with the noted Emily Mudd at the Philadelphia Marriage Council and wrote his doctoral dissertation on sexual foreplay only to learn that the university wouldn't put it on their shelves, is no stranger to American sexual mores. Now an associate professor of family relations at the University of Connecticut at Storrs, Humphrey says, "I think affairs mean many things, but they almost always mean danger to the marriage. If a person is in an affair, I'd call this a danger signal, even if the partner doesn't know about it."[11]

It may be unrealistic to expect that a marriage can meet all the needs of both spouses at all times. *Extra-Marital Relations,* edited by the University of Minnesota's outstanding teacher and marriage counselor Gerhard Neubeck, suggests the enormous gap between "faithfulness in the flesh," which most mates expect, and the numerous sexual involvements which disappoint but never seem to permanently alter the expectation of fidelity.[12] Even the sexual surrogate whose business was instructing and supporting other men to help them achieve sexual satisfaction found it difficult to deal with her mate's infidelity. Most men and women expect sexual fidelity of their mates, and the majority of husbands and wives, even in this day and age, do confine their sexual relations to their marital partners.

Keeping this in mind, it is not surprising that an affair can have a shattering impact on a marriage. The affair will either finish off a marriage which has been going downhill, or the stress will lead to a different, sometimes improved relationship between husband and wife.

AFFAIRS

Connie and Gus had been married for nine years. Gus was a factory foreman, often working a nightshift. As Connie put it, "I think two until ten are the very worst hours in the whole world. You get up in the morning and you feed your kids, then you feed your husband late. He goes out to mow the lawn. He comes in and goes to work. Then the kids come in from school, and then you lose your marbles. I guess I was lonesome. He was tied up at work and I was tied down with the three kids. I wasn't bored. I guess I needed more of a friend than anything else. After we went to Rabbi Goldberger for marriage counseling I realized a lot of the things we had been lacking, but that was after the affair, after Gus found out, after we were separated."

Connie's affair, which started out with walks in the park, lasted for six months. When she told Gus he was stunned. "I thought everything was fine. The husband went to work and made the money, brought it home. The wife stayed home, took care of the kids, and that was it. I didn't have any complaints. I mean, I was following along my little path. When I found out, it was almost too much. I don't know how to describe what I felt—anger, hatred, despair."

Connie thought of selling their house in Denver and moving to Oregon as an answer. But their hostility after the affair was out in the open became unbearable. They had both come from families in which bickering was the main form of communication—"conflict-habituated" families, as sociologists John Cuber and Peggy Harroff would label it.

During the first seven years of their marriage they had tried to avoid any fighting, even any difference of opinion, for fear of becoming like their parents. The affair created an explosion—the accumulated anger of seven years detonated by the news that all their efforts to keep the peace had been worthless. Connie didn't have much hope for the marriage, and Gus was convinced that Connie's affair, though arrested, was still going on.

Connie called the local mental health center, which sent two young women out to talk to the distraught couple. Gus disliked the pair more than Connie, but both agreed the counselors were too inexperienced and nondirective to offer them much help. As Connie puts it, "They were very nice, but it was just gruesome for us. We were really uptight. We were still together and didn't know why and didn't know if we wanted to be, didn't really care if we were or not. And they would come into our house and talk to us, or rather listen to us. No matter what we said, they'd ask, 'How do you feel about that?' And you're so mixed up at a point like that, you don't just need a listener. You also need somebody to say, 'Is it really that earth-shattering, what's happened between you?' "

Gus says, "I don't know whether I know anything about life or not, but I didn't feel that they did. They never imparted to me that they did know anything about life. They were just two younger women that went to college, took the classroom part of whatever counseling takes, and came out as if they knew it all. They never really had the experience or any insights into what our problem was as far as I was concerned. They could see Connie's side, no question about that. But they really couldn't see mine."

Even without being an expert at therapeutic matchmaking one could predict that a team of young women fresh out of college would not be suitable to counsel a thirty-year-old factory foreman with traditional notions of role responsibilities, whose wife had just had an extended affair. Predictably, this counseling effort, which lasted for twelve sessions and took place at their home, failed. Gus moved out and he and his wife each found a divorce lawyer. Fortunately the lawyers they contacted made an unusual effort to help them preserve their marriage.

"It wasn't just a passive divorce suit," says Gus. "I tried to get one on her, and she did get one on me because she got served first, and it was hot and heavy for a long time."

"But the lawyers kept insisting we cared about each other," adds Connie, still baffled at their insight. "We kept insisting we didn't care. We didn't give a darn. The lawyers did everything in their power to stall the divorce. They wouldn't set court dates. They wouldn't do anything; they just kept saying,

'You know you care,' while I would scream back on the phone, 'No, I don't!' They finally connived to have us see Rabbi Goldberger. I didn't want to go, but they told me Gus wanted to try it, and they told Gus that I was the one who wanted to try.''

"My lawyer said that if Connie and I made some kind of an attempt at reconciliation, things would go better in court. I never did deny the fact that I really cared a lot about Connie," Gus recalls. "It's just that I thought this thing she was involved in was never going to be over with, and I was just trying to call the whole thing off. When the lawyers told me Connie still cared, I really couldn't say no to giving counseling another try.''

The marriage counselor they went to was a rabbi who had given up the pulpit to devote his time to a secular practice. Gus and Connie had been raised in Polish-Catholic families but never even considered going to a priest when their marriage hit the rocks because, as Connie put it, "Priests aren't married; they've never been out in the world, and we didn't feel that priests knew anything about our problem or could even relate to it." But the rabbi they saw struck them as a man who "could relate to the dumb little things in a marriage that seem almost to eat away at you." There was an excellent rapport from the very beginning between the rabbi, Gus, and Connie. During the early sessions they aired their hostilities, screaming at each other right there in the office. Connie claims she screamed because she felt Gus would never change, and if he didn't change, she couldn't offer the fidelity—sexual and emotional—that Gus needed.

"Gus had a very passive attitude toward me. I like dumb things, like walking in the park—you know, really stupid things, and he thought they were—stupid. But they meant more to me than he realized. I bitched and nagged, and it didn't seem to do any good, so I quit bitching and nagging. Then it so happens somebody came along that also liked walks in parks and window-shopping and that kind of garbage. So rather than nag my husband, I made a substitute. But even when the affair came out, we fought constantly because Gus felt he had never ignored me, and I felt he totally had.''

Gus saw those early sessions with Rabbi Goldberger as a chance to unburden himself and at the same time gain reassurance that their problems could be handled. "It was a sounding board type of thing. When you're separated for a few months, you think all these hateful things. You can't say them. You keep them inside and then, when you get a chance, you just explode. I think we were trying to say that we didn't care about each other, and he kept saying that there was really something there that indicated we did. He kept saying every time we'd complain about something the other did, 'Well, that's something that's got to be worked out. That's just a problem. That isn't enough to completely call everything off. That's not insurmountable.''"

"Maybe that was the secret," says Connie. "We thought our problems were insurmountable, but he kept reassuring us that they weren't. Maybe that's why we were able to work it out. You know, you get to a point, you get so bogged down that you don't see any way clear. We couldn't see the forest for the trees.

"We got to the point where we were picking about money, picking about the kids. Something would happen to me that he had nothing to do with because he'd moved out, but I'd blame him. You know, dumb things, and then when I'd bring them up to the rabbi, he'd say, 'Well, that's not Gus' fault that the tire went flat on the car, for God's sake,' and, 'Why do you blame him?' and I'd say, 'Well, why do I blame him?' And at the time it seemed like things could never possibly get any better. They were just going straight downhill, as far as I was concerned. Evidently the rabbi saw us improving maybe by airing our thoughts."

"Both of us began to feel there was something to hang onto, enough common ground so we could start over to really be happy together," says Gus. The rabbi appealed to Gus because he asked many specific questions instead of just listening, as the two women counselors had, and periodically saying something vague like, "How do you feel about that?"

"The biggest help the rabbi offered," Gus continued, "was that he wasn't afraid to come out and say when someone was right and someone was wrong. The others would never comment if you were completely out in left field, but Rabbi Goldberger would come forward, like when we talked about the family, he might say, 'I don't care if you feel that way or not. You're wrong. If you let your mother enter into it that much, then you're wrong.' "

"A lot of the time was spent on family," says Connie. "Both of us moved from home and got married. We were eighteen, or barely nineteen. And both of us had a tendency to listen to our families. If my mother said something, even if I didn't consciously hear her or think I was paying attention to her, I did, and Gus was doing the same thing. And the rabbi would get ticked about that. Like Gus would say, 'My mother says it's still going on,' or, 'My mother says I don't keep close enough track of her.' And the rabbi would say, 'Who are you trying to please? You or your mother?' The rabbi said both of our families were right here, in on it at all times, and we were more dependent on the family than we realized.

"I can remember the rabbi saying to me, 'Have you made a decision if you want a divorce or not?' And that was the hardest thing for me to say yes or no to. I still cared enough about Gus, I didn't want to hurt him, and I cared what happened to him, and I cared about what he did and stuff like that. So I knew there was something there, but the word 'love' is such a hard word to pinpoint. But, anyway, I remember the day I told Rabbi Goldberger that I knew I could not make a decision that day, and he said, 'Well, then you have just made a decision, that you can't make a decision.' For some reason he made me feel better. As a matter of fact, I think it was less than two and a half weeks later that we got back together. After he told me that, it was very hard for me to make a decision. He told me I had to promise that if I ever saw this guy again in a store, I would walk right by and never say a word, and at that point I couldn't promise that because my feelings were still too mixed up, and I said, 'I can't promise that.' And he said, 'Well, now, that's two decisions you've made today.' He said, 'When you make the decision to either go through with the divorce or to forget it, it will be a steadfast decision, and you won't waver one way or the other.' And it was not even three weeks later, I don't think. Gus was at the house doing his laundry, which used to really tick me off. I'd been invited to a party and didn't want to go alone. I thought of asking Gus, but then I thought, 'No way, he's the quiet one. He hates parties with a passion.' Then he came down the hall after talking to one of the kids, and I just blurted it out, and he went with me and ended up going home at five o'clock in the morning to get his work clothes, and that was it. I don't know; something clicked.''

"Connie hadn't made the decision until then to call off this other thing, and that's why we continued to have problems. As soon as she made up her mind it was over, then I could see it. I don't know if I'm right or wrong, but this is the way I felt. When I could see that she had really decided on me, then I was willing to forget whatever had happened before that.''

Connie agrees that she had been wavering until then, that even though she had called off the affair, she still had thoughts of leaving with her ex-lover. Connie and Gus continued to see Rabbi Goldberger for five months, tapering off to a session once a month toward the end. They have been back together for two years now, and they feel they've grown up a lot through the counseling and the many things they learned about each other and themselves.

GUS: We had been leading our lives, I think, for other people and for what we thought we should do instead of just being ourselves.

CONNIE: And Gus was brought up that if the man goes to work, comes home and eats his dinner, and provides for his family, that that's a good father and a good husband. But that wasn't my idea. I live in a make-believe world, I guess. I wanted to do the things we did when we were still dating, kids and all. I wanted to be off alone with him. For a long time there was that terrible communication gap. Now if I say I want to go to the park or go away for a few days, even though it might not be his thing really, he realizes how much it means to me, and we go. Now even the nightshift wouldn't bother me; now I could handle it beautifully. Maybe this is more self-assurance on my part, but I also feel that much closer to him than I ever have. The last two years I have felt closer to Gus than I ever did because we were always—

GUS: I think playing roles.

CONNIE: Yeah, mommy and daddy roles, maybe that we had played when we were ten. You know what I mean?

GUS: Yeah. It wasn't life; it was a game.

The mates who are hit hardest by affairs tend to be those who have lived a symbiotic relationship. In biology symbiosis is an advantageous arrangement. Two dissimilar organisms live together and form a new whole. Fungus and algae together form the lichen. Two fungi will not effect this transformation. There are those who feel that husband and wife have exactly such clear-cut functions. Only by keeping to their assigned role and place will they effectively form that ideal known as the good marriage. Helen Andelin, founder of the course and author of the book *Fascinating Womanhood,* holds to this basic concept: "It was God who placed the man at the head of the family. . . . The father is a head or president or spokesman [not spokesperson] of the family. This arrangement is of Divine Origin."[13] Marabel Morgan hues to this line in *The Total Woman.*[14] Men should lead and be deferred to in all things. Half a million women have paid from $15 to $30 to take the Total Woman course or the Fascinating Womanhood program, and over a million people have purchased these books in hardbound and paperback editions. The traditional division of the sexes which both these books and courses advocate has these two things to recommend it: The system has worked, if one uses the criterion of keeping marriages and families together. The system is compatible with the religious teachings of the Western and even the Eastern world. At this moment in history, when marriages are less frequent and the divorce rate is at a record high, wouldn't it make sense to simply revert to this old system?

For some women, simply returning to a traditional sexist system may be the answer. But for an increasing number the assignment of separate psychological roles for male and female no longer makes sense. The religious and social supports for the old symbiotic system are crumbling.

Two women we interviewed epitomized the failure of the old system. One, named Leah, had been brought up "to take it, and take it." She never set limits on her husband, never made demands. When her husband's mistress called to discuss things, Leah took that too, turning any anger she felt into guilt and depression, even briefly contemplating suicide. Leah's husband eventually wanted a divorce—something Leah could never have initiated. "The idea that you might rock the boat toward divorce," said Leah, "was the most abhorrent thing to me. It was like death." But when the marriage broke up, Leah found she didn't die; in fact she flourished. She began to question the conclusions she had made as a young girl, that the world is a dangerous place, that life is a dangerous process. "It's strange," she says, "how we work from conclusions we drew when we were very small. I'm big now. I'm powerful. I'm in control."

Leah now works as social director at a large home for the aged. She can empathize with the residents' feelings of dependency—feelings she experienced throughout her marriage. "They feel they are just like a stone around somebody else's neck. The more dependent one feels, the more abhorrent, ugly, and unacceptable one finds oneself. That fact holds people riveted to one spot; it puts the whole world in a dangerous context. They don't see how much strength they have. Nobody sees how powerful they are. That's what I think is my greatest insight into myself—how powerful we can be.''

Leah had undergone a psychological lobotomy when she was a young girl, a common occurrence among female children. The clearest way to understand the logic of this operation is to use the TA model of parent/adult/child ego states and see how these states have been divided between male and female. The female ego is allowed a nurturing "parent" state, an "adult" state in which the computer function of the mind is limited to calculating the effect one's personal actions have on others. (*Fascinating Womanhood* advocates childlike behavior as a calculated ploy to get one's way by making the man appear to be stronger and wiser.) The "child" ego state normally includes anger, aggression, and inquisitiveness as well as affection, sadness, anxiety, and self-centeredness. The sexist system divides up these traits, with women allowed to be the touchers, the weepers, the worriers. Inquisitiveness is limited to the personal and family sphere and usually shows itself as gossip. Since aggression went to the men, female sexual drives are ideally reduced to flirtation, with the lead in sexual matters always taken by the male.

In this system, the model male has the judgmental and punitive portion of the parent state. In family life he supposedly lays down the law, or at least has the final word, while the wife comforts the children after he passes judgment, and provides emotional support for them while he is away. The male is encouraged to have an effective mental "computer" which processes information from the outside world. If the male's computer is faulty, this fact is masked by the women around him. Thus he always appears to be more of an adult than his wife, even when she computes most of the data.

The child in the man comes out in his aggressiveness, his outbursts of anger. He is supposed to be inquisitive and is allowed to give his sexuality free rein, but the type of creativity which depends on intuition and sensitivity to color, light, and sound is not encouraged. When he is sad or anxious he neither cries nor complains. When he feels passive or even defeated by the angry, aggressive outside world, his wife can calculate her actions to make him feel like a conqueror again. Thus marriage doesn't have to be a rich and stimulating meeting ground for two complicated, actualized individuals. It is rather a meshing of two partial people who together create an advantageous arrangement—a symbiotic existence which assures the continuation of the species.

This system has been as central to marriage as the Ptolemaic system was to our view of the universe. But like a Platonic ideal of a chair or a table, no living man or woman could perfectly fit the sex role models of the symbiotic, partial-people system. The more the persons departed from the model, however, the more conflicts they were likely to experience.

French-born Monique had always believed that a man should be dominant and capable. She met her husband during World War II when he was in uniform, having the title and the trappings of the dominant, capable male. But when the two married and settled in the United States, Monique realized she could make more money than he. Convent-educated and sexually naïve, Monique took longer to find out that her husband's savoir faire was a sham; he was as ignorant as she about sex. She feels her financial success ruined whatever chance there might have been for a successful sex relationship.

"I had already concluded that the roles with my husband and me had reversed, that I was playing the 'male' role and he was playing the 'female' role. This had gone on for a long time, and this was the basis of why I was so unhappy in the marriage, because I am a woman and I like being a woman and I don't want to dominate any man. I'm of an era where men were the dominant factor in a marriage. My background was that; my home life was that. I couldn't function where I was put in a role where I had to lead a man. I would lose respect and regard for that man. That's what happened in my marriage."

As Monique became more successful professionally, her husband became more resentful of her. The more honors she received, the more he resented her. This is the double bind of the successful woman in a marriage which still adheres to the symbiotic sex-role model. If she doesn't express her talents, she's frustrated; and if she does, she's resented. (Matina Horner would later examine this syndrome in research studies explaining why some capable women actually fear and try to avoid success.[15])

One night in bed with her husband, keenly aware of their incompatibility, Monique told him, " 'You know, Don, I've got it figured out that sex is here in our heads.' He laughed at me. He made me feel like an idiot. He said, 'I never heard anything so stupid in my whole life.' "

Monique, like Leah, felt no affinity for the group she calls the women's libbers. She saw her dissatisfaction as a private and personal matter. "Ultimately, one day, I raised my head from my desk and thought, 'I'm not getting any younger.' I have never felt old, ever. I'm approaching fifty. I've never been on skis. I haven't played tennis since I was out of school. I love to swim. I enjoy playing bridge. I'm not doing any of these things. All I'm doing is working and being a household drudge besides. Where's my lollipop?" Not surprisingly, Monique fell in love that year with somebody else, a married man. The affair finished off the last vestiges of what she had called, rather euphemistically, her "marriage."

Most of us straddle the old and the new. As products of the symbiotic system, we still feel incomplete on our own. Indeed, Leah and Monique, for whom divorce was a good thing, still had to deal with the loneliness and moments of feeling that they had failed to be the right kind of woman. The new system—which we would call the "personhood" system—is also imperfect. If the old approach to male and female roles made biology synonymous with identity and thus too constricting the new approach may give too little credit to our biological and psychological needs to share our lives with a mate. The self-centeredness of the personhood system makes such sharing very difficult.

AN AFFAIR WITH HERSELF

The greatest threats to today's marriages come not from affairs women are having with other men, but from affairs women are having with themselves. The strict monogamy of the past has enforced an altruism and self-abnegation which an increasing number of wives are finding intolerable. As Claude Steiner puts it, "Monogamy usually means the woman can't even love herself." The husband who comes home and is greeted by a wife saying, "I'm taking care of me now," could be as jealous and resentful as the husband who comes home and finds his wife with another man. The three aspects of the marital relationship—the me, the you, the us—become like a lovers'triangle. If the wife wants to bring the "me" into the forefront when the "us" and the "you" were comfortably in control, there will be conflict.

What we are beginning to see is a violent reaction on the part of some women who have ignored their own needs in marriage. They are so intent on satisfying the "me," they feel they no longer have room in their lives for anyone else—no husband, no family, no one that might impinge on the affair with the self. Of course, men have been deserting their wives for centuries. But "husband dumping" and "runaway wives"—these are recent, and to many, startling phenomena.

Perhaps one of the most revealing statistics about this new "role reversal" can be found in the offices of private detective agencies. In 1961 Tracers Company of America, a nationwide private detective agency, was asked to find one runaway wife for every 300 husbands who were reported missing. By 1973 the company was searching for one vanished wife for every one husband who had disappeared. And in 1974 they were searching for more runaway wives than husbands.

Husband dumping, which often entails leaving one's children with the husband—chucking it all—has not been evaluated statistically. We know that there is a small increase in the number of fathers awarded custody of their children and a gradual change in the importance of fathers' participation in child rearing. But one tends to think of the husband dumpers as eccentric or deviant characters. What woman could leave her children after years of nurturing them? Bambi and Sloan illustrate the genesis of what seems a radical, even unnatural departure of wife from husband and children.

Sloan's grandfather had gone to Harvard, founded his own corporation, and become a pillar of the community. Sloan's father went to Harvard and became an executive in a chain of newspapers. Sloan went to Harvard and then into the State Department. Bambi's father had gone to Harvard with Sloan's father and the two met at a cocktail party. As Sloan put it, "We both had the same scripts in our heads and it all seemed to unreel like clockwork except for a minor embarrassment about having a shotgun wedding."

Sloan's career at the State Department was meteoric. "I didn't have enough security to question anything that went on there and bought the whole competition thing. Since I was essentially insecure, my strategy was that if I'm not as good as those sharpshooters, I can keep up with them if I work twice as hard." So Sloan worked from eight in the morning until one in the morning six, sometimes seven days a week. Their first child, a daughter, was born seven and a half months after they were married, and eleven months later Bambi gave birth to a son. Sloan's ambitions entailed concomitant social obligations, so at twenty-five Bambi was giving sit-down dinner parties for the famous and near-famous. After two years in Washington, Sloan was transferred to work on a special United Nations project in New York.

Their marriage began to disintegrate. The pressures from the two young children, Sloan's long hours at work and frequent five-day trips to faraway countries was more than Bambi could take. Even when he was home, their sexual relationship was unsatisfactory; he was often too mentally or physically exhausted to enjoy sex and she rarely achieved orgasm. She tried to tell Sloan about her problems, but Sloan found them not as interesting as the problems he was trying to solve at the State Department, so he would nod or occasionally grunt while Bambi talked, his mind focusing on Moscow or Peking or Cairo. Finally the two agreed to see a family confidant, a minister who told them to just "spend time with each other"—clearly impossible, given the greater and greater responsibility Sloan assumed in State Department matters.

Bambi became pregnant in New York just at the time her older daughter began to display behavior which was close to autism. After bitter arguments Bambi finally convinced Sloan that the child needed therapy. When Sloan discovered that child psychiatry in New York was heavily dominated by Jews, he felt even more insecure. "It was all threatening to me," Sloan remembers. "All the Jews at school, at the State Department, were smarter than me. They were the epitome of all the people who were smarter and more successful than I, the people I had to work twice as hard to stay even with, so it was tough on me that I had to send my child to a Jewish psychiatrist."

Then Bambi became pregnant again. She vowed to have an abortion, but in New York then, as elsewhere around the nation, abortions were illegal unless three doctors would certify that she would be likely to become severely mentally disturbed upon the birth of the child. It was, as Bambi put it, "like *Catch-22*. The psychiatrists I saw said, 'Well, you're not crazy enough to have an abortion, so have the child and if it makes you crazy, come back and see us.'" So Bambi went alone to Puerto Rico and had her abortion. "I became a raging feminist in the space of about three weeks," she recalls.

Finally, much to the dismay of Sloan, the two of them went to a psychiatrist about their marriage difficulties. This time it was a gentile psychiatrist. Nevertheless, Sloan had difficulties admitting that he was receiving psychotherapy. "That was a dirty word to me. We ran into a couple on the street one time and Bambi said, 'Oh, our shrink said . . .' Well, I just about shriveled up. I was furious at her afterwards, and I said, 'That's a dirty secret. You don't just go around telling something like that to people on the street.' I just thought that any admission of anything like that was taboo. I also think another ingredient was just fear. I felt so powerless inside, so insecure and unsettled and unsure of myself that I couldn't bring myself to admit that I had any weaknesses. You see, I knew I had weaknesses, but to admit them to somebody else was just unthinkable. People would think less of me." Which, of course, was an impossible position for a third-generation Harvard graduate from a "terribly Waspy family line," as Sloan calls his background.

Sloan spent two years working on his United Nations projects and two years in therapy, trying to piece together the reasons he was uptight. Not once was the unsatisfactory sexual relationship between Sloan and Bambi discussed, because the two of them felt uncomfortable and they believed the discussion would upset the psychiatrist.

Finally, after the UN projects were complete, Sloan was offered a leave of absence to study at Stanford University. Sloan jumped at the chance, but Bambi was not enthusiastic. She wanted to stay in New York and continue taking courses for a masters degree at the New School for Social Research. But Sloan said they were going and they did.

This marked a new period in Sloan's life. "I got out there, and I bought a pair of blue jeans and started hanging around with the shaggies and a teacher who had dropped out of a straight career. I started having conversations with people instead of just picking their brains. I came home two or three nights a week, saw the kids and Bambi, and all the time thought, 'Gee, I really don't want to go back to the grind in Washington.'" Bambi felt alone and isolated. "It wasn't a mutual agreement. I didn't want to be in California, but there I was, with no way back to New York or Washington, and I woke up in the middle of one night thinking, 'Hey, I'm being used! I need to break that cycle.'" Sloan loved the freedom of California; Bambi felt "dumped on." "I was ready for a role model of my own," she recalls. "I needed a woman therapist. There were some things that I wanted to work with by myself and didn't want to share in a marriage context. I wanted some stuff for me as a person and not connected to my vocational training as a mommy or a wife."

Sloan spent a couple of months agonizing about what he would do if he left the State Department when a friend suggested he write up a résumé. The next morning, instead of working on his résumé, he called an acquaintance who was head of the political science department at a small but prestigious college nearby. The acquaintance immediately offered him a teaching position in his department.

Bambi was assigned the task of closing the New York apartment. She flew back and took care of her "obligation," spending half the time contemplating an affair with a mutual friend. "I was still feeling hollow and reverberating that this marriage just wasn't going to work for me," she remembers after returning from New York. "Sloan and I had one of our usually unsatisfying for me and very distancing love-making evenings, and I woke up in the middle of the night just paralyzed with fear. What I had seen was the shell of myself, and I thought that I needed to rescue that person. I just wouldn't go around being a shell any longer."

Bambi began to see a feminist therapist and after a fairly short time informed Sloan that she was "thinking about moving out." One month later she put together two cartons of minimal possessions, had Sloan drive her to a rooming house, and said good-bye. After a few months of separation Sloan became jealous of the relationship between Bambi and her therapist and decided he needed some help also. The two of them agreed to interview therapists together, but Bambi would not participate in Sloan's therapy. (The therapist they finally chose as the most simpatico, interestingly, turned out to be Jewish.)

For two years their relationship continued in this manner. Sloan was home with his two children; Bambi lived nearby in a rooming house, dropping over to see the children four or five times a week, spending several hours and, perhaps on the weekends, entire days.

One day Bambi came over to the house, the same day that Sloan accepted a teaching position in New York City. Bambi had come home to tell him that she had filed the legal papers for a divorce.

Somehow this ending to a tale of "personhood" is just as unsatisfactory as the old dependency situation with the wife kept servile and unfulfilled. One can't help feeling that there could have been a better way for Sloan and Bambi to resolve their marital problems, something between the old self-abnegation and the new infatuation with the self. What might have happened if they had gone to an enrichment program early in the marriage, one that might have helped Bambi to express her feelings of frustration with the heavy domestic burden and the insufficient opportunity for personal challenge? Sloan wound up making a great deal of progress from his uptight Ivy League days. Couldn't a sensitive counselor have cut through the veneer of chauvinism and insecurity to bring out the basically decent and reasonably compassionate husband and father before Bambi left for the rooming house? Our experience and research comparing couple therapy and individual counseling suggest that Bambi's choice of a separate therapist weighted the outcome in favor of divorce.

It is too late for Bambi and Sloan to ask what might have been. But for couples whose marital problems are just becoming apparent, this is the time to check enrichment, prevention, and other avenues for couples to grow together.

7

Saving Yourself from the
Wrong Marriage Counselor

In these perilous times a couple needn't be sick or abnormal to feel that they might be in need of guidance and counseling. Beyond the general malaise, the predictable marital woes brought on by pregnancy, mobility, children's adolescence, middle-aged crises, retirement—there are certain danger signs that might alert couples to seek help before they reach a point of no return.

DANGER SIGNS

Dr. Michael Solomon of Denver, Colorado, notes these "marital red flags." "The simplest things to identify are consistent arguments over what appear to be insignificant issues," says Dr. Solomon, citing several examples from his career as a family therapist. "Parents arguing consistently about the children. That's usually a clue to the fact that the children are about to be indoctrinated into the role of 'spacer' between marital partners." As we saw in Chapter 2, Ruth, the child with severe asthma, used her illness to save her mother and father from having to face each other and from dealing with their real, adult problems.

A second red flag goes up for Dr. Solomon when "people begin to see themselves as not lovable in relation to their family." He calls this the "lovability factor" and it indicates, not that these persons are actually unlovable, but that something in the family interactions isn't filling that person's need for approval, his or her need to be loved.

Avoidance is another red flag. There are an amazing number of ways in which families (and couples) can remain together and yet avoid each other. Sometimes the family/couple "overrelates" to other people by always having people around, never permitting themselves the opportunity to be alone. Dr. Solomon relates the case of one family that was overrelating to such an extent, they seemed to be running a hotel. "There was always a friend who stayed in the house with them. They were never guest-free. Their friends thought they were wonderful, happy people. But what they were really doing was using other people to avoid opportunities to be alone. Even on vacations they would go with three or four other couples. By the time they were actually alone, they were too exhausted to give to each other."

The television set provides one of the most convenient barriers for couples who would rather look away than at each other. Some couples or families have the television set on constantly; others have a TV set in their bedroom. As we noted in the chapter on sex therapy, one of the first steps in treating dysfunction is to banish the TV. A surprising number of husbands and wives will listen, night after night, to the *double entendres* and blue humor of late-night talk shows; they'll watch Hepburn and Tracy, Gable and Lombard, Bogart and Bergman, then turn the other way without giving their own lover so much as a peck on the cheek.

Individual members of a family need "space," a chance to be alone. Housewives, particularly, hunger for just a half hour to relax and read a book or listen to music. But "distance" can occur when everyone is physically close. Continual arguments during suppertime keep husband and wife miles apart. If Janie's bad manners are always the subject of conversation, Mom and Dad never have to engage in any meaningful give and take. Some families have to eat at different times during the week, but those who can never share a meal together are obviously avoiding any interchange. Dr. Solomon believes many families simply can't stand to be face to face because it makes them feel so lonely.

Lonely Together, the record album title, describes many marriages, particularly those couples who once looked forward to every moment together. As one couple told Dr. Solomon, "Being together makes us twice as lonely as being apart." That horrible feeling of being in the same room with one's spouse and feeling achingly lonely is a signal that neither partner is able to supply the other with what is needed. They have a double sense of inadequacy and failure.

Among the behavior patterns which can lead to divorce, family therapist Virginia Satir finds one of the most common to be the oblivious husband and the overburdened wife.

Being overburdened is nothing new to women—colonial or contemporary. But the burdens seem more onerous when they are no longer obligatory. A contemporary wife and mother could cook, clean, see that her children are fed, clothed, and reasonably contented, but she is keenly aware of all the other women who are no longer doing those things, no longer taking them seriously. There is all that potential, which she is only now seeing as ripe for expression, the talents and training aching to be put to use in the kind of "fulfilling" work *Ms.* magazine features. Such a woman feels more overburdened than her ancestral counterpart whose labors may have been more strenuous. Such a woman feels, to use the words of a salty mother of four young children who wound up running one of Chicago's top art galleries— "They all want something from you, and you feel as if you have six pairs of teats with someone sucking on each one." Or there is the runaway wife, who left a family of six lazy children and one chauvinistic husband because she was fed up with housework only to find herself working as a housekeeper in another city because she had no other means of supporting herself. Asked why she left, the woman replied, "I did it because I couldn't look at another dish." It's a question of perceived burdens rather than actual burdens. We perceive burdens within marriage to be unbearable when our society and our mates offer no sense of actual or sympathetic support.

When the pressing needs of children dissipate and the economic crunch of early marriage eases, boredom becomes the primary cause of divorce. Our awareness of other, perhaps more exciting life-styles, may give the ordinary life an even duller look by contrast to the psychedelic pinks and purples of our more swinging neighbors. After years of marriage, partners become predictable. They find it difficult to surprise each other, in many cases because they no longer try to put romance in their lives.

"We don't excite each other anymore." This is the complaint of a woman in her late thirties describing the monotony of her marriage. "Ten years, every three days, the same old routine. I knew exactly what approach he was going to make to me when he wanted to make love. And I thought, 'Oh, again?' "

Edward Rydman, Dallas marriage counselor and past director of the American Association of Marriage and Family Counselors, sees many couples in their middle years, and he too finds that boredom for men and lack of intimacy for women are significant causes of marital dissatisfaction. The question Rydman often asks is, "What's it like being married to you?" The wife or husband may try to get out of answering that one by telling the therapist to ask their spouse, but Rydman insists they answer. Then, for many individuals, the answer will be, "It's deadly dull being married to me. It's a drag. It's lonely." The union of two dull people is not likely to produce an exciting marriage. The union of one dull person and one stimulating person is likely to produce dissatisfaction.

There are women who have lost all their major jobs of being wife, mother, and homemaker and feel they're not needed anymore. Even a good marriage can't absorb all the shocks of personal disenchantment that middle-aged couples are heir to. Even though a woman may feel that her personal life is just a series of "no help wanted" signs, she is also aware that there may be other options. As Satir puts it, "People have a new awakening of what life can be for them, and they haven't got a context in which that can happen. So they try to find it.'' Finding it, for a woman, may just mean that she will have to grow in her own right before her marital relationship can improve. She may go back to school, start a new career, open a small business.

The woman who has known economic and sexual freedom and has "given it up" for the security of marriage is in a particularly vulnerable position. Rydman sees a significant number of pilots and their wives. Some of these women can live with the awareness that their husbands are having other sources of pleasure and excitement. Others find their own sources of intimacy and stimulation. A certain proportion may use the new no-fault Texas divorce laws to say no to the marriage. In most cases Rydman finds that only one of the spouses really wants out. "The other one doesn't want out but wants to maintain the marriage, though not necessarily for healthy reasons. It's primarily for security: 'What am I going to do if he leaves? I never educated myself. I've never been responsible for myself.' I think this is producing a counterpart movement to women's lib among women who are not women's libbers, but who are simply finding that they have to become individuals rather than just appendages to their husbands."

The husband who chivalrously told his wife, "I will take care of you; I'll marry you and you'll never have to do anything again," is encouraging a dependency that may result in marital unhappiness for both. Carrying someone for years can become an intolerable burden, even to the most broad-shouldered of men. When the woman is coming from a dependent place, the kind of mutual sharing that produces intimate relations is impossible. One can't be intimate with a mink coat, a ranch house, or a white Cadillac. Wives who are treated as possessions have similar limitations.

Ask yourself what is it like to be married to you? If the answer is bad news, consider that another marital red flag.

Sex and other forms of communication are the most common presenting problems, but they are often signs of sterile relations, marriages which lack warmth, intimacy, and spontaneity. Our survey of sex clinics and couples who have participated in sex dysfunction therapy shows that changes in sexual behavior often bring about profound improvements in the marriage. Greater tenderness and sensitivity in sexual relations usually meant greater tenderness and sensitivity in other areas of the marriage. Women who could "let go" in bed felt less need to nag and control their mates outside the bedroom. If sex is the presenting problem, a couple should not be alarmed. If they find the right therapist, they have an excellent chance of finding greater satisfaction.

We have cited many danger signals—and there are an infinite number of variations—but it would be a mistake for a couple to become alarmed over short-lived, shallow dips in domestic satisfaction. One day's argument over the children, a few days of melancholy or self-pity, a jolt of envy—these are not definite signposts that there is trouble in the marriage. The key is the repetition of signals—a continual sense of boredom, lovelessness, overburdening responsibility, and sexual dissatisfaction. The normal strains of living in this complex and often debilitating society take their toll.

The distinguished psychotherapist Carl Rogers, in his book *Becoming Partners: Marriage and Its Alternatives*, provides a rare and sensitive description of a forty-seven-year marriage (his own) which has withstood periods of individual pain and torment. This involved the strains of his work with schizophrenic patients and the painful personality changes of his wife's aging mother, who suffered a series of strokes and threw a pall of guilt and sadness over his wife. Dr. Rogers also cites this example of marital steadfastness: "During my forties," he writes, "there was a period of nearly a year when I felt absolutely no sexual desire—for anyone. No medical cause was found. Helen [Rogers' wife] was confident that my normal urges would return and simply 'stood with me' in my predicament. . . . Her quiet continuing love meant a great deal to me and probably was the best therapy I could have had. At any rate, I gradually became sexually normal once more."[1]

One of the advantages of marriage over cohabitation, open or secret affairs, swapping and communal relations, can be the greater degree of patience and security in the relationship. At least you don't have to be "on" with your husband or wife; you can relax. You can be reasonably sure that your spouse won't desert you at the first sign of inadequacy. How do the hostile, indifferent, lonely, or bored spells of your marriage balance out against the intimate, tender, and spontaneous moments? If you think the balance leans heavily toward "spiritual divorce," this may be the right time to communicate your concerns. If you find these concerns are shared by your spouse, or if discussion and communication of marital anxieties are impossible for the two of you, that in itself is the most important signal that your marriage could stand the services of a marriage counselor.

DON'T LET YOUR FINGERS DO THE WALKING

In our travels during the two-year period in which this book was written, we have encountered advertisements in the Yellow Pages which boggled the mind. In Chicago we found the "Counselor of Life" who unequivocally stated in his ad, "Do You Have a Problem? I Have the Solution." There was a "Dr." David M. Berry who, when queried about his approach to therapy, said he was primarily interested in the "astrological aspects of marriaging [*sic*]." Sister Bell (no relation to Ma Bell) was also in the Yellow Pages in Chicago. Her approach was rather unique in that she said she "reads the minds and when you reads the minds it helps the problems." In Denver, leafing through the Yellow Pages, we found the Holy Ghost Repair Service.

Without passing judgment, and not having visited Universal Freedom, Inc., in Boston, the appellation of "universal freedom" doesn't provide much information as to what kind of therapy is practiced. The same can be said of the Abundant Life Counseling Service in St. Louis or the ad for the Drake Institute of Hypnosis which read "Psychology is Wonderful/Philosophy Is Great/Hypnosis Makes Them Work Better" (which may be something like "Therapy Goes Better with Coke").

The marriage counselor who is best is not likely to be the one with a universal set of rules or a panacea or technique, but rather the person equipped with a range of approaches, a person responsive to your needs and compatible with your values and tastes. Even our "rules" for finding a reputable counselor have their exceptions.

Sources

1. Ask friends—ones with whom you share some common values and preferences. Your married friends may have had similar problems. Your divorced friends may offer valuable references or warnings.

2. Inquire at the local chapter of established professional associations. Membership in organizations such as AAMFC, the Family Service Association of America and others listed here (see Appendix A) indicates academic credentials and practical experience.

3. Call a teaching hospital or university, preferably asking for the name

Exceptions

1. Just because a therapist worked for your friend doesn't mean he/she will be effective for you. Reserve the final decision until you and your mate have checked out this recommendation.

2. Integrity is not necessarily related to diplomas and official organizations. Therapists with the most outstanding reputations tend to have MD's, PHD's or at the very least masters degrees in social work or psychology in addition to many years of experience. Virginia Johnson Masters has no graduate degree, but her pioneering research with Dr. Masters, her unique and extensive experience, more than compensate. The most effective therapists also tend to have "talent"—natural empathy, awareness, insight—but in therapy as in other endeavors, talent must be accompanied by discipline, study, and experience.

3. Therapists with such affiliations are not likely to be harmful, but they

of a department head or staff member. Affiliation with such places offers accountability. People recommended have typically fulfilled minimal requirements and received some supervision.

may be ineffective or unsuitable in temperament or training to your needs. If you ask for two or three affiliated therapists, you will increase your options.

4. Call the nonprofit social service agency in your city, town, or suburb. Some religious denominations are in charge of major agencies of this type. If you live in a large city, there may be a council which coordinates community services of this kind.

4. Nonprofit agencies customarily require an intake interview to help them assign an available therapist. Some agencies will have a battery of tests or a number of interviews. The available therapist may be inexperienced or inappropriate. Paying on a sliding scale does not diminish your right to a suitable therapist.

5. Ask a professional person—doctor, lawyer, clergyman—whose integrity you respect to recommend two marriage counselors.

5. Here again, as with hospital or university affiliated therapists, you have no guarantee of effectiveness. You are the best and final authority on your problems.

Finding a therapist is obviously going to require some adultlike confidence about your own judgments. As family therapist Elsa Leichter so aptly put it, "When you go to a doctor, a therapist, a lawyer—anybody in authority—the child in you comes out. I know that feeling. All of a sudden I'm very dumb—I don't quite know. Is my head operating well or am I just resisting? So that's the little child who doesn't trust his own judgment."

We hope we have convinced you that it is necessary and possible to behave like an adult consumer when seeking a suitable marriage counselor.

Let's assume you now have in hand a shopping list of potential marriage counselors and have eliminated the mind readers, astrologists, palmists, and the noncredentialed therapists. But there are two major categories you still want to rule out—the exploiters and the mismatches. The only way you can strike them from your list is by asking necessary questions and being on guard during the initial interview.

SHOPPING FOR A THERAPIST

One of the first considerations for most couples, but one which some couples fail to clarify at the outset, is how much the counseling will cost. Why are we so reticent about money when it comes to hiring a therapist?

Our society used to have two dirty little secrets. One of them, sex, is now being brought into the open, no longer dirty and rarely confidential. That leaves one secret—money. No one, except for the IRS, questions the ordinary man's right to keep private his financial affairs.

This reticence about personal finance is characteristic of many therapists. They don't immediately tell prospective clients what their fees will be and the clients feel they shouldn't ask. This makes the financial aspects of seeing a therapist even more perplexing than the business of understanding different therapies and seeing through the more dangerous approaches.

The range of professional fees we have encountered is extremely broad and does not seem to be a clear indication of ability. At one end of the spectrum is Claude Steiner in Berkeley, who charges patients $40 a month, or agencies like the Henderson Clinic in Hollywood, Florida, with a sliding scale averaging $8 a visit, or the Giordanos in New York City with their multiple family therapy at $40 a weekend per family. In the middle range of $25 to $35 per visit there is the Philadelphia Marriage Council, and in Los Angeles the American Institute of Family Relations, as well as many excellent social workers and psychologists. Psychiatrists working individually may be getting as much as $50 or $60 for their fifty-minute hour. Co-therapy, as we have seen, is more expensive since there are two therapists to be paid. Intensive co-therapy programs such as sex dysfunction treatment tend to be the most costly. The reputable sex clinic at Chicago's Loyola University Medical School, directed by Dr. Domeena Renshaw, charges $350 for their twenty-eight-hour couple therapy program, and Masters and Johnson in St. Louis get $2,500 for their twelve-day intensive dysfunction therapy. Groups of four to eight couples pay the lowest rates, often spending $25 per session for a therapy team which charges $75 per individual session. In short, we have found effective therapists at almost every financial level. (Interestingly, the most damaging psychiatrist we encountered charges $100 an hour.)

Edward Rydman of Dallas, himself a moderately priced counselor, is one of many therapists we encountered who is concerned about the often inequitable fee system. "The whole fee-for-service system in therapy and in medicine is based on the premise that getting people well is unprofitable. If you get people well, they don't pay you anymore," he says.

"I'm involved right now in a situation with a psychiatrist who has been milking a couple, particularly the man," Edward Rydman told us. "He has been seeing them for over two years and has taken four thousand dollars in fees. The therapist is working out his own need to be a swinging single because he is encouraging the man to live alone. The couple has just become aware of this. They are now going back together *against* the advice of the psychiatrist."

Another way of milking the client is to avoid termination of the therapy by placing the "well" individual or couple in a group therapy situation which then goes on for years. Dr. Rydman cites one therapist who kept people in his groups for as long as seven years. "It becomes a way of life. It becomes their only social life. It becomes an extended family." When it comes to the so-called experts on human behavior, many of whom have questionable expertise, we keep them in cars, condominiums, and cashmere long after they have rendered their services.

Rydman is not sure how to change this system. "I don't know whether it becomes a socialized system whereby therapists have to be prepared to be on some government payroll or social service system—but fee for service, hour by hour, is going to have to go."

Claude Steiner is also an outspoken critic of the pay-for-help situation. "If I go to a therapist," says Steiner, "and the therapist is charging twenty-five dollars a session and there are eight people in the group, and he does four groups a day, five days a week, then figure it out. If you want to contribute to someone making one hundred thousand dollars a year, okay. I think that's outrageous. If you're a guy who makes over one hundred thousand dollars a year, also okay. But if you make ten thousand dollars and he makes one hundred thousand dollars, there's no place he can fit in your life. I think a good therapist should make as much as a good plumber. If he makes more he's probably ripping people off."

Dr. Milton Berger of New York City, one of the pioneers in the use of videotape and psychotherapy and past president of the highly regarded American Group Psychotherapy Association, probably wouldn't agree with Steiner, or even with Rydman. Dr. Berger is not ashamed of the yacht he owns; in fact, he has a picture of it on the mantel in the office where he conducts his therapy sessions. Berger's average fee is $50 a session although some patients pay $75. His fee for groups is $30 a session (in contrast with Steiner's charge of $40 *a month* for group therapy). Berger says he may raise his rates, although he is concerned, as he put it, with "killing off the goose that lays the golden egg."

Berger is very straightforward about where he stands as a therapist. "I've given to the public and I've given to the profession and they've given to me. In my lifetime I fortunately am one of the people who has been rewarded. I earn a nice living. I've been to the top of the podium many times. There on the wall is what is the peak in our society—a full page in *Time*. I've got books. I've got movies going around, some I get money for, fifty bucks a rental. I've been adulated, I've been cursed. I've been envied. People say I'm on an ego trip. When they say that, I say, 'Well, it took me a long time to grow this ego.' Nine years I was in treatment and I suffered a lifetime. So if you want to feel it's pure ego trip or unhealthy, that's your decision. If you stick around and get to know me, you'll find a pretty decent sort of guy."

Dr. Lawrence Laycob of Denver, a psychiatrist, has been practicing on his own for six years. He does a great deal of work with married couples, including sexual dysfunction therapy. During the first session, near the completion of the hour, Laycob tries to deal with the money situation by saying this to the prospective patients: "Look, one of the things that is really important for us to discuss—a lot of patients don't like to talk about it and a lot of doctors don't like to talk about it, but I think that it's important that we settle it very clearly between the two of us—is what my charges are, how I charge, and how I expect to be paid. Let's also talk about if there are going to be any difficulties there."

But Laycob expects to be paid for his work. "I don't think I've ever let someone stop therapy because of financial problems," he says. "However, I don't let people start therapy with me if I don't think that there's a reasonable chance that they can afford it without it being too much of a bind." Laycob says he is flexible about his $45 fee for a forty-five minute session but he wants everything open and up-front before therapy starts "because what you pay me and what I receive is something that gets to be part of our relationship and has to be dealt with like any other part of our relationship."

Laycob opposes an end to the fee-for-services system because he feels even the modified socialized system would fail to provide the incentives that push therapists to do their best work. "When you work for a state institution, your paycheck has nothing to do with whether you get people better or not. If you're working with me and pay me forty-five dollars a session and in two months you say, 'I still feel shitty,' you're going to demand something from me, and I'm on the spot to help you feel better."

The whole problem of fees is a subject which *must* be totally spelled out during the very first session of therapy. And from the experience of many couples around the country, you had better cross every *t* and dot every *i*.

ASKING THE RIGHT QUESTIONS

To avoid costly misunderstandings you can ask a few brief, pointed questions over the phone. If the receptionist balks at letting you speak to "the doctor" before setting up an interview, firmly insist that your questions will take only five minutes of his/her time and are essential. Some therapists are busy, but one needn't be overly intimidated.

Here is a sample of this type of brief phone query:

1. State who recommended you and very succinctly why you will be coming. (We have a serious marital problem, a family problem which includes our two teen-age sons, a sexual problem, etc.) Do not go into a lengthy history of the problem or a detailed description of how it manifests itself.

2. Will you have time to see the two of us within the next few weeks?

3. How much do you charge per visit and how long is each session?

4. If the therapist states that he/she is too busy to take on any additional clients, ask him/her to recommend two other therapists.

5. If you do not know what affiliations this therapist has, ask the therapist if he/she is connected with a hospital, professional association, or university in the area. Write this information down and check to be sure the therapist has been accurate.

If most of your questions are answered on the phone, you will still have the most important question to answer when you meet the therapist(s). Do you trust this person? If you spend the initial hour feeling wary and uncomfortable your chances of opening up and taking care of the problems at hand are slim. You may want to feed back any adverse reactions to the therapist and see if that leads to better rapport. Both you and your spouse should have positive feelings about the therapist, otherwise the visit to the marriage counselor can itself become another source of marital conflict. Even among the reputable people we have quoted in the book, there are many personality differences. The same therapist who seemed to work wonders for one couple may be offensive or ineffective for another. So the "gut reaction"—while not the only test—is ultimately a deciding factor.

Once you have been reasonably careful in selecting a therapist, once you are convinced that this marriage counselor has suitable experience and training and charges a fee you can afford, you should be able to lower your guard and concentrate on your marital problems. You may want to know what you should expect in the way of therapy techniques from this point forward. One of the techniques is a benevolent form of manipulation. This word has so many connotations and so much significance in the field of therapy that it is worth dwelling on for a moment.

GOOD MANIPULATION VERSUS BAD MANIPULATION

Every effective therapist exercises some form of artful management of his clients. In a sense, that is one of the services you are paying for. The therapist manipulates the office sessions in such a way that communication is facilitated. For example, associate professor of family relations at the University of Connecticut and marriage counselor Fred Humphrey uses a technique called "pseudo stupidity" which he learned from Hilda Godwin at the Philadelphia Marriage Council. Says Humphrey, "It's nothing more than pretending you don't understand what they're saying because you want them to explain it more clearly so they know it or so their partner clearly knows it." Humphrey gives this example of a therapy session with husband and wife using "pseudo stupidity."

HUSBAND: Well, I don't get excited as much about coming home anymore after a hard day's work.

HUMPHREY: I don't understand. What do you mean by "not excited"?

HUSBAND: Well I just don't look forward to it.

HUMPHREY: You don't look forward to it, in what sense?

Of course Humphrey understands what the husband is talking about, but through "pseudo stupidity" he draws the husband out so that he—the husband—will be very clear about his complaints and hopefully, says Humphrey, "his wife will then know her husband's feelings. She may be distressed to hear those feelings but nevertheless she will know what's going on."

In effect it's nothing more complicated than a technique to get the center of the message clear, that he or she knows what they're saying or feeling and that the receiver of the message, the marital partner, is quite clear about it.

Virginia Satir uses a rephrasing technique which we'll call "What I'm hearing is . . ." Satir has a hunch—based on body language, family history, past experience—that a particular issue is troubling someone. She asks a question about it: "How do you feel about your son's stealing?" The woman may answer, "How do you *think* I feel? Terrible, of course!" Satir may reply, "What I'm hearing is that you feel guilty too about his stealing, as if you might have caused it or at least avoided it." Now that is not what the woman stated, but there is a strong probability that these are some of her true feelings. If so, the therapist's articulation will help further the therapy.

These are instances of useful manipulation, benign actions which may further communication but will do no harm to the client. What about malignant manipulation?

Contracts are an important means of avoiding the more dangerous forms of manipulation. As Claude Steiner puts it, "Once the therapist frankly admits that he expects to manipulate his patient . . . it becomes extremely important that the therapist obtain a previous, clear-cut agreement or contract, delineating what the patient wishes to change in his behavior. Practicing therapy without such an agreement or contract leaves the choice of changes to the therapist, who will then be clearly overstepping the boundaries of his patient's right for self-determination. No human being has the right, even if he is in the superior position as therapist, to make decisions for another human being, and to do so is more aptly described as brainwashing than as psychotherapy."[2]

You may not know which behaviors need to be changed, which patterns need to be altered, but after a degree of comfort and trust is established, the therapist and the two partners should be able to agree that they generally feel dissatisfied with the relationship and they specifically want to change certain behaviors.

The "specific discomfort contract," as Dr. Michael Solomon calls it, will vary from couple to couple. One pair may want to begin by changing the dinner hour behavior—who cooks the food, who serves it, who clears, how the conversation goes, what is discussed, who gets a chance to talk, etc. Another couple may decide to start by taking the TV out of the bedroom and being sure they have a half hour each night to communicate. If the woman is a harried homemaker, she may change her schedule to have a brief rest in the afternoon so she will *feel* like talking. He may need his quiet half hour when he comes home from work. The point is they have made a start. They have agreed that change is needed and they have agreed to take action in concert.

There are an infinite number of variations on the details that are handled in therapy, but once the therapist has managed the sessions so that such an agreement for change is possible, he/she may encourage change by offering "permission."

In sex therapy particularly, the word "permission" comes up again and again. Individuals needed permission from a parent or authority figure to enjoy sex, to pleasure themselves, to expose their emotions, to be naked and vulnerable. There were many versions of sexual problems, but in most cases at least one of the partners needed to have the sanction and support of the therapist. They wanted to hear an expert tell them: "Even though people told you when you were a child not to do this, not to feel those angry feelings, not to imagine that you are anything but a good girl, a respectable boy—in spite of these old injunctions, I, the therapist, am telling you that it is okay to experiment with these new kinds of behaviors."

We saw what happened when Ben Parks and his wife were encouraged by their therapist to engage in affairs and discuss those relationships openly. Wasn't this "permission"? First, their therapist was not sure that both partners wanted to engage in this experiment. Sexually open marriage was a panacea, in this therapist's mind, for marital ills. When Ben Parks reported that the news of his wife's affair had rendered him impotent, the therapist's reply was, "You'll get over it," small comfort to a man who is feeling sexually and psychologically powerless.

In therapy there is a difference between permission and coercion. Permission is a sanction given by an authority figure. It allows a person to do what they have expressed a wish to do. "You may take three giant steps. You may go to the washroom. You may masturbate. You may have a Superman fantasy while making love to your wife." Permission is a supportive response to an implied or overt request. It is quite different from, "You should" masturbate "You should" have fantasies, "You should" experiment with partners other than your husband.

"Shoulds" and "should nots" are the consumer's province. A therapist shouldn't give permission (1) unless he is reasonably sure that the new behavior will enhance the client's marriage and increase his/her self-esteem, and (2) he is convinced that both partners would like to try this new behavior—that it doesn't violate their core of moral or spiritual beliefs, that it is "egosyntonic."

"Anytime a marriage counselor recommends a potential course of action for an individual or couple," notes Fred Humphrey, "this course has to be egosyntonic. It has to be compatible with that person's basic value system (egosyntonic as compared to ego-alien). If the behavior is incompatible with their values, or ego-alien, we risk helping them bring about guilt, severe guilt, in their personal life which could lead to depression, even suicide. . . . If a counselor promotes, let's say, a good, firm, typical Christian, religiously-oriented person to get into couple swapping when all the evidence should be that this person has a rigid conscience or superego, that's like saying to a little kid, 'That hut over there is filled with gasoline fumes. Would you like to play with some matches?' "

Some counselors will make such suggestions, will give such permission, out of ignorance or lack of sensitivity. Others, like Ben Parks' therapist, are so sold on their new panacea for the world's ills, that they are oblivious to the dangers to the individual. Like the snake cult members in Kentucky, their religious fervor blinds them to the fact that they are wrapping a cobra around their necks.

Even with a carefully chosen therapist who is judicious about permission and protection and deals with a couple with sensitivity and integrity, things often have to get worse before they can get better. When dealing with two people, progress is usually uneven. One of the partners risks opening up; the other rebuffs. In this circumstance an effective therapist will be able to support the rebuffed partner, encouraging that partner not to give up while helping the other to be more responsive.

While the couple should feel comfort and trust at the outset of therapy, they should not expect to continue feeling comfortable throughout therapy. It is not comfortable to change old habits, particularly if the couple has the notion that things *must* remain the same or the marriage will not survive. Martin Blinder and Martin Kirschenbaum call this prevalent misconception "the survival myth" because "the partners see any alteration in the marital equilibrium as a dire threat to their continued existence."[3]

The survival myth makes couples resist and fear change and openness. Part of the marriage counselor's job is to help a couple realize that they have never learned or have rejected the reality of marital survival.

> A marriage is a union of two separate *individuals* who, though they frequently come to amicable agreement and compromise, nevertheless bring to the marriage different sets of values and a potential for different kinds of growth. Honest expression of these differences and the opportunity for independent growth are essential to a viable, healthy relationship. Marriage is a unique, dynamic, and flexible interpersonal exchange subject to constant variation, many-layered shifts, and the ebb and flow of feeling.[4]

This then is the survival reality of marriage. If the couple chooses to move from the myth to the reality, the chances are good that their marriage will survive and flourish.

But if they choose to move from the survival myth to the survival reality, husband and wife are likely to experience some discomfort, even some pain. The discomfort in this situation is a product of changes occurring in the marital relationship.

You may want to run away rather than face issues which you have tried for years to avoid. You can ask yourself, if you feel this urge to flee, Am I running away from the therapist or am I running away from our marital problem?

Do you change your dentist frequently because you can't stand the selfish way he treats you—his bad jokes, his suggestive remarks? Or do you break dental appointments and change dentists because you've had a series of toothaches and are afraid the pain might be a symptom of a serious and expensive dental problem?

In therapy, more than in other professional services you may buy, the personal qualities of the therapist are of paramount importance. You can learn to distinguish between growing pains and a therapist who gives you a pain. As a couple with a marital problem—unless either of you has a history of serious mental illness—you are not a child, and you are not sick. Start taking responsibility for your choices. Learn to terminate a therapeutic relationship if it's a mismatch or if you sniff exploitation. But be prepared to risk the discomfort of change. Ultimately the choice to risk change is the first decision to make yourself a marriage saver.

In the process of writing this book, traveling from one end of the country to the other, interviewing and talking with hundreds of people in the therapeutic community as well as an equal number of people who had been through marriage counseling, we found ourselves being asked about the standards by which we were going to "judge" marriage counselors. On one occasion a militant lesbian who claimed she was a marriage counselor demanded to know how journalists could possibly write such a book since they had never actually done any marriage counseling. We wondered how a woman with a homosexual preference could counsel heterosexual couples.

We both have our limitations and our personal biases. Even as we tried to remain openminded throughout our research, we were forming certain standards. After each interview we would ask ourselves this question, "If we were having problems with *our* marriage, if things were continually out of whack, if the pain of our relationship outweighed the pleasure, would we, *personally*, go to this therapist for help?"

PORTRAIT OF AN EFFECTIVE MARRIAGE COUNSELOR

F. Theodore Reid, MD, is one of the therapists we would be able to trust and a person whose views are particularly congenial to ours. We feel it is important to share his ideas and feelings about marriage and therapy so you will have a gauge by which to "judge" our standards.

Dr. Reid has not written startlingly innovative books on psychotherapy, nor has he engaged in self-aggrandizement by appearing on television talk shows or by being endlessly quoted in newspapers or magazines. But he gives honor to the profession of counseling.

He was born in New York forty-five years ago. He spent his childhood in the intellectual poverty of New York 's Harlem, yet he was able to attend the enriching Bronx School of Science. He went on to Columbia and to McGill University Medical School since, at that time, blacks were just not being admitted to United States medical schools. Internship followed, then two years in the Navy, residency, private practice, and teaching at the prestigious University of Chicago's Pritzker School of Medicine, and a staff position at Michael Reese Hospital. Dr. Reid sees individuals, couples, and groups, working with several co-therapists including his wife, Diane.

Here are his observations about marriage and marriage counseling.

It has been relatively rare, in Ted's experience, for couples who have a "tolerable" situation to come for counseling or therapy in order to change the "tolerable" to something "good." By far the vast majority of couples he sees wait until their marital situation has become intolerable and then seek help to make their lives at least tolerable. In most cases Ted believes that can be accomplished in short order—in from two to eight sessions.

"At that point," Ted says, "at least to my way of thinking, you have to make one of the biggest choices in your life, which is, do you take your marbles and leave, which is what most people do since they're able to stay with that which is tolerable, or do you take a step which is basically revolutionary, one which says, 'I will gamble with what's basically tolerable in hopes that I can make it really good'?

"That, from a psychological point of view, is one of the most profound shifts that anybody can make. Some people can make it; some can't. But it is a decision with which most people flirt for a while before they move one way or the other."

It is for this reason that Ted does not like to establish a specific contract defining the spelled-out goals of therapy. He wants couples to have a freedom of choice after they've arrived at that "tolerable place to do something different, really profoundly different with their lives." Thus, the couple who has come to him because they have one major fight a night, and after four or five weeks of therapy report they've gone one full week without a fight, are now offered a choice by Ted: "Things are better. This is what you came in for. You've got a choice now, whether you want to stop therapy because you've got what you came here for, or whether you want to go on further and look at the relationship and how you got there and where you want to go with it."

Personally Ted is much more interested in where couples want to go rather than how they got there. He is interested in having couples consciously look at their behavior and perhaps, for the first time in their lives, establish new ways of relating.

It is in this manner that Ted Reid is in sync with what seems to be a profound shift in the attitude of many married couples: many no longer wish to live a "tolerable" life, much as their parents did, but instead to live more fully, to drink more of the cup.

But if that shift in attitude represents a kind of sophistication, so too is there an equally sophisticated understanding that the world of singlehood is not all *Playboy* or *Viva* would lead you to believe. The profoundly important ingredient missing from singlehood is the inability to be vulnerable. It was Dr. William Masters who defined marriage as the only place where couples could establish "the exquisite interchange of vulnerabilities," a concept which fits exactly into Ted Reid's theory of personality construction.

Ted puts it this way. "People tend to relate from three positions of "V"—*victim, vindictive,* or *vulnerable.* But basically you only have fruitful relationships when both people try to stay vulnerable."

Ted feels there are lots of societal models for setting oneself as a victim: the long-suffering mother, the long-suffering wife, and so on. "And, of course," he says, "every victim needs a victimizer. During an argument partners may flip back and forth—first the husband is the victimizer, then the victim, and the wife, the same thing. You almost need a scorecard."

Carefully, through several different kinds of techniques, Ted will try to lead a couple to the vulnerable position. "Most people tend to confuse vulnerable with helpless. They click into their memory of helplessness and needing to be taken care of, needing to be loved and fed—all those things." But when a person actually connects with being vulnerable, says Ted, it's a very exciting thing. "There is something whole and powerful about feeling vulnerable because you're saying, 'Yeah, you can hurt me. But you're not able to destroy me.' So you never lose touch with the fact that you're an intact human being when you're in a vulnerable place."

Getting to that vulnerable place is difficult. "A lot of couples come in and present 'position papers.' They've been over the turf so often, it's not an argument; it's a position paper and nobody listens to position papers because everybody knows what the other person is going to say. But once you start talking from a new place, a vulnerable, spontaneous place, the other person's got to listen because they don't know what's going to be said. They might miss something important. They're going to be free to explore new places for themselves. One of the fears about vulnerability is that you're going to be out there, all by your lonesome—but what in fact tends to happen is that one person's vulnerability hooks the other."

A couple came to Ted ostensibly for help with a sexual problem. After a short time that cleared up and the couple was given the opportunity to do some work on their relationship. Something in that relationship was missing, almost like a missing sprocket in a cog, because the wife always expressed her caring for her husband from an angry, victimizer place. It seems that his parents always depreciated him. This infuriated her because she loved her husband very much. But what she expressed to her husband came out as an angry attack on his parents, and he was then forced into the position of having to defend his parents against his wife. At this one session Ted spent a great deal of time working with the wife on how she could literally express her tenderness and caring. "She invited her husband to put his head in her lap, which triggered all kinds of new experiences for her. Then, surprisingly, with his head in her lap, he started talking about how tired he was of being shit on by his parents—the first time she's ever heard him say that and the first time he's ever dared to say it. You see, vulnerability hooks the vulnerability in the other, so you no longer have to defend or attack."

Ted Reid feels that many of the difficulties experienced by couples today come from the fact that they are caught between two very different and conflicting worlds—one past, one present. The past belongs to their parents, people who looked for stability and achievement points in life. It is a past which is described in terms of going to school, graduating, getting married, having a child, getting promoted, a world of if-I-get-to-this-point, *then*-I'll-be-happy; if-I-get-there, *then-I'll* . . .

The other world is one in which the *process* of living, the act of striving together and separately, of stretching to reach the possible and beyond is the stuff of life, the joy.

"It is not that one gets married and lives happily ever after. One gets married and starts a process of marriage, family, growth, and change, an evolving kind of relationship. It is not enough to have people comfortable with each other today. They've got to face the fact that tomorrow they're going to be different people, and their confidence in moving to tomorrow with each other and being available as helpers for each other is the end goal of therapy. My notion is that therapy approximately ends when people have some confidence in managing the process of change themselves, whether it's individually or as a couple. It's when they feel comfortable with managing that change, not unduly frightened by it, either in themselves or in their partner, that the point has come at which therapy should end."

Where does a couple find a "marriage saver"? Everywhere and nowhere.

The quick-guided tour you have just taken with us through the maze of therapies should suggest that everywhere there is a responsible therapist—Gestaltist, TA, behavior mod, pastoral, psychodrama-oriented, Freudian—there is a possibility that you and your mate will acquire coping equipment. Nowhere that a therapist seeks to exploit, nowhere that a therapist seeks to proselytize, nowhere that a therapist lacks training and sensitivity, are two individuals likely to grow in awareness and intimacy. Finding the therapist that has the resources to fit your situation—whether those resources spring from Moses, Jesus Christ, Sigmund Freud, Eric Berne, Fritz Perls, Don Jackson, Jacob Moreno, Nathan Ackerman—is possible once you realize that the best authority on saving your marriage is you.

How does a couple save their marriage?

They find out if it's worth saving, with the help of a trained, experienced therapist or co-therapists whom they have chosen with care and caution.

Marriage counseling at its best is no insurance against divorce. It does prevent a hasty decision to divorce, and at the very least, it can prevent individuals from making the same mistakes in their next marriage. No-fault divorce laws and impulse affairs make a quick dissolution of a marriage possible for most Americans. If you have already invested several years in marriage, why not invest another few months finding out about yourself and your spouse, learning the dynamics of your present family and the one from which you came, taking care of unresolved sexual or emotional conflicts? Successful marriage counseling does not always keep the marriage together; it is not always marriage-saving, but it reveals the possibilities for more satisfying ways of relating. Sometimes that superior relationship can come about within the marriage by evolutionary stages. Sometimes the new way of relating can only spring forth phoenix-like, on the ashes of the old.

We have given a nationwide range of reputable therapists, concentrating on a few individuals, teams, and agencies in order to give a more vivid picture of what a couple should expect—what they should, in fact, demand.

But the disadvantage of being a marriage-counseling consumer is that you take responsibility for the outcome. Even the most effective therapist can do nothing without the cooperation of husband and wife.

The couple must realize that to change a long-term relationship they will have to suspend their disbelief in each other. They will have to abandon blaming—each other, their in-laws, the children, even chauvinism and women's lib. They will have to interact not as host and parasite, but as individuals capable of generating their own self-esteem. Each will have to give up something, letting go of some old behaviors that have become habitual and destructive.

The psychic cost is great. Self-discovery can come dearer in pairs. And there is always the possibility of falling back into old ways with a new and frightening vulnerability.

But there is also the possibility of a new warmth, honesty, and intimacy, as so many of the couples in these pages can testify.

If you decide to take the risk, we hope we have made your course a little less risky.

Appendix: How to Find a
Marriage Counselor

Contents

Behavior Modification	252
Bioenergetics	252
Family Therapists	252–55
Feminist Therapists	255–56
Gestalt Therapists	256
Humanistic	256–57
Marriage Encounter/Marriage Enrichment Programs	257
Pastoral Counselors	258
Psychiatrists	258–59
Psychoanalytic Referrals	259–62
Psychodrama	262
Psychologists	262–63
Psychotherapists	263–64
Sex Therapists/Sex Clinics	264–67
Social Service Organizations	267
Social Workers	268
Transactional Analysis	268–69

"Marriage counselor" is a general term which can include persons who think they are qualified to help couples deal with marital problems, and persons who really are qualified. Only five states have specific regulations concerning marriage counseling. They are California, Michigan, New Jersey, Utah, and Nevada. A marriage counselor may describe himself/herself as a social worker, psychologist, psychiatrist, psychotherapist, or sex therapist, or the counselor may use any number of terms referring to a particular approach to therapy—Gestaltist, TA, therapist, etc. Some of these labels imply licensing and specific academic standards; some don't.

The foremost organization in the nation for accrediting and certifying marriage counselors is the

American Association of Marriage and Family Counselors
225 Yale Avenue
Claremont, California 91711
(714) 621-4749

The AAMFC will supply a caller with a list of three (or more) accredited marriage counselors in their area over the phone and at no charge. Marriage counselors who belong to this association often list the initials AAMFC after their names in the Yellow Pages of the phone book.

The AAMFC requires its members to have at least a masters degree in one of the behavioral sciences (psychology, sociology, education, etc.) plus two years of clinical experience in marriage counseling under the supervision of an approved agency or a member of the AAMFC.

BEHAVIOR MODIFICATION

Although there is no central organization for behavior modification therapists, those who do use this technique are primarily psychologists or psychiatrists. (See definitions of both categories in this Appendix.)

A roster of evaluated behavior modification therapists called Clinical Fellows can be obtained from

The Behavior Therapy and Research Society
Temple University Medical School
Eastern Pennsylvania Psychiatric Institute
Henry Avenue and Abbottsford Road
Philadelphia, Pennsylvania 19129

BIOENERGETICS

The Institute for Bioenergetic Analysis conducts a training and certification program and will make referrals. Be sure to state an interest in marriage counseling in order to get the most suitable therapist.

The Institute for Bioenergetic Analysis
144 East 36th Street
New York, New York 10016
(212) LE 2-7742

FAMILY THERAPISTS

The term family therapist designates a therapist who sees human problems in the context of family interactions. A family therapist believes that the individual cannot change unless the context or system of relationships changes. Family therapy often involves the participation of all members of the family at some point in the treatment. The family therapist may be a psychologist, social worker, psychiatrist, or psychiatric nurse who has had special training and experience working with families.

There is no central clearing house, national association, or accrediting organization for family therapists, per se. Many family therapists belong to the associations of their particular discipline—psychiatrists may be members of the American Psychiatric Association; social workers may belong to the National Association of Social Workers. Many family therapists work for social service agencies, special "family institutes," or various university-affiliated family therapy programs. The list of names and addresses we have compiled includes some of the leaders in the field of family therapy and a number of the institutes which train family therapists.

Names of Family Therapists

Nathan W. Ackerman Family Institute
149 East 78th Street
New York, New York 10021

Ian Alger, MD
Visiting Associate Professor
Albert Einstein College of Medicine
1300 Morris Park Avenue
Bronx, New York 10461

Boston Family Institute
Frederick Duhl, MD, Director
1170 Commonwealth Avenue
Boston, Massachusetts 02134

Murray Bowen, MD
Department of Psychiatry
Georgetown University
3800 Reservoir Road NW
Washington, D.C. 20007

Brief Therapy Center, Mental Research Institute
555 Middlefield Road
Palo Alto, California 94301
Paul Watzlawick, PhD, John H. Weakland, ChE, and
  Richard Fisch, MD

Center for the Study of the Family
521 West Saint Catherine Street
Louisville, Kentucky 40203

Eastern Pennsylvania Psychiatric Institute
Dr. David Rubinstein and Ivan Boszormenyi-Nagy, MD
Henry Ave and Abbottsford Road
Philadelphia, Pennsylvania 19129

Family Institute of Chicago
Charles Kramer, MD, Director
Division of Northwestern University, Department of Psychiatry
20 East Huron Street
Chicago, Illinois 60611

Family Institute of Marin
Shirley Luthman, PhD, and
  Martin Kirschenbaum, PhD, Directors
1353 Lincoln Avenue
San Rafael, California 94901

James L. Framo, PhD
Temple University, Department of Psychiatry
Philadelphia, Pennsylvania 19122

Joseph Giordano, PhD
Director National Project on Ethnicity and Mental Health
American Jewish Committee
165 E. 56th Street
New York, New York 10022

Alfred Messer, MD
Department of Psychiatry
Emory University
Atlanta, Georgia 30322

Philadelphia Child Guidance Clinic
Salvador Minuchin, MD, Director
Jay Haley, Director of Family Research
Two Children's Center
34th Street and Civic Center Boulevard
Philadelphia, Pennsylvania 19104

Virginia Satir
PO Box 11457
Palo Alto, California 94306

Michael A. Solomon, MD
University of Colorado Medical Center, Department of Psychiatry
Denver, Colorado 80220

Ross V. Speck MD
221 Delancy Street
Philadelphia, Pennsylvania 19106

Carl A. Whitaker, MD
University of Wisconsin Medical School
Madison, Wisconsin 53703

FEMINIST THERAPISTS

Several national groups can supply the names of therapists who are particularly sensitive to the limitations which sex stereotypes have imposed on women and men. These names are usually volunteered by psychologists, social workers, and other therapists who consider themselves feminist but there is no guarantee with the referral of the academic background or experience of the feminist therapist. Women who want to break out of old stereotypes may wish to start the process by joining a women's group, but they will eventually have to bring their partners through some consciousness-raising if they want to maintain the partnership.

Association for Women in Psychology
Feminist Therapy Roster Coordinator,
    Nechama Liss-Levinson
The University Counseling Center
Colorado State University
Fort Collins, Colorado 80521

National Organization for Women
Coordinator of Task Force on Marriage,
    Divorce, Family Relations
Elizabeth Cox Spaulding
7 Hill Road
Greenwich, Connecticut 06830

Local centers for women's liberation, YWCA's and local NOW chapters may also be helpful in guiding you to a feminist therapist in your area.

GESTALT THERAPISTS

There are no accrediting associations for Gestalt therapy, perhaps because it is an approach to therapy which emphasizes the freedom of the therapist to improvise and experiment. There are, however, five major teaching institutes which may provide information about a Gestalt therapist in your area:

Gestalt Institute of Chicago
609 Davis Street
Evanston, Illinois 60101
(312) 866-7977

Gestalt Institute of Cleveland, Inc.
12921 Euclid Avenue
Cleveland, Ohio 44112
(216) 421-0469

Gestalt Institute of San Francisco
1719 Union Street
San Francisco, California 94123
(415) 775-4500

Gestalt Therapy Institute of Los Angeles
337 South Beverly Drive
Beverly Hills, California 90212
(213) 277-2918

New York Institute for Gestalt Therapy
7 West 96th Street
New York, New York 10025
(212) 850-5080

HUMANISTIC

A number of the newer branches of therapy have not organized any referral services. However, they do have associations which may be helpful.
Association for Humanistic Psychology
325 Ninth Street
San Francisco, California 94103

Anyone can join this association and judging from their conventions, anyone does. There are some well-qualified Gestalt, TA, and bioenergetic therapists in the association, and some who are mainly interested in being on the fringe of the latest psychological fad.

MARRIAGE ENCOUNTER

A number of organizations now offer the weekend experience for couples known as the Marriage Encounter weekend. Although the religious aspects of these weekends are not stressed and people of all denominations are welcome, couples still may prefer to choose weekends conducted in the expression closest to their religious beliefs. National Marriage Encounter and Worldwide Marriage Encounter are conducted in the Catholic expression, though they estimate that 30 to 40 percent of their couples are not Catholic.

Episcopal Expression
6 Commonwealth Boulevard
Bellerose, New York 11426

Jewish Marriage Experience
199 Boston Avenue
Massapequa, New York 11758

National Marriage Encounter
5305 West Foster Avenue
Chicago, Illinois 60630

Worldwide Marriage Encounter
(the largest of the encounter groups, with affiliates in 40 states including some Protestant groups)
Suite 108
10059 Manchester Road
Warson Woods, Missouri 63122

MARRIAGE ENRICHMENT

Programs to teach communication skills and generally perk up marriages are proliferating under the auspices of churches, community organizations, growth centers, and universities. One association serves as an umbrella group, but does not serve as a guarantor of academic training, experience, or the effectiveness of any particular group.

Association of Couples for Marriage Enrichment
403 S. Hawthorne Road
Winston-Salem, North Carolina 27013
David Mace, PhD, Director

PASTORAL COUNSELORS

Not every priest, rabbi, or minister is educated or trained to do marriage counseling. To find one who has this kind of academic background coupled with supervised experience contact

The American Association of Pastoral Counselors
3 West 29th Street
New York, New York 10001
(212) 889-7663

You can also contact a specific religious agency for other referrals. These national offices can refer you to an appropriate agency or clergyman in your area.

Catholic

National Conference of Catholic Charities
1346 Connecticut Avenue
Washington, D.C. 20036
(202) 785-2757

Jewish

Council of Jewish Federations and Welfare Funds
315 Park Avenue South
New York, New York 10010
(212) 673-8200

Protestant

Joint Department of Family Life
National Council of the Churches of Christ
475 Riverside Drive
New York, New York 10027
(212) 870-2200

PSYCHIATRISTS

A psychiatrist is a medical doctor with at least three years of training in a psychiatric residency program. Of all the professional groups involved in marriage counseling, psychiatrists undergo the most extensive training and charge the highest fees. Some psychiatrists are avilable at moderate fees through agencies, clinics, or community mental health programs. But couples going to a private psychiatrist or team of therapists which include a psychiatrist will pay an average of $75 to $80 per hour. At these prices, one wants to be assured that the psychiatrist in question is well qualifed.

A "board-certified psychiatrist" has taken a special examination in psychiatry, completed three years of residency at an approved hospital in the United States or Canada, and spent at least two years in practice after residency. Certification is granted by

American Board of Psychiatry and Neurology
1603 Orrington Avenue
Evanston, Illinois 60201

One may write the ABPN to see if a psychiatrist is actually board-certified or one may go the public library or the library of a large hospital or medical school and consult a volume called *The Directory of Medical Specialists* which lists certified psychiatrists. The American Board office in Evanston will make *no* referrals.

County medical societies will usually give three names of psychiatrists located near the caller's residence or place of work.

A medical doctor with at least three years of training in an approved psychiatric residency program may become a member of the

American Psychiatric Association
1700 18th Street, NW
Washington, D.C. 20009

The association has established a code of ethics (one of which forbids sexual relations between psychiatrist and patient, even if the patient encourages such relations). The APA does not give any special certifying exams, nor do they make referrals. They will direct people seeking a member psychiatrist to one of their seventy district branch offices around the country. These branch offices may make a referral or they will direct the caller to the county medical society, which will make a referral.

Other sources of psychiatric referrals are reputable medical schools or the psychiatric section of any large teaching hospital.

PSYCHOANALYTIC REFERRALS

Psychoanalysis as a method of treatment for marital problems has been discouraged in this book because it requires husband and wife to be treated separately; it is costly in terms of time (minimum three years, three times a week) and money (minimum $75 per week, average $150 per week). The twenty-three Institutes for Psychoanalysis in various parts of the country offer excellent referral services which include referrals for marriage/couples counseling. Some of the institutes listed below may give referrals over the phone. Others may suggest an evaluation of the problem for a fee which averages $25. When contacting one of the institutes, be clear about requesting a therapist who does marriage counseling as opposed to an analyst or psychotherapist who is committed to individual therapy. As with other referrals, a recommendation by the institute should not prevent a couple from asking direct questions of the referred therapist.

Baltimore-District of Columbia Institute for Psychoanalysis
821 N. Charles Street
Baltimore, Maryland 21201
(301) 727-1740

Boston Psychoanalytic Society and Institute, Inc.
15 Commonwealth Avenue
Boston, Massachusetts 02116
(617) 266-0953

Chicago Institute for Psychoanalysis
180 North Michigan Avenue
Chicago, Illinois 60601
(312) 726-6300

Cincinnati Psychoanalytic Institute
2600 Euclid Avenue
Cincinnati, Ohio 45219
(513) 961-1319

The Cleveland Psychoanalytic Institute
11328 Euclid Avenue
Cleveland, Ohio 44106
(216) 229-5959

Columbia University Psychoanalytic Clinic For
Training and Research
Psychiatric Institute
722 W. 168th Street
New York, New York 10032
(212) 927-5000

Denver Institute for Psychoanalysis
University of Colorado School of Medicine
4200 East Ninth Avenue
Denver, Colorado 80220
(303) 394-8505

Division of Psychoanalytic Education, State University of New York,
College of Medicine at New York City
606 Winthrop Street
Brooklyn, New York 11203
(212) 630-3816

Institute of the Philadelphia Association for Psychoanalysis
15 St. Asaph's Road
Bala Cynwyd, Pennsylvania 19004
(215) 839-3966

Los Angeles Psychoanalytic Society and Institute
344 North Bedford Drive
Beverly Hills, California 90210
(213) 271-1368, 272-1434

Michigan Psychoanalytic Institute
16310 W. 12 Mile Road, No. 204
Southfield, Michigan 48076
(313) 559-5855

New Orleans Psychoanalytic Institute, Inc.
3624 Coliseum Street
New Orleans, Louisiana 70155
(504) 899-5815

New York Psychoanalytic Institute
247 East 82nd Street
New York, New York 10028
(212) 879-6900

Philadelphia Psychoanalytic Institute
111 North Forty-Ninth Street
Philadelphia, Pennsylvania 19139
(215) 474-5748

Pittsburgh Psychoanalytic Center, Inc. School of Medicine
The University of Pittsburgh
4617 Winthrop Street
Pittsburgh, Pennsylvania 15213

St. Louis Psychoanalytic Institute
4524 Forest Park Avenue
St. Louis, Missouri 63108
(314) 361-7075

San Francisco Psychoanalytic Institute
2420 Sutter Street
San Francisco, California 94115
(415) 931-4205

Seattle Psychoanalytic Institute
4033 East Madison Street
Seattle, Washington 98112
(206) 323-1706

Southern California Psychoanalytic Institute
9024 Olympic Boulevard
Beverly Hills, California 90211
(213) 276-2455

Topeka Institute for Psychoanalysis
Box 829
Topeka, Kansas 66601
(913) 234-9566

University of North Carolina-Duke University
Psychoanalytic Training Program
Department of Psychiatry, UNC School of Medicine
239 Old Nurses Dorm
Chapel Hill, North Carolina 27514
(919) 966-4224

Washington Psychoanalytic Institute
4925 MacArthur Boulevard, NW
Washington, D.C. 20007
(202) 338-5453

Western New England Institute for Psychoanalysis
340 Whitney Avenue
New Haven, Connecticut 06511
(203) 562-2103

PSYCHODRAMA

Psychodrama continues to influence many therapists, but therapists who use this approach have no central agency. Many psychodrama courses and programs emanate from the
Moreno Institute
259 Wolcott Avenue
Beacon, New York 12508

PSYCHOLOGISTS

A psychologist may have a masters degree or a doctor of philosophy. Some states require in addition that psychologists pass a state written or oral examination. While all psychologists are concerned with the dynamics of personality and behavior, their training varies considerably. Some may have a strong background in experimental psychology, which includes testing theories of behavior on rates and mice. Others focus on industrial psychology, personnel management, and efficiency—fields which have little relevance to marriage counseling. So it's wise to question a psychologist as to his/her specific experience. Generally, a background in either clinical or counseling psychology is what you are looking for. Sometimes those trained in educational psychology who have clinical experience also make fine marriage counselors.

Many psychologists belong to the national organization of psychologists called

The American Psychological Association
1200 17th Street, NW
Washington, D.C. 20036
(202) 833-7600

Membership in the APA simply means that the psychologist in question has paid dues and earned his PhD. The APA gives no written or oral exams, and the association considers it unethical to use membership as a standard for competence.

Some state branches of the APA, however, will suggest names of psychologists who specialize in the field of marriage counseling: Illinois, New York, California, Ohio, Pennsylvania, Texas, District of Columbia, Washington, and Massachusetts. (For example, if asked for a referral, the Illinois Psychological Association will recommend two psychologists.) For those who do not have access to a local office, the Office of Professional Affairs of the American Psychological Association in Washington, D.C., will offer recommendations in a particular geographical area.

PSYCHOTHERAPISTS

"Psychotherapist" is a term, like "counselor" or "marriage counselor," which does not clearly indicate a particular kind or even any kind, of graduate training or experience. One way of finding out if a "psychotherapist" is qualified is to ask what formal training, degrees, and experience he has. Is he a licensed psychologist? Does he have a master's degree in sociology? Is his training in psychiatry?

Membership in the American Group Psychotherapy Association is one assurance of training and experience. Members of the AGPA must have 1,800 hours of supervised experience in a combination of therapies involving individuals, groups, and family therapy. The AGPA is comprised of therapists from a number of disciplines—psychiatrists, psychologists, and social workers. All must have fulfilled the necessary requirements for degrees in their fields. Psychologists and social workers must have at least a masters degree.

The AGPA will make a referral to one of its twenty-two affiliate societies throughout the nation. The referral will be to the area president, who in turn will make a recommendation of an AGPA member located in your area.

American Group Psychotherapy Association
1865 Broadway
New York, New York 10023
(212) 245-7732

Group therapy varies in price but is always less expensive than individual therapy or couple therapy. Many couples and professionals find the group situation highly effective for treating marital problems.

SEX THERAPISTS/SEX CLINICS

There are absolutely no academic or experiential qualifications assured by the label "sex therapist." While most states have some licensing and certification covering psychologists, social workers, psychiatrists, and nurses, there are as yet no legal barriers to setting oneself up as a sex therapist. To seek a reliable practitioner, the best way to proceed is to find out if there is a sex clinic or sex dysfunction treatment program attached to a large hospital or medical school in your vicinity.

Therapy at university-or medical school-affiliated clinics is usually handled by a medical doctor or psychiatrist who may be working in partnership with a psychiatric nurse, psychiatric social workers, or psychologist. Therapists at these clinics are usually supervised by a highly qualified professional director who is accountable to the parent institution. Programs are usually scaled to the couple's ability to pay. A few outstanding examples of such programs are:

Loyola University Foster McGaw Hospital Sexual Dysfunction Clinic
Domeena Renshaw, MD, Director
2160 S. First Avenue
Maywood, Illinois 60153
(315) 531-7350

Mount Sinai Medical School, Program in Human Sexuality
Dr. Raul Schiavi, Director
11 East 110th Street
New York, New York 10029

Payne Whitney Clinic of New York Hospital
Sex Therapy and Education Program
Helen Singer Kaplan, MD, PhD, Director
525 East 68th Street
New York, New York 10021
(212) 472-5033

Human Sexuality Program
University of California Medical Center
San Francisco, California 94143

The Reproductive Biology Research Clinic run by Dr. William Masters and Virginia Johnson usually charges $2,500 per couple for the intensive twelve-fourteen day program. Twenty percent of the couples going through the Masters and Johnson program are on what Dr. Masters calls "scholarships," or reduced rates. A good deal of the money earned from the therapy program goes into research conducted by the foundation.

Reproductive Biology Research Foundation
4910 Forest Park Boulevard
St. Louis, Missouri 63108
(314) 361-2377

Many sex therapists bill themselves as "Masters & Johnson-trained," which may mean simply that the therapist spent a weekend or a ten-day workshop with that team or have read their books. We are listing the addresses of the teams trained by Masters and Johnson to date, not only to prevent misrepresentation but because these people are among the best and most experienced sex therapists in the country.

Alexandra Fauntleroy, psychiatric nurse
Oxford, Maryland 21654

Alexander N. Levay, MD
161 Fort Washington Avenue
New York, New York 10032
(212) 579-5392

Virginia Lozzi, MD
480 Park Avenue
New York, New York 10022
(212) 751-0272

Armando de Moya, MD, and Dorothy de Moya, MSN
11016 Ticasso Lane
Potomac, Maryland 20854
(301) 365-0297 or (301) 365-0299
(The de Moyas are also on the Sex Therapy Certification Committee of the American Association of Sex Educators and Counselors)

John B. Reckless, MD, and Eileen Sullivan, BSN
John Reckless Clinic
5504 Durham-Chapel Hill Boulevard
Durham, North Carolina 22707
(919) 489-1661

Harvey L. Resnik, MD, and Audrey R. Resnik, RN
Suite 201, Chevy Chase Medical Center
4740 Chevy Chase Drive
Chevy Chase, Maryland 20015
(301) 656-4774

Philip M. Sarrel, MD, and Lorna J. Sarrel, MSW,
Directors, Sex Therapy Clinic, Yale Medical School
333 Cedar Street
New Haven, Connecticut 06510
(203) 436-3592

Marshall Shearer, MD, and Marguerite Shearer, MD
13A Tower Plaza
555 East William
Ann Arbor, Michigan 48108
(313) 668-6341

Philip E. Veenhuis, MD, and Joanne Veenhuis, MA
1220 Dewey Avenue
Wauwatosa, Wisconsin 53213
(414) 258-2600

Nonprofit social service agencies that specialize in marriage counseling often have responsible sex therapy programs. An excellent example is the Center for Sex Education and Medicine, affiliated with the Philadelphia Marriage Council and the University of Pennsylvania.

Center for Sex Education and Medicine
4025 Chestnut Street
Director, Dr. Harold Lief
Philadelphia, Pennsylvania 19104

The proliferation of sex therapists has prompted several groups to consider ways of regulating the field. The American Association of Sex Educators and Counselors has recently established certification standards for sex therapists. If you wish to receive a copy of their standards and a list of sex therapists in your area whom AASEC has qualified, write:

Sex Therapy Certification Committee
American Association of Sex Educators and Counselors
5010 Wisconsin Avenue, NW
Suite 304
Washington, D.C. 20016
(202) 686-2523

Because the AASEC certification program is new and does not represent a comprehensive and uniformly accepted standard, do not assume that an individual sex therapist who has not received their certification is not qualified. But do set your own standards, particularly for a private therapist. Demand an academic degree (MA, PhD, MD, MSW) from a reputable school and supervised experience at a reputable agency, including specific supervised experience in sex therapy.

Another organization which has strict certification and membership requirements for sex therapists is

Eastern Association of Sex Therapy (EAST)
10 East 88th Street
New York, New York 10028

EAST has approximately 100 members and twenty-six medical schools which have associated themselves with the organization. Its members must have either a PhD or an MD, 200 hours of supervised training by a sex therapist previously certified by EAST, as well as other educational requirements. EAST's limitation is geographic, covering only the eastern section of the United States as far south as South Carolina. EAST will make referrals.

SOCIAL SERVICE ORGANIZATIONS

More than 350 marriage- and family-oriented, nonprofit social service organizations throughout the nation are affiliated with the

Family Service Association of America
44 East 23rd Street
New York, New York 10010
(212) 674-6100

Member agencies in any local community may or may not have some other affiliation as well, such as a religious one, but broadly, the purpose of an agency affiliated with FSAA is to provide support for marriages and for families with problems.

Member agencies may offer programs of therapeutic services which range from adequate to outstanding, but an agency which is affiliated with the FSAA can be relied upon to have marriage counselors/therapists who are qualified in their field. Because of their nonprofit status and their subsidy through religious or national charitable organizations, the cost of marriage counseling at these agencies is always reasonable.

SOCIAL WORKERS

There are various kinds of licensing and certification for social workers. A degree in social work may or may not include specialized courses and training in marriage and family counseling. Thus, a degree in social work per se does not a marriage counselor make.

1. *CSW.* In some states a person may qualify as a social worker if he has a bachelors degree in any field and has taken a state certification exam. Although these exams vary in difficulty from state to state, we think this background does *not* qualify a person to deal effectively with marital problems, unless the certified social worker (CSW) has additional supervised clinical experience and some specialized training in the psychiatric field.

2. *MSW.* Some social workers use the initials MSW or MA after their names, noting that they have been granted their masters degree, which means they have had approximately two years of graduate training. This indicates greater knowledge and skill than a CSW. But a couple will want to ask a social worker with an MSW specifically what kind of experience he has had with psychological counseling. Since marital problems often involve sexual difficulties, problems with children, and personality conflicts of various types, we prefer a social worker with additional psychological training.

3. *ACSW.* Social workers with an ACSW have been certified by the National Association of Social Workers. This title guarantees that the social worker has had two years of supervised work and has passed an examination which is far more difficult than the average state certification exam. The National Association has recently designed an examination for clinical social workers which involves oral and written tests and grants the title of Certified Clinical Social Worker (CCSW).

Try not to be confused by all these initials. Ask if the social worker in question has been certified by the National Association—your best safeguard against inexperience and ignorance. In order to check qualifications or find a nationally certified social worker near you, write:

National Association of Social Workers
1425 H Street, NW
Suite 600
Washington, D.C. 20005
(202) 628-6800

TRANSACTIONAL ANALYSIS

There are 10,000 members worldwide of the
International Transactional Analysis Association
1772 Vallejo Street
San Francisco, California 94123
(415) 885-5992

The ITAA has a geographical membership directory which lists the members of this organization who have conformed to the professional standards of training and ethical practices of TA. The minimum category is "regular member," which one can achieve after taking and completing a TA introductory course from a teaching member. With more instruction, supervision, and experience one may become a "clinical member," a "special field member," a "clinical provisional training member," or the highest category, a "clinical teaching member."

The ITAA will refer you to TA therapists in your local area if you write or phone them. Many therapists use TA techniques in their marriage counseling but are not members of ITAA. What membership implies is that an ITAA member has a basic, intellectual commitment to transactional analysis as the chosen method of therapy and has completed special courses on the TA approach.

Notes

Chapter 2

1. Robert Resnick, *Chicken Soup is Poison.* Pamphlet (1974), p. 5. Available from Renaissance Integrated Workshops, P.O. Box 3094, San Diego, California 92103.

2. *Ibid.*, p. 2.

3. Philip Nobile, "Conversations." *Midwest,* Magazine of the Chicago *Sun-Times.*

4. George and Nena O'Neill, *Open Marriage* (New York, M. Evans, 1972).

5. Gustave LeBon, *The Crowd* (New York, Viking Press, 1960), p. 43. Le Bon's study was first published in 1895 and is now a classic in social psychology.

6. Morton A. Lieberman, Irvin D. Yalom and Matthew B. Miles, *Encounter Groups: First Facts* (New York, Basic Books, 1973).

7. ———, "Change Induction in Small Groups." Scheduled for publication in *Annual Review of Psychology,* 1976.

8. Kurt Bach, *Beyond Words* (Baltimore, Penguin Books, 1972), pp. 78-80. In this brilliant history of the encounter movement and sensitivity training, Bach explains the tenets of the "here and now" and the value shift it represents.

9. Donald Baer, "Let's Take Another Look at Punishment." *Psychology Today* (October, 1971), p. 36.

10. Joanne Koch, "It'll All Come Out on the Ravich Flyer." Chicago *Tribune,* Sunday Magazine, March 28, 1971.

11. Sigmund Freud, *The Psychopathology of Everyday Life* (New York, W. W. Norton, 1965), p. 279.

12. Robert O. Blood and Donald M. Wolfe, *Husbands & Wives* (New York, Macmillan, 1960).

13. Claude M. Steiner, *Scripts People Live: Transactional Analysis of Life Scripts* (New York, Grove Press, 1974), pp. 1-2.

14. A clear and comprehensive explanation of transactional analysis which therapists often recommend to couples is *Born to Win* by Muriel James and Dorothy Jongeward (Reading, Massachusetts, Addison-Wesley, 1971). We have culled basic concepts from James and Jongeward, Claude Steiner and Eric Berne. But this highly concentrated explanation is only a sample of a creative, and despite its clarity, complicated view of human nature.

15. Claude M. Steiner, *Games Alcoholics Play* (New York, Ballantine Books, 1971), p. 188.

16. *Ibid.*

17. Marabel Morgan, *Total Woman* (Tappan, New Jersey, Fleming H. Revell, 1974).

18. Linda Wolfe, *Playing Around: Women and Extramarital Sex* (New York, William Morrow, 1975), pp. 10-11.

19. Hogie Wyckoff, "Banal Scripts of Women," a chapter in *Scripts People Live: Transactional Analysis of Life Scripts,* Claude Steiner. (New York, Grove Press, 1974), pp. 176-96.

20. The best explanations of strokes and the part they play in psychological development are provided in Eric Berne's chapter on strokes in *Transactional Analysis in Psychotherapy* (New York, Grove Press, 1961), and Claude Steiner's chapter entitled Basic Training: Training in Lovelessness, which includes details on "the stroke economy," in *Scripts People Live.*

21. Robert J. and Amy Levin, "Sexual Pleasure: The Surprising Preferences of 100,000 Women." *Redbook* (September, 1975), p. 52.

Chapter 3

1. James L. Framo, remarks delivered during the American Association of Marriage and Family Counselors' Annual Convention, 1974. Available on tape through AAMFC, 225 Yale Avenue, Claremont, California 91711.

2. Ivan Boszormenyi-Nagy, *Invisible Loyalties* (New York, Harper & Row, 1973).

3. Virginia Satir, *Peoplemaking* (Palo Alto, California, Science and Behavior Books, 1972), p. 114.

4. *Ibid.*, p. 59.

5. Jay Haley, and Lynn Hoffman, *Techniques of Family Therapy* (New York, Basic Books, 1967), p. 289.

6. *Ibid*, p. 301.

7. *Ibid.*, p. 309.

8. For further information on kin network therapy, see R.V. Speck, "Psychotherapy of the social network of a schizophrenic family." *Family*

Process 6, 1967, pp. 208-14; also R.V. Speck and U. Rueveni, "Network Therapy—a developing concept," *Family Process* 8, 1969, pp. 182–91.

9. This case is described in greater detail in a book devoted to explaining the theory and practice of the paradoxical approach, *Change: Principles of Problem Formation and Problem Resolution* by Paul Watzlawick, PhD, John Weakland, ChE, and Richard Fisch, MD (New York, W.W. Norton, 1974), pp. 116–19.

10. Virginia Satir, *Conjoint Family Therapy,* (Palo Alto, California, Science and Behavior Books, 1967).

11. E. James Anthony, MD, and Cyrille Koupernik, MD, eds., *The Child and His Family: Children at Psychiatric Risk,* (New York, John Wiley, 1974), p. 477.

Chapter 4

1. William H. Masters, MD, "Phony Sex Clinics—Medicine's Newest Nightmare." *Today's Health,* (November, 1974), p. 24.

2. *Ibid.;* p. 26.

3. 1972 Hearings on Abuses by Unregulated Therapists in New York State.

4. *Ibid.*

5. William H. Masters and Virginia Johnson, *Human Sexual Response,* (Boston, Little Brown & Co., 1954).

6. Helen Singer Kaplan, MD, PhD, *The New Sex Therapy,* (New York, The New York Times Book Company), p. 29.

7. While a book is unlikely to have sufficient power to remedy a sexual dysfunction, Dr. Masters may underestimate the enrichment and educational value of some of the more recent publications. For example SAR [Sexual Attitude Restructuring] *Guide for a Better Sex Life: A Self-Help Program for Personal Sexual Enrichment/Education,* designed by the National Sex Forum, is used in conjunction with a number of sex dysfunction and sex education programs around the country. The guide is based on a program widely used in medical schools and other professional courses for people who will be consulted about sexual matters. The manual is available from the National Sex Forum, 540 Powell Street, San Francisco, California 94108.

8. William H. Masters and Virginia Johnson, *Human Sexual Response* (1954), *Human Sexual Inadequacy* (1959), and *The Pleasure Bond,* with Robert J. Levin (1975) (Boston, Little Brown).

9. Helen Singer Kaplan, *op.cit.,* p. 204.

10. William E. Hartman, PhD, and Marilyn A. Fithian, *Treatment of Sexual Dysfunction,* (Center for Marital & Sexual Studies, 5199 E. Pacific Coast Highway, Long Beach, California, 1972).

11. "The trend towards explicit participation of the therapist in his pa-

tient's sexual experiences in the treatment of sexual dysfunction has been exploited by a number of opportunistic 'therapists' who engage in sexual activities with their patients and/or conduct group sex experiences and provide specially trained 'sex-therapists'—prostitutes—for this purpose. The ethics of some of these practices are highly questionable and the effectiveness of these methods has not been demonstrated." Helen Singer Kaplan, *The New Sex Therapy*, p. 204.

12. Lonnie Garfield Barbach, *For Yourself: The Fulfillment of Female Sexuality* (New York, Doubleday, 1975).

13. *Ibid.*, p. 115. Barbach's use of masturbation as a learning tool is based on three solid pieces of evidence: (1) Masters and Johnson found that the physiological response during orgasm was the same whether orgasm was produced by masturbation or intercourse. (Remember, Freud thought the two were different, the former being immature, the latter mature.) (2) Kinsey had reported in his study of female sexual behavior that 62 percent of the women in his sample masturbated. Of those who masturbated, Kinsey reported that 96 percent achieved orgasm. (3) Drs. Charles Lobitz and Joseph LoPiccolo had developed a nine-step masturbation desensitization program for preorgasmic women. Working with the women individually in conjunction with a couple program, Lobitz and LoPiccolo reported 100 percent success. Lonnie Garfield Barbach, "Group Treatment of Preorgasmic Women," *Journal of Sex & Marital Therapy* 1, no. 2 (Winter, 1974), pp. 134–44.

"Preorgasmic Group Treatment." *Journal of Sex & Marital Therapy* 1, no. 2 (Winter, 1974), p. 146.

15. At a New York City sex conference sponsored by the National Organization for Women masturbation was the password. One militant feminist proclaimed that men will have to learn to make love as women, with their mouths and fingers, with intercourse permitted only with a flaccid penis.

16. Helen Singer Kaplan, *op.cit.*, p. 204.

17. Joanne and Lew Koch, "The Marriage Savers," *Chicago Guide* (now *Chicago*), (February, 1974), p. 96.

18. *Ibid.*

19. Helen Singer Kaplan, *op.cit.*, p. 209.

20. The top ten marital complaints cited in 1972 by psychiatrist Bernard L. Greene, author of *A Clinical Approach to Marital Problems*, are: (1) lack of communication; (2) constant arguments; (3) unfulfilled emotional needs; (4) sexual dissatisfaction; (5) financial disagreements; (6) in-law trouble; (7) infidelity; (8) conflicts about the children; (9) domineering spouse; (10) suspicious spouse. (Martha Weiman Lear, "Save the Spouses, Rather Than the Marriage." *The New York Times Magazine,* August 13, 1972.) In their nationwide study of family service agencies, based on 3,646 cases, the Family Service Association reports communication to be the presenting complaint in 86.6 percent of the couples. Problems concerning children and sex were

cited in 40 percent of the families who sought help. Money, leisure, relatives, infidelity, housekeeping, physical abuse, and other problems including alcoholism followed in descending order. (Dorothy Beck and Mary Ann Jones, *Progress on Family Problems* [New York, Family Service Association of America, 1973], p. 148.)

21. Cliford J. Sager, MD, "Sexual Dysfunction and Marital Discord," a chapter in *The New Sex Therapy*, pp. 501–16.

22. *Ibid.*, p. 504.

Chapter 5

1. Roger Gould, "The Phases of Adult Life," *Psychology Today* (February, 1975), pp. 74–78.

2. Gail Sheehy, "Catch-30 and Other Predictable Crises of Growing Up Adult, *New York* (February 18, 1974), p. 34.

3. Gould, *op.cit.*

4. Dorothy Fahs Beck and Mary Ann Jones, *Progress on Family Problems*, (New York, Family Service Association of America, 1973), Chapter 10, "Profiles of Special Groups: Couples with Marital Problems," pp. 148–54.

5. "About 15 percent who were separated when they first applied shifted toward reuniting during treatment. A smaller group—8 percent—moved in the course of treatment from staying together toward separating. The proportion who made any legal change in their marriage during the treatment period was even smaller—7 percent. About one in seven of these moved toward remarriage; the other six, in the direction of separation or divorce." (*Ibid.*)

6. Beck and Jones, *op. cit.*

Chapter 6

1. Chicago *Tribune* Poll of Women's Attitudes (February 9, 1975).

2. Urie Bronfenbrenner, "Who Cares for America's Children," a paper presented for the symposium on "The Family—Can It Be Saved?" sponsored by St. Christopher's Hospital for Children, Boston Children's Hospital Medical Center, and the Johnson & Johnson Institute for Pediatric Service, Philadelphia, April 25, 1975. Bronfenbrenner's primary sources are government statistics, principally *Current Population Reports*, published by the Bureau of the Census; *Special Labor Force Reports*, issued by the Department of Labor; and *Vital and Health Statistics Reports*, prepared by the National Center of Health Statistics.

3. John F. Cuber and Peggy B. Harroff used five categories to describe

the different types of marriages in their study of 437 upper-middle-class couples: *devitalized, conflict-habituated, passive congenial, vital,* and *total.* The study was first published as *The Significant Americans* by Appleton-Century in 1965 and is now available in paperback under the title *Sex and the Significant Americans* (Baltimore, Penguin Books, 1966).

4. Sherod Miller, Elam Nunnally, and Daniel Wackman, Interpersonal Communication Programs, Inc., 2001 Riverside, Minneapolis, Minnesota 55454.

5. The booklet *Twelve Years of Development,* put out by the Minnesota Family Study Center, documents the important contributions made during the years 1957–1969. Under the directorship of Dr. Ira Reiss, the center continues to be a training ground for leaders in the field of family-life education.

6. Sherod Miller and Elam Nunnally, "A Family Developmental Program of Communication Training for Engaged Couples." Monograph, Family Study Center, University of Minnesota, 1970.

7. David Olson, "Marriage of the Future: Revolutionary or Evolutionary Change?" *The Family Coordinator* (October, 1972), p. 390.

8. Linda Wolfe, *op. cit.*

9. Robert N. Whitehurst's study is included in *Extra-Marital Relations,* edited by Gerhard Neubeck, (Englewood Cliffs, New Jersey, Prentice-Hall, 1969), "Extra-Marital Sex: Alienation or Extension of Normal Behavior," pp. 129–44.

10. Ralph E. Johnson, "Some Correlates of Extramarital Coitus," *Journal of Marriage and the Family* (1970), Volume 32, pp. 449–56.

11. As for mate swapping to juice up the marriage, Humphrey cites a study by Dwayne Denfield called "Dropout from Swinging," which surveyed marriage counselors around the country and revealed that they are seeing a number of former swingers whose attempts to liven up their relationships have backfired. In the book *Group Sex,* Gilbert Bartell suggests that there may be as many as one million couples experimenting with the brief sexual contacts referred to as swinging. Bartell's study of 280 of these couples reveals the swinging life to be a short-lived episode and usually a disappointing one. The pursuit of sexual partners requires more time and energy than even the most libidinous husband and wife have to spare. (Gilbert D. Bartell, *Group Sex* [New York: Peter H. Wyden, 1971])

12. Gerhard Neubeck, editor. *Extra-Marital Relations* (Englewood Cliffs, New Jersey, Prentice-Hall, 1969).

13. Helen B. Andelin, *Fascinating Womanhood* (New York, Bantam Books, 1974), pp. 129–31.

14. Marabel Morgan, *op cit.*

15. Matina S. Horner, "Toward an Understanding of Achievement Related Conflicts in Women," *Journal of Social Sciences* 28, no. 2 (1972), pp. 157–74.

Chapter 7

1. Carl Rogers, *Becoming Partners: Marriage and Its Alternatives* (New York, Houghton Mifflin, 1970), p. 25.

2. Claude Steiner, *Games Alcoholics Play*, p. 122.

3. M.G. Blinder and M. Kirschenbaum, "The Technique of Married Couple Group Therapy." *Archives of General Psychiatry* (July, 1967), p. 51.

4. *Ibid.*

Index

Abundant Life Counseling Service, 236

Ackerman, Nathan, 68, 69, 106, 174, 249

Ackerman Family Institute. *See* Nathan W. Ackerman Family Institute

ACME (Association for Couple and Marital Enrichment), 47, 214

Action, in psychodrama, 46·

"Adjustment," of wife to husband, 163, 168, 190

Adjustment therapy, 19

Adler, Alfred, 131

Adult ego state, in transactional analysis, 48, 49–50, 223

Adult life stages, 161

Adulthood, developmental view of, 160–62

problems of, 160–61

Affair(s), 216–25; as symptom of marital problems, 77 ff. *See also* Extramarital sex

"Age-specific problems," 160

Alcoholism, 50–52

Alger, Ian, 103–5, 253

Alimony, 204

Alive and Aware: Improving Communication in Relationships, 210

Allison, Harry, 42, 44

Allison, Sarah, 42, 43–45

Alternative life-styles, 203,

American Association of Marriage and Family Counselors (AAMFC), 22, 42, 43, 61, 233, 236

American Association of Pastoral Counselors, 258

American Association of Sex Educators and Counselors, 156, 266–67

American Board of Psychiatry and Neurology, 259

American Group Psychotherapy Association, 239, 263–64

American Institute of Family Relations, 163–68, 238

American Medical Association, 146

American Psychiatric Association, 27, 253, 259

American Psychological Association, 263

Amy/Ted (case), 205–6

Andelin, Helen, 222

Anger, expressing, 148–49, 152

Anxiety, 86

Assertiveness training, 148

Association for Couple and Marital Enrichment (ACME), 47, 214

Association of Couples for Marriage Enrichment, 257

Association for Women in Psychology, 255

Automobile, effect of, 167–68

Avoidance, 231–32

Baer, Donald M., 37–38

Bambi/Sloan (case), 225–29

Barbach, Lonnie Garfield, 144–45, 147

Barbara/Rick (case), 164–65

Barnham, Pamela (case), 175
Beck, Dorothy Fabs, 191–92, 193
Beck-Jones Study, 191
Becoming Partners: Marriage and Its Alternatives (Rogers), 235
Behavior, changing, 22
Behaviorists, 24–25
Behavior modification therapist, how to find, 252
Behavior modification therapy, 37–42, 248
Belden, Benjamin C., 40
Bell, Robert R., 216
Berger, Milton, 239
Berkeley Sex Therapy Group, 137–38
Berne, Eric, 48, 68, 249
Berry, David M., 235
Bioenergetics, 37, 42–46
Bioenergetic therapist, how to find, 252
Bioenergetic therapy, 21
Blinder, Martin, 244
Blood, Margaret, 46–48
Blood, Robert O., Jr., 46–48
"Body language," 45
Bonaparte, Marie, 91
Boredom, 233, 235
Born to Win (James/Jongeward), 21, 64
Boston Family Institute, 253
Boszormenyi-Nagy, Ivan, 69, 70–71, 254
Bowen, Murray, 253
Brief Therapy Center of the Mental Health Institute (Palo Alto, California), 87, 93, 253
Bronfenbrenner, Urie, 204
Brown, Allen J., 167–68
Burt/Marie (case), 206
Byron/Emily (case), 167–68

Calvo, Father, 209

"Can This Marriage Be Saved?" (Popenoe) (column), 163
Carlyle, Sharon and Dave (case), 113–24, 133, 152, 154
"Casualties," psychological, 28–29, 36
Catharsis, in psychodrama, 46
Center for Family Learning (New Rochelle, New York), 212–14
Center for Marital and Sexual Studies (Long Beach, California), 134
Center for Sex Education and Medicine, 266
Center for the Study of the Family (Louisville, Kentucky), 254
Certification: of marriage counselors, 252; of social workers, 268. *See also* Licensing
"Change Induction in Small Groups" (Lieberman), 35
Charismatic Leaders, 35
Chicago Center for Behavior Modification, 40
Chicago Marriage Encounter, 207
Chicago *Tribune* marriage poll, 203–4
Child ego state, in transactional analysis, 48, 49–50, 223
Child-rearing, men and, 225
Children, involvement of, in marital problems, 17–18, 192–93, 231
Child-support payments, 204
Christian Family Movement, 209
Cindy/Frank (case), 173–74
Clergyman, and marriage counseling, 60–64
Client(s): responsibility, 175; rights of, 175–77
Clitoral orgasms, 126–27
Closed family system, 71–72, 97
Communication, in marriage, 165, 174, 178–79, 192, 209–12,

234–35; "leveling," 72–73; masked, 51, 52; straight talking, 51, 52, 53; television as barrier to, 232

Concentrated therapy, 132

"Conflict-habituated" marriage, 205, 218

Conjoint Family Therapy (Satir), 97

Conjoint therapy, 20

Connie/Gus (case), 217–21

Consciousness raising, 205

Consumer accountability, social service agencies and, 160

Contracts, 242–43, 246; in behavior modification, 39, 40, 41; in transactional analysis, 50, 51

Co-therapy, 117, 129, 131; fees, 238

Council of Jewish Federations and Welfare Funds, 258

Culture, and sexual stereotyping, 185–86

Davis, Darlene, 149

Davis, Jack, 149

De Moya, Armanda, 265

De Moya, Dorothy, 265

Dependence, on therapist, 14–15

Developmental view of adulthood, 160

"Devitalized" marriage, 205

"Dialoguing," 209

Divorce, 20, 156, 174, 190, 203, 218–19; actions, liberalization of, 204; as alternative, 191–92; boredom as cause of, 233; and family therapy, 70, 71; marriage counseling as insurance against, 249; no-fault, 204, 249; rate, 18; and remarriage, 204; and separation therapy, 162; spiritual, 205, 208

Double standard, sexual responsibility and, 128

"Doubling," in psychodrama, 46–47

Drake Institute of Hypnosis, 236

Duhl, Frederick, 253

Eastern Association of Sex Therapists (EAST), 156, 267

Economic survival problems, 17

Ego-alien, 244

Ego states, in transactional analysis, 49, 150, 223

Ego-syntonic, 243–44

Eli (case), 29–33, 215

Ellis, Albert, 181

Emerson, Ralph Waldo, 181

Emotional monogamy, 56–57

Encounter groups, 31–37, 210

Encounter Groups: First Facts (Yalom/Miles/Lieberman), 34

Erhard Seminars Training (est), 174

Erickson, Milton, 92

Erikson, Erik, 131, 160

Ethnicity, and neuroses, 108, 109–10

Extended family, 209; social service agency as, 179–85; therapy as, 239

Extra-Marital Relations (ed. Neubeck), 217

Extramarital sex (EMS), 16, 56–57, 130, 187–90, 216–25; in open marriage, 216; as symptom of marital problems, 77 ff.; women and, 55

Fair fighting, 148

Fallon, Tony, 186–87

Family, 17; as dynamic system, 69, 71–74, 97–103; and mobility, 179–80; modern, and need for community, 112; of origin, and marriage, 67–68; power of, 68, 70–71; single-parent head of, 204

Family Counseling Service (Evanston, Illinois), 175
Family Encounter weekends, 209
Family Institute of Chicago, 254
Family Institute of Marin, 254
Family Institute (New York), 69, 74
"Family lib," 203
Family of origin sessions, 70
Family reconstruction, 70, 102–3
Family retreats, 97–103
Family Service Association of America, 159, 188, 236, 267
Family sculpting, 69–70, 105–6
"Family-stress ballet," 100, 103
Family Study Center (University of Minnesota), 211
Family system, 69, 71–74, 97–103
Family therapists: how to find, 252–55; training, 108
Family therapy, 19, 68–112, 177–79: family sculpting, 105–6; family as system, 71–74, 97–103; innovations in, 86; multiple, 109–12; as opposed to individual therapy, 84; paradoxical intention, 86–97; process, 106–8; scapegoating, 74–75; techniques, 69–70, 103 ff.
Family Therapy Institute of Marin (San Rafael, California), 106
Fascinating Womanhood (Andelin), 222, 223
Fascinating Womanhood program, 222
Fauntleroy, Alexandra, 265
Fees, 15, 59–60, 204, 237–40; exorbitant, 14; for family retreats, 98; for family therapy, 88; Marriage Encounter, 209; Masters and Johnson, 132, 265; Minnesota Couples Communication Program, 211; for multiple family session, 109; psychiatrists', 258; for psychoanalysis, 259; sex clinics, 135, 138, 148, 157; of social service agencies, 159–60, 170, 193
Fellatio, 152, 153
Female sexuality, vs. male, 128–29. *See also* Woman
Feminine Mystique, The (Friedan), 214
Feminism, 56, 109, 111; militant, 145
Feminist groups, 56
Feminist therapists, 185, 189, 228; how to find, 255–56
Feminists, separatist, 56
Fisch, Richard, 87, 88–93, 94, 108, 253
Fithian, Marilyn A., 134–36, 137, 147
For Yourself (Barbach), 144
Forest Hospital Sexual Dysfunction Clinic, 114 ff., 134, 148
Fort, Joel, 170–75
Fort Help, 170–75
Framo, James L., 69, 70–71, 254
Franklin, Benjamin, 16
Freud, Sigmund, 20, 21, 28, 46, 68, 126, 131, 249
Freudian analysis, 43, 248

Games: grown-up, 183; in transactional analysis, 49–50, 53
Games People Play (Berne), 21
Gardner, Jill, 34
Gaylin, Willard, 27–28
Gestalt Institute (Chicago), 72
Gestalt therapists, how to find, 256
Gestalt therapy, 21, 22–24, 46, 57, 60, 174, 248
Giordano, Grace, 108–12, 238
Giordano, Joseph, 108–12, 238, 254
Glick, Paul C., 204
Godwin, Hilda, 241

Goffman, Erving, 104
Goldberger, Rabbi, 217, 219–21
Goldiamond, Israel, 39, 40, 41
Gould, Roger, 160–61
"Gripe-feedback" method, 64
Group euphoria, 33
Group marriages, 16
Group therapy: bioenergetic, 45; feminist, 56; sex, 144–45; in transactional analysis, 49, 51, 52, 53, 60
Growth model, 107
Guttman, David, 162
Gynecologists, 14

Halbert, Mike, 35–36
Haley, Jay, 69, 84, 108, 174, 254
Hallucinations, 33
Hartman, William, 134–36, 137, 147
Hartogs, Renatus, 27
Helen (case), 192–93
Henderson Clinic (Hollywood, Florida), 180 ff., 185 ff., 192, 238
Hill, Reuben, 210–12
Hoffman, Lynn, 84
Hollander, Carl E., 46
Holy Ghost Repair Service, 236
Horner, Matina, 224
Humanistic therapies, 19, 36
Humanistic therapists, 24; how to find, 256–57
Human Potential Movement, 19, 26
Human Reproductive Biology Foundation, 129–30, 157, 265
Human Sexual Inadequacy (Masters/Johnson), 120, 125, 131
Human sexual response 14; research into, 126–28
Human Sexual Response (Masters/Johnson), 126, 131
Humphrey, Fred, 216–17, 241–42, 243
"Husband dumping," 225–29

I'm O.K.—You're O.K. (Harris), 21
Impotence, 54
Inadequacy syndrome, 128
Individuation, process of, 132
Infidelity, 187–90. *See also* Extramarital sex
Innovative therapies, 170–75
Institute for Bioenergetic Analysis, 252
Institutes for Psychoanalysis, 259
Integration, in psychodrama, 46
International Transactional Analysis Association, 48, 268–69

Jacobs, Leo, 117 ff.
Jackson, Dan, 181–85, 194
Jackson, Don D., 68, 69, 97, 107–8, 169, 174, 249
James, Muriel, 64
Jefferson, Thomas, 16
Jewish Family Service Agency (New York), 177
Jewish Marriage Encounter, 206, 209
John/Patricia (case), 174
Johnson, Virginia, 14, 94, 153. *See also* Masters and Johnson
Johnson study, 216
Joint awareness, 205
Joint Department of Family Life, 258
Jones, Mary Ann, 191–92, 193
Jongeward, Dorothy, 64
Jung, C. G., 102, 131

Kaplan, Helen Singer, 14, 127, 129, 132, 134, 138, 147, 151–52, 264
Kennedy, Margaret (case), 181–82, 185
"Kin network therapy," 86
Kinsey, Alfred, 62, 126, 216
Kirschenbaum, Martin, 69, 106, 108, 244, 254

Krafft-Ebing, Richard, 126
Kramer, Charles, 69, 74, 93–97, 254
Kramer, Jan, 93–97
Kuhn, Jerold R., 163–65
Ladies' Home Journal, 163
Lana (sexual surrogate), 138–44
Landers, George and Cynthia (case), 93–97
Larry/Ann (case), 43
Laycob, Lawrence, 239–40
Leah (case), 222–23, 224
Learning theory, 24
LeBon, Gustave, 33
Lefkowitz, Louis, 126
Lefkowitz–Mendell Hearings into Abuses by Unregulated Therapists in the Mental Health Field, 148
Leichter, Elsa, 177–79, 237
Leila/Bruce (case), 77–86
Levay, Alexander N., 265
Levin, Amy, 62
Levin, Joseph, 146
Levin, Robert, 62
Levinson, Daniel, 161
Licensing, 125, 146, 156–57. *See also* Certification
Lieberman, Morton A., 34–35
Lief, Harold I., 162
Lilli/Craig (case), 194–201
Liss-Levinson, Nechama, 255
Lobitz, W. Charles, 145
Logical extreme, 86
Loneliness, in marriage, 232
Look, 211
LoPiccolo, Joseph, 145
"Lovability factor," 231
"Love lists," 165–66
Lowen, Alexander, 43
Lozzi, Virginia, 265
Luthman, Shirley, 69, 106–8, 254

Mace, David, 47, 214

Mace, Vera, 214
Male(s): chauvinism, 51; and childrearing, 225; dominance of, in marriage, 53–54; and extramarital sex, 216–17; without female, psychological state of, 204; role of, in sexist system, 223; sexuality of, 128–29, 145;
Male Caressing the Female, The (film), 121
Male-female therapy teams, 117, 129, 131
Malpractice suits, 27–28
Manipulation by therapist, 241–45
Manson, Charles, 171
Maria (case), 188
Marital problems, 15, 17, 20, 41; affairs as symptom of, 77 ff.; children and, 17–18, 76–77, 192–93; danger signs, 231–35; economic survival and, 17; and family therapy, 69; and normal crises, 160–63; scapegoats for, 74–75; sex therapy and, 154–56; as sign of change, 162; and sociopolitical forces, 162
Marriage: advantages of, 235; alternatives to dull, 203–29; conflict-habituated, 204, 218; devitalized, 205; and extramarital sex, 216–25; and family background, 67–68; group, 16; as "impossible" institution, 179, 180; loneliness in, 232; male dominance in, 53–54; modern, 15–18; and mobility, 180; normal crises in, 206; open, 56, 57, 214–216, 243; partnership-style, 203; passive-congenial, 205; as preferable life-style, 203; problem periods in, 161; and religion, 62; single "sexual standard in, 54–55; security in, 234; sexism in, 63; survival reality of, 244–

45; traditional, 214; unconsummated, 130

Marriage counseling, 13, 19; client-responsibility, 175; and divorce, 190–92, 205, 249; effect of, 190–94; for family, 68–112; fees, *See separate entry*; rights of clients, 175–77; sex-role stereotyping in, 165; and social service agencies, 159, 201; studies of, 191; technology, 38–39; types of, 19–65

Marriage counselor(s), 13, 15; certification of, 252; choosing the right, 13–14, 15, 235–49; exploitative, 14, 15, 21, 26–27; fees, 14, 59–60; fraudulent, 13, 15; how to find, 251–69; licensing, 125

Marriage Encounter, 205–9, 210, 211; how to find, 257

Marriage enrichment programs, 193, 205, 209; ACME, 214; Center for Family Learning, 212–14; how to find, 257; Marriage Encounter, 205–9; Minnesota Couples Communication Program, 210–12; open marriage, 214–16

"Marriage of the Future" (Olson), 214

Masked communications, 51, 52

Masters, William, 14, 94, 153, 247

Masters and Johnson, 54, 117, 120, 127, 134, 137, 138, 146, 147, 156, 163, 238, 265; on exploitation in sex therapy, 125–26; fees, 132, 265; *Human Sexual Response*, 126; human sexual response research, 127–33; program, 131

Masturbation, 144–45, 148 ff.

Mate swapping, 16

Maureen/Vic (case), 207–8

Medical model, 107

Medical schools, and sex education, 128, 146

Menopause, 18

Mental illness: and divorce, 204; psychiatrist's definition of, 172

Messer, Alfred, 254

"Midolescence," 18

Miles, Matthew, 34

Miller, Sherod, 209–11, 215

Millman, Eileen, 206–7, 109

Millman, Marty, 206–7, 209

Mind-fucking, 22

Minneapolis Family and Children Services, 211

Minnesota Couples Communication Program (MCCP), 210–12

Minnesota, University of, Family Study Center, 211

Minuchin, Salvador, 69, 254

Mirror technique, 147

Mitchell, Faye, 185–86, 187, 190, 192, 194, 201

Monique (case), 224

Monogamy, 57, 225; emotional, 56–57

Moreno, Jacob, 46, 249

Morgan, Marabel, 53, 222

Mudd, Emily, 216–17

Multiple family therapy groups, 109–12, 181

Nathan W. Ackerman Family Institute, 105, 212, 253

National Association of Social Workers, 253, 268

National Conference of Catholic Charities, 258

National Organization for Women, 255

National Marriage Encounter, 207, 209, 257

Nestor, Hugh, 186

Network therapists, 86

Neubeck, Gerhard, 211, 217

Neugarten, Bernice, 161

New Sex Therapy, The (Kaplan),

127, 134
Nobile, Philip, 27
No-fault divorce, 204, 249
Nunnally, Elam, 210, 211

Olson, David, 214
O'Neill, George, 29, 214
O'Neill, Nena, 29, 214
Open family system, 97–103
Open marriage, 56, 57, 214–16, 243
Open Marriage (O'Neill/O'Neill), 29, 215
Orgasms, clitoral vs. vaginal, 126–27
Overrelating, 231–32

Packard, Vance, 179
Pain: change and, 177–79; and punishment in therapy, 37–38
Palo Alto Veterans Administration Hospital, 168–70
Papp, Peggy, 105–6, 212–14
Paradoxical intention, 86–97
Parentectomy, 74
Parent Effectiveness Training, 207, 211
Parent ego state, in transactional analysis, 48, 49–50, 68, 223
Parenting, styles of, 67, 68
Parents, distorted perspective of, 70
Parks, Ben and Brenda (case), 29–34, 215, 243, 244
"Parts party," 101, 102
"Passive-congenial" marriage, 205
Pastoral counselors, 258
Patient(s): manipulation of, 241–45; rights, 175–77
Payne Whitney Clinic, 134
Peltz, Dorothy Ann, 216
Peoplemaking (Satir), 71
Perls, Fritz, 22, 24, 26, 29, 46, 61, 249
Permission vs. coercion, 243–44

Personal power, 108
"Personhood" system, 225
Philadelphia Marriage Council, 160, 161, 162, 163, 217, 238
Physiological causes of sexual dysfunction, 133
Playboy foundation, 216
Playing Around (Wolfe), 55
"Pleasure bond," 120, 147
Pleasure Bond, The (Masters/Johnson), 131
Pomeroy, Ward, 126
Popenoe, Paul, 163, 168
Potter, Jessie, 146–47
Pounds, David, 165–66, 167
Progress on Family Problems (Beck/Jones), 191
"Pseudo stupidity" technique, 241–42
Psychiatrist(s), 13–14; definition of mental illness, 172; fees, 238; how to find, 258–59
Psychoanalysis, 19, 20, 60–61, 107
Psychoanalytical referral, how to find, 259–62
Psychodrama, 46–48, 248
Psychodrama therapist, how to find, 262
Psychological pain, 76
Psychologists, how to find, 262–63
Psychology Today, 37, 161
Psychosexual history, 164
Psychotherapist, how to find, 263–64
Psychotherapy, 173; importance of family in, 68

Quackery, in sex therapy, 125

Ralph/Dorothy (case), 50–53
Ravich, Robert, 38
Ravich Interpersonal Game Test, 38
Reckless, John B., 266

Redbook, 62
Rediger, Lloyd, 62–65
Redl, Fritz, 20
"Reductionistic" therapies, 163
Reich, Wilhelm, 131
Reid, Diane, 246
Reid, F. Theodore, 177, 245–48
Religion, and modern marriage, 62
Renshaw, Domeena, 147, 238, 264
Reproductive Biology Research Foundation, 129–30, 157, 265
Resnick, Robert, 22–23
Resnik, Audrey R., 266
Resnik, Harvey L., 266
"Reversal," 106
Reverse psychology, 86
Reverse role playing, 48
Ridker, Claire, 72, 73
Ridker, Mike, 72–73
Rights, client, 175–77
Rimel, Carolyn, 57–60
Rimel, Warden, 57–60
Robinson, Ralph, 173–75
Rogers, Carl, 181, 235
Role playing, 46, 48, 101–2. See also Sex roles
Role reversals, 225
Rooney, Bob and Betty (case), 99–103
Roy, Julie, 27–28
Rubinstein, David, 254
"Runaway wives," 225, 233
Ryder, Charles, 167
Rydman, Edward, 61–62, 233–34, 238–39

Sager, Clifford, 154–56
Sally/Sam (case), 55
Saltmarsh, Robert, 22–25
SAM (Signal System for the Assessment and Modification of Behavior), 38
Sarrel, Lorna J., 266
Sarrel, Philip M., 266

Satir, Virginia, 14, 36–37, 54, 69, 71–72, 97–103, 107–8, 169, 174, 177, 209, 232, 233, 242, 255
Satori, 21, 23, 24
Scapegoating, 74–75
Schiavi, Raul, 264
"Script," in transactional analysis, 49, 50, 52
Security, and marriage, 234
Sensate focus exercises, 131, 134, 152, 155
Sensitivity training, 210
Sensory exercises, 120–21
"Separatist feminist," 56
Sex: and marital problems, 234–35; as natural function, 128; and power, 154, 155; between therapist and patient, 26–28
Sex clinics, 15, 19, 113–57; affiliated, 133; controversial procedures, 134–44; exploitative, 19, 125–28, 133, 134, 156–57; fees, 135, 138, 148, 157, 238; group sex therapy, 144–45; how to find, 264–67; standards, 146–52. See also Sex therapy
Sex education, 136; in medical schools, 128, 146
Sex manuals, 129
Sex roles, 225; Judeo-Christian divisions in, 63; reversal of, 225; and sexist system, 222–24; stereotyping, and marriage counseling, 165
Sex therapist(s): exploitative, 14, 125–28, 133, 148, 153, 156–57; how to find, 264–67; licensing, 146, 156–57; male-female team, 117, 129; relationship with patients, 130; standards for, 146–57; training, 131, 133
Sex therapy, 113–57; drawbacks and limitations of, 154–56; exploitation in, 125–28; failures,

153, 156; group, 144–45; length of, 153; Masters and Johnson, 129–33; and patient "permission," 243; setting goals in, 152–54

Sexism, 63

Sexist system, traditional, 222–24

Sexological examination, 135–36, 147

Sexual dysfunction, 127, 128, 131, 147, 162; causes of, 133; change in attitude toward, 162; and male dominance, 54–55

Sexual fidelity, 217. *See also* Extramarital sex

Sexual positions, 127

Sexual problems. *See* Sexual dysfunction

Sexual responsibility, 128–29, 132–33

Sexual satisfaction, religion and, 62

Sexual stereotyping, 189; culture and, 185–86. *See also* Sex roles

Sexual surrogates, 130, 137–44, 146, 217; training, 137

Sexual techniques, demonstrating, coaching or observing, 134–36

Sexuality, male vs. female, 128–29. *See also* Human sexual relations

Shearer, Marguerite, 266

Shearer, Marshall, 266

Sheehy, Gail, 161

Sheila (case), 188–89

Sherfey, Mary Jane, 129

Singlehood, 247

Single parent, as head of family, 204

Six Characters in Search of an Author (Pirandello), 104

Skinner, B. F., 40

Social Service agencies, 19, 159 –201, 237; avant-garde, 170–75; consumer accountability and,

160; diversity of therapies, 185; as extended family, 179–85; fees, 159–60, 193; how to find, 267; and innovative therapy, 168–70; normal crises, treating, 160–70; services, 159; therapists, 159, 160, 175–77

Social workers, how to find, 268

Sociopolitical forces, and marital problems, 162

Socrates, 181

Solomon, Michael, 74–77, 177, 231–32, 242, 255

Spaulding, Elizabeth Cox, 255

"Specific discomfort contract," 242–43

Speck, Ross, 69, 86, 255

Spiritual divorce, 205, 208, 235

Squeeze technique, 134

Star, Sheldon, 168–70

Steiner, Claude, 48–49, 50–57, 163, 225, 238, 239, 242

Stewart, Richard, 166

"Straight-talking" technique, 51, 52, 53

"Stroke deficit," 58

Stroke strategy, 58

Strokes, in transactional analysis, 48, 49, 58–59

Success avoidance syndrome, 224

Sullivan, Eileen, 266

Surrogate sexual partners, 130, 137–44, 146, 217; training, 137

"Survival myth," 244

Swinging couples, 16

Sylvia (case), 166

Symbiotic relationships, 58, 222–24

Szasz, Thomas, 172, 181

Techniques of Family Therapy, 84

Technology, and marriage counseling, 38–39

Television, as barrier to communication, 232

Therapeutic match, 175–76
Therapist(s), 13, 19–65; checking credentials of, 41, 156–57; choosing a, 235–49; dependence on, 14–15; exploitative, 13, 125–28, 133, 134, 156–57, 238–39; flexibility of, 25; manipulation by, 241–45; and patient "casualties," 28–29; sex between patient and, 26–28; in social service agencies, 159, 160, 163; sources for, 236–37; and termination, 238–39. *See also* Marriage counselor
Therapy marketplace, 20, 22
Therapy team, 13
Therapy. *See specific types of therapy*
Thomas, Edwin J., 38
Today's Health, 125
Tom/Bernice (case), 165–66
Tom/Sara (case), 148–51, 153, 154
Total Woman, The (Morgan), 53, 222
Total Woman Courses, 211, 222
"Total woman" philosophy, 54
Tracers Company of America, 225
Train game (Ravich Interpersonal Game Test), 38
Transactional analysis, 21–22, 48–60, 150, 163, 223, 248
Transactional analysts, how to find, 268–69
Treatment of Sexual Dysfunction (Hartman/Fithian), 135

Unconsummated marriages, 130
Universal Freedom, Inc., 236

Vaginal orgasms, 126–27
Vander Voort, Nicole, 207
Vander Voort, Steve, 207
Veenhuis, Joan, 266
Veenhuis, Philip, 266

Victimization, 247
Videotape therapy technique, 103–5, 169, 239
Vindictiveness, 247
Vines, Neville, 160
Virginia Slims-Roper Poll, 203
Vulnerability, 247

Wackman, Daniel, 210, 211
Walters, Norma, 165–66, 167
Warm-up, in psychodrama, 46
Warnack, Jean, 117 ff.
Watzlawick, Paul, 87–92, 94, 108, 253
Wayne, Diane (case), 26–27, 28
Weakland, John H., 87, 90, 253
Weir, Ann, 210, 215
"Well-family" clinics, 212
Whitaker, Carl, 14, 69, 77–87, 94, 98–99, 255
Whitaker, Muriel, 82–83
Whitehead, Alfred North, 16
Whitehurst, Robert, 216
Wife: overburdened, 232–33; runaway, 225, 233
Williams, Martin, 138
Wisconsin Council of Churches, Office of Pastoral Services, 62
Wolfe, Linda, 55
Women: affairs with themselves, 225–29; divorced, 204; and extramarital sex, 55, 216–17; group therapy, 55–56, 185–90, 192, 194; sexual needs of, 152
Women's liberation movement, 54, 162, 188, 205, 224
Work, addiction to, 60, 206
World Wide Marriage Encounter, 209, 257
Wyckoff, Hogie, 53, 55–56, 57

Yalom, Irvin, 34

Zilbergeld, Bernie, 145